AMERICAN EDITIONS
HEIDELBERG

Other books by Alan Goldfein

HEADS

JEWS AND GERMANS
GERMANS AND JEWS

Alan Goldfein

EUROPE'S MACADAM
AMERICA'S TAR

How America Really

Compares to "Old Europe"

m

AMERICAN EDITIONS
HEIDELBERG

Die Deutsche Bibliothek – CIP-Einheitsaufnahme

Alan Goldfein:

Europe's Macadam – America's Tar:
How America Really Compares to "Old Europe" / Alan Goldfein. – Heidelberg:
American Editions, 2004
ISBN 3-00-014357-2

ISBN 3-00-014357-2

© Alan Goldfein
American Editions
Heidelberg 2004
http://www.americaneditions.com
Alle Rechte vorbehalten.

Titelabbildungen: "Eiffel Tower": Microsoft-Clip; Mercedes-Stern „Gottlieb":
© --helmi- | Helmut Fischer | digital graphix & design! | WWW.PlanetMensch.de |
www.Art42.de; "Empire State Building": © totem graphics inc.

Printed in Germany

for Ute

CONTENTS

INTRODUCTION

America is a shambles.

Compared to "old Europe", brick-for-brick, America is skyscrapers overshadowing shacks.

I debated with myself over whether or not to launch this book with such a provocative hull-crack of the Château La Pouilly bottle. After all, we in America are at the fulcrum of pushbutton interconnection, of globalization. We are The World's Model. But this book *is* about denial-- We are *not* The World's Model-- and, as the saying says, "Denial is not just a river in Egypt." At a time where it seems plain commonplace to compare America to an empire, albeit with self-flattering modesty no conquering Rome nor proud colonizing Brittania, but a "reluctant" empire, a do-good empire (although "do-good" is a sobriquet that we reserve contempt for at home) we may just be bugling with too much brio. "Americanism" has become such an Old Glory flying given, a kind of perverse bargain basement White Magic, that to affirm any homegrown inferiority seems sourpuss, unAmerican. . . . So, we whisper it. Within our brains.

Or, it whispers itself to us.

Shambles. . . Skyscrapers shadowing shacks.

Ugly compared to that "old Europe"-- which isn't as Great as us.

Then our whisper fades and again we hear the suspicious megaphone: Greatness (In fact, if you wish to hear our Greatness-bellow first, begin then at Chapter Seven).

In any case, ricocheting between our magnificence and our moulder we don't fix up much-- of the Greatness that is a Shambles.

Europe does. Or tries.

We are Not The World's Model.

*   *   *

Indelicate to say, comical to picture, but this book had its origin on a German toilet. One of those widebody power jobs more suitable for an NFL linebacker than an ectomorphic writer. Toilet symbolism is of course embarrassingly cheap and easy and obvious: A prow, basically, expanding to a wide top not unlike Atlas in spreadarmed support of the world; or the Queen Mary spreading out from its long narrow underbuoy; this reminder of both our inescapable animal being and our civilized "triumph" over "gross" animal nature: the pensive face, so gone-oblique, the solitude on spare porcelain. Diane Arbus person, it cries out, or an uncropped Helmut Newton -- quirky art-photo. Or Martin Luther famously aseat in Worms and constipationally recriminating against the far south Holy See in Rome. Still, I was on the toilet. Which is how a European would describe it. An American might too, although the American's inclination, his instinct, would be to declare, "I was in the bathroom," or "I was in the restroom." "You were *resting*?" a German or Frenchman might inquire with bemusement. "You felt the need to rest-- on the *toilet*?" Or bathe?

In "the little boys' room"?

In "the little girls' room"?

To "freshen-up"?

We Americans do seem to need the euphemisms.

Anyway: I was in Germany, where I have lived half each year for the past ten years, my wife being a German professor. I sat now upon plush pads, pontoons that might keep you afloat if your ship went down. A throne, not as in the ironic American pun, "I'm on the *throne* now, honey," but as in, well, literally, a throne. When I flushed I became aware there was no sound. Well, only the barest muffled sizzle, a Mercedes engine under a solid Mercedes hood. No jalopy jiggle-jangle, no Niagara Falls. No worry (if you are a home owner); no disturbing intimations of the RotoRooter man. And the operation of flushing itself on that German toilet, the surefire compressing, not of a flimsy gimcrack-gibbet handle, as in America, but a reliable Louisville Slugger of a panel built smoothly into the water tank's lid. Why you could toss in five dozen squares of two-ply Charmin-- I don't know why you'd want to; maybe for lonely psychotic entertainment-- and this Germanic baby would handle that bunchup with no-reflux dispatch. By way of comparison, and despite the bizarre obsession, I have conjured many times my toilet in Berkeley. Its small and flimsy cocklebox with its flakey wire works that sometimes dribbled water on my "*bath*"room's linoleum tile floor (and, let me say, I have never even seen a linoleum bathroom floor in Germany. They all seem to be solid tile.). The copper float ball in my Berkeley toilet was so tissue thin, its striations formed like drunk-spun spiderwebs, often allowing in water so it did not float, so the rubber shutoff puck would never fully drop and halt the dribbling water. A cackling hen was what it sounded like-- through I suppose a thinner coat of porcelain than this Daimler-Benzey toilet I now marvelled at in Germany. This hen, my American toilet. This utter rooster.

> The pumps don't work,
> But no vandals took no handles.

Nope, can't blame it on anybody but ourselves. But my oldtimey Berkeley shuttlecock ball and chain had been replaced now in The Old World, the Euro-World, by an adjustable cantilever that wedged into and out of a watertight socket. Burp and burple free.

Why was the American toilet so thin and iffy? This shouldn't be so, as the first full-fledged "water closets" were invented and then placed in use in America, not in Germany, not England-- and certainly not in France; the veritable premier was installed in 1851, in President Millard Fillmore's White House, and the "*rest*"room centerpieces we made immediately after that were luxurious enough to be installed in Buckingham Palace and in the privies of Versailles and Sanssouci. *We* made the toilets for continental royalty. America! *We* brought the outhouse in-house. But now? My god: Even the flange screws and screwcaps on my German toilet were more attractively designed and more reassuringly sturdy. No need to ever worry about its collapsation through the floor, and me endup in the cellar with a flange unintentionally serving as suppository. Even the toilet paper dispenser in Deutschland put my crummy American wall roller to shame, as it released the paper with an ingenious L-shaped hook, capped by an automatic paper cutter. Well, to endure a jalopy of a toilet seemed now to me to disrespect *oneself,* right at the fulcrum of civilization. Just American perfunction.

American Denial.
American Devolution.
Shambles.

Skyscrapers over shacks.

No, it wasn't so perverse of me then to think about toilets. Actually, I thought too about American radiators, invented here in the U.S. for the world in 1874, but then alas to become, eventually, the world's worst steam-asizzle clangers. Our radiators too often sound out like Santa's elves puckishly clanking out metal *chatchkies* for all the children of the world. Fateful coincidence, my house in Berkeley was built in the same year as my house in the Black Forest-- 1950. The Berkeley radiators are burly; as I say, they hiss and send up corrugations and isobars of hot warped air, as in a demonic funhouse. I sometimes expect Beelzebub himself to be sitting atop its lumpy ridges crosslegged and grinning with devil savvy. The controlling knob of my Berkeley radiator is loose and feckless. Spin it-- it doesn't matter. But the *Schwarzwald* radiators, also fifty-five years old, are streamlined and controllable; under rich marmor-stone shelves their piping can still manage to resemble a Rolls Royce grill. No visible steam stream, as from a locomotive engine: *I think I can/ I think I can/ I think I can.* But enough: I'll stick now with the more essential latrine, as you seldom hear anyone declare, "I've got to go to the radiator."

Note: And it's not just German toilets. The French too have caught up and surpassed America-- the *French*!?-- for as late as the early 'eighties many Frenchmen (and poor tourists) were compelled to squat, or stand, on what they called "the Turkish toilet", metal placements soldered to the floor and shaped like shoe heels and soles, to each side of-- there is no other way to say this-- a *hole*. The human being as shoed horse. Man Toiletless. But now the once beholed French, a nation happily (seemingly) attached to "The Franco-French Solution" in all things, have, toiletwise, gone and eclipsed us too. Well, no total surprise: they did cleverly give the world the bidet.

In a way that we at the top don't usually conceive, globalization can be a backfiring deficit as well as benefit: Compared to all the world, it really illustrates for us how not-so-great we're doing. How we, the world's whirling economic dervishes, may be in danger of becoming stationary dervishes, while we believe we are yet awhirl. . . In the main however I have not forced my comparisons here to all-the-world, but to Europe-- and really to Germany and France, the two largest nations in the EU and therefore the nations most comparable to us in variety and in variety's dilemmas.

CHART ONE

THE GREAT AMERICA-EUROPE

WEALTH-POVERTY FACE-OFF

(also see Chapter Seven)

America Poverty   **Europe Wealth**

The Poverty of Poverty
The Poverty of Community
The Poverty of Perception
The Poverty of Longevity and Height and Health
The Poverty of Companionability (friendship)*

Europe Poverty   **America Wealth**

The Wealth of Wealth
The Wealth of Optimism (blind, cockeyed and real)
The Wealth of Energy (entrepreneurial)
The Wealth of Flexibility (creativity)**
The Wealth of The Kindly***

---

*   A friend in Europe, once becoming a friend, remains a friend.
           Trust: secrets of the soul can be shared.
**   Language slips and slides; rules change; new slang ever born,
           old slang slung away.
***   Stratagems of personal superiority less prevalent.

1

YOU DON'T HEAR *THE TRAMS*

Twice, not once, I was almost clobbered by one of the silent, barely sibilant, streetcars of Strasbourg. The original location of my being whalloped to the next world was downtown, near the famous *Cathedral de Strasbourg*-- the most intricate non-Gaul Gothic (non-Notre Dame gothic) structure I have ever seen. The second time that I and a Strasbourg streetcar nearly butted heads was along the sycamore-threaded boulevard that leads to the shimmery wide-winged headquarters of the new European parliament and just across the Rhine from our home in Germany. As there are no borders within the new European community (well, trade-and-travelwise anyway; otherwise, countries are still countries and borders are yet borders), passing over the Rhine into France is no different than looping over the Hudson on the George Washington bridge and landing in New Jersey-- except for the moderate differences between France and The Garden State. At any rate, crossing *La Rue de la Forêt Noire*, preoccupied by a grapple with the French that my recent learning of German was supplanting into a garbled Deutsche-Franceusisch *("Monsieur, pardon, aber voh ist la mitte von diese ville?")* I heard screaming, a serious, urgent yawp, and as a good well-inured American I paid no attention, until an overmastering forearm swept me off the streetcar tracks, the owner of the arm regarding me with the contemptuous sympathy one reserves for the brain damaged or aboriginals just in from the outback. And this latter had its truth: I am from the boonies: Baltimore, then DC, then Pittsburgh, then New York, then LA, then (and now) Berkeley. The center of the world, the USA, alas aka The Outback (In Europe, the "*pampa*") as, amazingly, we really don't know what's going on. For example, my halftime home, the Bay Area: Where the Muni, San Francisco streetcars, clatter and shimmy on their steel rims, the doors cackle rather duckishly-- or not unlike our toilets-- the brakes are great nails on great slate blackboards (and no, I am not talking about the fabled cable cars-- which are *supposed* to be clangy-noisy, for tourist charm). It is of course out of the realm of possibility for a tourist to be clobbered by a streetcar in America unless he is deaf or drunk-- or already moribund on the tracks-- because one is attuned to the drum and cymbal of American public transport: Grade B stuff. Category C scrap. A Strasbourger, or even a Viennese, or even a noise-aware Berliner could never be done in by the Fisherman's Wharf Line, as I just missed being-- twice by a quiet whisk-- by the Strasbourg tram. And those European cars, with their impressively bevelled jetstream anteater snouts, are not just smooth as murmurs; they are longer conveyances, sometimes six linked lengthy carriages, stretching a full city block: twice the reach then of the most capacious klankery American streetcar-- and with the conductor reposited inside his or her own glass-enclosed cabin (a jewel in a showcase?) and a recording announcing each stop: "*Nexta halt—Alexander-platz.*" Then, at Berlin's *Alexanderplatz*, or at Zurich's *Hauptbahnhof*, or at Munich's *Leopoldstrasse*, as at just about every "halt", a computerized ticket machine; a computerized sign system indicating time and destination of each next tram; a computerized traffic light system that stops motor cars, to allow this city train-tram the speedy right-of-way. Then, once outside city limits, these carriages muscle-up and zip along at about ninety miles per hour. And no, these really are not trains. Not even subways. Just plain local transport (An envious LA friend, visiting me, marvelling at the many attractive, fashionably-dressed patrons, dubbed these "Hooterville Trolleys". Reason obvious). But I had read in *The San Francisco Chronicle* when the city announced its Muni purchase of modern rail conveyances, from ABB, a nifty manufacturer based I believe in Switzlerland, that these were to be the best money could buy, top-of-the-line. Well, likely it was top-of-the-*affordable*-line ("Hey, Ludwig, another order here for the chickensheisse American shoddies!"), which might work out to bottom-of-the-line for Europe, which *makes its own trams*-- even if Europe is not richer than us (Except, it is. Europe *is* richer than us, folks. Few skyscrapers, fewer shacks). Perhaps these bargain-basement San Francisco trolley purchases were also reserved for Tirana, Albania? Or Tbilisi, Georgia? Or terror-torn Kashmir? Or Chechnya? Well, why fret? It doesn't matter: We Americans commute by public transport one-eighth as frequently as Europeans do: Europe-- half its commuters (even considering their, unheard of here, walking and bicycling commuters-- on nice bike lanes); America-- less than one-tenth, and specific figures of population use of mass transit are even more dramatic:

Stockholm---------- 70%
Berlin---------------- 40%
Helsinki------------- 55%
USA------------------ 2%

Translation: USA-- one in *fifty*, folks. One American in fifty going shopping or to work boards a, "Yuch", bus or trolley or subway car (I know: So at least there are seats!). Now this super-shunning of public transport transpires because, for one thing, Americans live in a big, beautiful, drive-beckoning land, a drive-demanding land, and we have a character to match that expanse. But there are other reasons we don't Do The Tram: Like our gasoline is cheap. What!? What did that nut say? Yes, you read me: Our auto fuel is priced-to-go. Even as it has recently risen to $2.20 per gallon regular at the pump. Well, peanuts compared to what those dumb sucker-dupe Europeans tolerate. The average price per gallon of regular is over $5 in England, France and Germany. Of course our American-refined gasoline is of lower quality, lower octane-- You didn't know that one, did you? Well, business is business -- cost and revenue: you want cheap cost gas you get that crumbum gas, along with your crumbum trolleycars. Your neighborhood fuel-distillery is not the Department of Welfare and Social Services. No kindly social workers at Gulf and Chevron and Enco-- not that I've heard tell. So now you hear that chronic ping of your guzzling SUV-- which they are about to ban from the streets of urban France-- (or your Mustang or Grand Prix) with enlightened ears, eh Charlie. Angry chumpsville ears. So now you'll demand higher quality gas, Euro-quality gas, hang the Euro-quality-price. No you wont. Of course you wont. Damned if you're going to ride to work in a TROLLEY-- even in Hurricane Zeno with golfball hailstones popping your windshield and your defogger not up to it. Although if you did go Public (Hey, only now and then), you might work up some moderate interest in influencing your mayor and your city council to-- *purchase better, unklanky, trolleys*. Pleasant Grade A paraphernalia. You should move on that, you know, because fuel prices will be heading higher and higher anyway, as the less-developed world-- China, India, Singapore-- dramatically ups its own fuel importation, as that world becomes more developed. Supply and demand really should be called demand and supply. Hasn't anyone ever thought of adjusting that in the textbooks!? ("Supply-side economics" is for super-rich guys, CEOs, and tenured conservatives at the Hoover Institute). But whoah-- back to trams. There are other reasons why we don't have sleek sluicers with aerodynamic arrow snouts. Like the, you know, *profit* reason? In the U.S. what we do is we focus solely on profitability-per-rail-construction-mile, or cost-recovery from the fare box; whereas in Europe, where light rail is seen as a public good, private (fare box) profit isn't the shining Excalibur. Sure, profit is there, it's considered, and many in Europe complain that it should be there with greater weight, to compete with profit-obsessed, growth-rate crazy America; but social profit across the Atlantic still does win out. Government may have to dig down deep for social profit, but part of that social profit is the pleasant windfall that you get fashionable ladies on the trams reading *Elle*, so unsnooty as to leave their Mercedeses at home. Sometimes. That's a nice, unembarrassed perk of living too. The tram as the Excalibur. Public Good gives private, not a whipping, but a run for its private money.

No, on second thought, a whipping.

So it really is rueful in retrospect, as with the aforementioned toilets (and radiators), that the first streetcars were made, not in Europe but here in America, in the nineteenth century. "The Detroit Edison", one Charles J. van Depoele, a Belgian immigrant, created the mechanized urban carriage on tracks. The Detroit Edison had come here to benefit from the innovating American climate, which he did not find under the clouds of old diamond-cutting Brussels: van Depoele could not have-- in what really *was* "old Europe" then-- self-made himself into "The Brussels Edison". Too many rules and regulations. An entire trolley system was soon after developed here in America (and not yet in Europe) by Frank Julian Sprague, an Annapolis graduate, who actually did work with the real Edison-- *and* with The Detroit Edison. Obsessive American workhound tinkerers hooking up. Again and again we *were* top-of-the-line here.

But now: well, it's a different story now. What we desperately need today in America are social benefit Edisons. Community-oriented minds, with clout. Europe has these, as their societies lean in that direction. Europe has good public amenities. But, here's the rub: Europe knows this requires taxes. Taxes: *Americans simply don't pay very high taxes.* As one economist puts it, we "starve the beast"-- the "beast" being the social wellbeing slice of the government pie, the "mommy"-stuff in bills and legislation that pass far more easily when they are American "poppies": anti-social payloads, hardware like bunker-buster bombs (See Tables 1, 2). Percentagewise we Americans are the least taxpaying citizens in the developed world. Least taxes, largest economy. Pretty slick accomplishment. Pretty bizarre accomplish-ment.

Except, you get what you pay for.

Or, what you don't pay for.

And it's not just public transportation and radiators and toilets. It's plenty.

Example: At one time America led in The Mother-of-All-Machines: Machine tools. Those metal pressers and precision parts produced for industries from cars to trains to planes to computers. Germany these days has the top ten companies in such basic sine qua non firms, prime-mover firms-- an over ten billion dollar business. America doesn't boast one top company in machine tools. When you give up on The Good Stuff for society at large, all else follows downward.

Now we don't even *make* The Good Stuff *for* the Good Stuff.

Example: By the mid-eighties France had the Minitel-- an early Web, e-mail and Google type black-box contraption installed for a pittance in apartments and homes. State subsidy supported Minitel purchases. Nothing major hi-tech, mind you, but still, *France!?*-- those recalcitrant-backward fops and fancydan boulevardiers? *Them!?* Ninety-nine percent of Americans might have identified the Internet back then in the mid-eighties as a net interns used to play tennis.

Sadly, the jokes going around Europe these days are American put-downs, not Polish:

How many Americans does it take to figure out they are behind?

Answer: What's the population of America?

Yes-- the constant theme of this book-- we Americans believe, and continue to believe despite the evidence, that-- Hallelujah!-- we are the most advanced, richest, happiest, most fortunate nation. Envied by the world. Even by Europeans.

You ask anybody.

In America, that is.

Well, almost anybody, not residing on the coasts. Northern coasts, that is. Otherwise, *80 percent* of Americans know about Europe, says Gallup, "little or nothing".

Nobody in Europe-- nobody!-- walks around overcompensating by wearing his nation's flag stickpin on his lapel, like a sixth grader or a Cub Scout on Independence Day. Probably nobody even down in Zimbabwe wears a plastic Zimbabwe flag-- and they *have* reasons to overcompensate.

So folks, could we just give Old Glory a break from the ridiculous which negates the sublime? This America-The-Most malarkey is just not true. I swear it. It was once true. Then somewhat true. Then not true. Germany, "*le coeur de l'Europe*" (Madame de Stael) is more admired. Germany, which has recently been labeled "The Sick Man of Europe", as it has dug deeply into its pockets to absorb its long-sovietted East. Germany, which has throughout history been vilified as barbaric and cold and dull. The Russians called the reserved Germans "*Niemets*"-- the people who do not speak; Stendahl commented, foreordaining the comedians' put-down of Philadelphia, "*Il me semble que l'on fait plus de plaisanteries in Paris pendant une seule soiree que dans toute l'Allemagne en un mois.*" But those Deutsch grimsbies are now more admired than we the mobile-faced chattery nice guys. And the French, always envied for their "civilized" way of life, have always been, for their "civilized" way of life, despised. But now we have got even the French contempt-topped. Would any European but an exhibitionist showoff purchase a Cadillac? Are you kidding? Maybe a wiseguy hobbyist mechanic in Wolfsburg would import one. Maybe the kind of Eurodude who would prance around with an ocelot on his leash would buy himself a pink Cadillac, or even a white one-- as he sports a plastic Euroflag on his lapel. That's about it (Nobody in Europe even recognizes what an EU flag looks like). Surveys have shown a very troubling fact for over a decade now. Recent Pew polls (sure, always an amusing descriptive moniker for a poll) have revealed the attractiveness of the U.S. to have dropped by *thirty* points in European countries.

This The Greatest routine that we do and we do to death, it's The Doctrine of the Twofold Truth, isn't it? You believe as you don't believe; you even have to not-believe in a corner of your mind to preserve some anchoring semblance of reason that-- ah, paradox-- again allows you to Believe:

CHART TWO
WHO WANTS TO LIVE IN AMERICA?

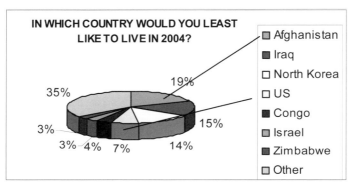

Source: The Economist Poll -1/04

CHART THREE

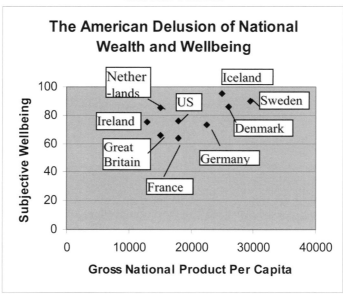

Source: Ronald Inglehart: *Modernization and Postmodernization*

Now from Chart Three we may draw one of two conclusions: One: we Americans deny so magnificently, so boldface majestically, we actually see in the mirror a happy, satisfied, well-off, admired people.[*] Being an optimistic nation, we would be committing an act tantamount to high treason if we did not behold a sunny present, a shining future (In these days of the paranoid Patriot Act and its hallucinatory enactors, such sedition well might land us "disappeared"). Isn't Optimism why we created ourselves?-- for Ronald Reagan's City-on-the-Hill. I have in fact seen quite a few towns perched up yonder on hills in Germany and France; never such magic vista in America, however; a regimented suburb on a hill perhaps. Especially after 9/11 we proclaim WE loudly. More than ever. Sociologists have taken to calling this yodeling the "halo effect": The What, *Me* Worry? physiognomy of George W. Bush, that give-em-a-wink-smirk-boy-man MO. But the chart above, although it indicates total national wealth divided by population, does not show wealth *distribution*. If it did, we would be down-rated beneath Ireland. No, beneath the whole crowd. So it would be an error to conclude that money buys much happiness: the homily that money doesn't procure (or secure) satisfaction is true, even though it be wielded by the well-off, like that Marxist opiate, religion. Even money's prospect doesn't warrant you a bundle in the peace-of-mind department. Or even money's delusion that you have it when you don't. . .

But then, another survey (See Chart Four) shows that Americans are not after all happiness-wealth deluded. We do after all see it like it is, and therein we came out undeludedly (and Pyrrhicly intelligently?) down there with Bulgaria. Sociology is some curious social science-- like all social sciences.

Okay, before the mind goes pingponging, it is probably best to decide from these two contradicting charts that both are correct, as the factors involved are so varied for each nation, each culture:

---

[*] Actually, another study showed that 86% of the French claimed that they were happy. But for certain reasons that study-- or all studies in this area on France-- may be skewed: 1. The French consume alcohol on average 5 liters per person per year. 2. The French claim to be at the top of the sexual activity league: 20% report affairs on a regular basis, and nearly one half of all French pensioners swear to sexual activity, 17.5 % over sixties enjoying sex at least once per week.

CHART FOUR

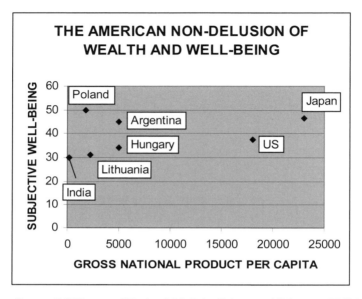

Source: Ed Diener and Eunkook M. Suh: *Culture and Subjective Well-Being*

You've got "individualism", whatever that holy-unholy amalgam is; you've got "communitarianism", whatever that less self-embracing ideal is; you've got individualistic communitarianism and communitarian individualism; you've got liars; you've got deluders and deludees; you have, in America, the highest percentage of people *in the world* who attempt to contact their dead, which is probably not a sign of terrific happiness or contentment on this plain of existence (never mind intelligence); you've got people afraid of the interviewer wielding his/her officialish clipboard; you have expectations of wealth and happiness, which may be worth more in a society which at a particular time has neither much wealth nor happiness; and you have fears of wealth-loss and depression's descent like a black curtain in a society which is yet enjoying prosperity and pleasure-- but at one time did not enjoy it. And, finally, you have cultures which just like to kvetch. Even competitively. And cultures which enjoy denying and condemn kvetching competitively. What you have is a Rubik's Cube of happiness-- which is why the "folks" who study these attitudes (for a living!) call them by the acronym SWB.

Subjective Well-Being.

True, in America we still do have the heaviest hitter GDP. Of the entire euro area it was only sixty percent of America's in 2001 (France and Germany together, forty percent). But we are nowhere near the peak in gross product per capita-- that is, if you weight down the average, semi-canceling the imbalance caused by our super-duper rich like Bill Gates, the Ellisons and Murdochs and Buffetts and a few thousand others profiled in *Business Week* and *Forbes*. And true we have the most entrepreneurs. (See Chart Five and Comment, for the monkey-wrench there). But Big China in two to three decades may likely top even our GDP. And although it may constitute bragging rights to unfurl the banner of our winning the entrepreneurial software patent olympics, that victory can also be seen as a shackling in the land-of-the-free, a sign of Jealous Guarding, a restraint of competition: The EU does not even issue software patents. By the way, many of our patents are to Europeans schooled here (and Indians), who may eventually develop an active homesickness listening to the whassups and the guns of Silicon San Jose, or just particularly craving Home.

From automobiles to cellphones to aircraft, America has fallen behind its European competitors in technological development, and in the smooth sophistication of production technique. With all too growing passivity, or indifference, we seem to readily accept the fragile-klunk inferiority of our Chevvies and Fords as god-given, or as a metaphysical phenomenon as primary as The Big Bang, as if we can do no better, and don't much care to. I would have to conduct a pretty intensive search to find a GM or Ford product parked in any carport in my neighborhood; but then again I do live in The Free Zone of Berkeley, and Detroit sales do seem to pass the breakeven point in the mountain and central zones-- and perhaps east of the coastal range. As I've said, you would however be hard-pressed to lay your eyes on an American import in Europe, except for the isolated hippish pickup-- a trophy of some perverse Euro-cracker-redneck (and not unusually with a Germanesque bumper-sticker on the "tasteful" order of something like *Women Bin Fuckists*). Our export figure here (i.e., there) is probably down in the cellar at .001 percent. American automakers' share *of our own North American market* has been descending for decades, from eighty percent in the seventies to sixty percent now, as Europe's share-- and Asia's-- has of course risen. And you need not drive a handleably challenged Cadillac or

Lincoln-- Chrysler now owning-up to being German-owned-- after operating a Mercedes or BMW (although admittedly our luxury cars are less techno-challenged than they once were, and the German ones-- being "over-engineered"-- are a little more[*]) to experience our American failings first-hand. Just pick up your "handy", what Europeans call a cellphone (believing we call it that too). Recently Nokia owned thirty-nine percent of the world mobile phone market,[**] more than double Motorola's, and this success is despite Nokia's high Finnish corporate taxation rate. Could it be the reason for that Finnish triumph was that Nokia made a better "handy"? And Boeing's commercial sales have now fallen behind Europe's Airbus; Boeing survives as a formidable megalith from our Defense Department support-- military aircraft as American welfare to its corporations. By the way, U.S. industrial productivity in terms of output per worker is now lower than in Germany, Belgium, Holland-- and even France; and this sad fact is not because American labor is lazy or indifferent or dumber. It is a consequence of Europeans viewing corporations not merely as profit machines from which every last drop of value must be extracted in the immediate present for stockholders, but as-- you should excuse the expression-- organisms, alive with human relationships, thriving to serve the public as much as serving those corporations. In Europe, ploughed-back earnings are far greater in commerce and industry, and this mercantile investment ultimately makes for a highly skilled workforce-- motivated too. Although U.S. Department of Labor statistics belie the truth, unemployment tends to be lower in Europe in general than in the US. Our "numbers" consistently spin away this truism, as we only count those unemployed who are registered with the Department of Employment Security, and whom our shallow pockets unregister for com-pensation after a brief six months-- compared in various "mollycoddling" European nations to *years*. And our-- "unemployed"-- prison dwellers dwarf Europe's. And then it is trumpeted in our media that our six percent unemployment rate is *lower* than Europe's-- which is of late ('91-'93 recession) nearly ten... But honestly reported.

Our rate isn't lower. There is a concept called, for want of a better concept, "disguised unemployment"-- or for want of a phrase even that apt,

---

[*] Porsche and VW finished 35th. and 36th of 37 brands ranked in a 2003 J.D. Power survey of vehicle dependability. Hummer was 37.

[**] Cut into in the last year, however, by Asia's SONY and Samsung, and Sweden's Ericsson.

"labor underutilization"; or, for cynical positivism, "early retirement" (at *twenty-five?!*); or for super cynical American optimism, "consultant work"; or, for reality: You know, like, "Sir, you want the McBurger or the McFish?" (It has occured to me-- at offbeat moments-- that with our unemployment rates deceptively low, misleadingly low, it is easier for the The American Religioso to cavalierly attack abortion rights and the morning-after-pill-- available in Europe-- not to mention their condom-condemnations: Population swelling becomes less a crucial issue, an economic issue, a moral issue, when you believe "full employment" means "everyone" is actually employed).

There ought to be a law against some of our superspin-stats-of-self-congrat: for example, that fact that we are the most entrepreneured-up of the advanced nations: Partially yes, that is our energy thrumming, our work-hard-think-up-things attitude, our un-mollycoddling econ-religion, if you will (and oughtn't sink-or-swim be swim-or-sink?); but partially these numerous American undertakings, as praiseworthy as many may be, are due to the compulsion to do *something*, when there are no jobs and no more unemployment compensation in the works. Fear of the poorhouse (street or squat or prison) may create quite the entrepreneurial motive too-- not unincluding the criminal; sometimes these two being indistinguishable. Case in point: Improverished Uganda has a much higher entrepreneurial rate than the US. *Uganda*, you heard me right. And many other Third World nations. Coming at our national silhouette from the other side, the perspective starts to take on a shape that harks us back to the way historians once referred to nineteenth century immigration to "wide-open" America as pull-- our attraction (gold-paved streets)-- rather than to its equal and opposite push: the potato famine, dust streets, pogroms. The narrow closed and ugly count as well. The detritus equals the attribute. That's elementary Newtonian.

That American "push" entrepreneurialism: Because my wife and I live half-American, half-German, we need a car in both places, a car that will have to lay fallow six months each year. In Karlsruhe we purchased a small new inexpensive Volkswagen Lupo (unavailable in America), easily extracting from the Croatian immigrant salesman the promise that we might store our auto at the dealership during our away months. This has worked out well. But both my wife and I fear American dealers, their snappy-smooth-sincerity and used slicker-suit eagerness (or "lowkey"-slick unslicker suitedness-- passive as a psychiatrist), their unctuous, grabby smiles, their Old Glories glistening on their lapels as if they are about to run for congress in a heavily Republican district. Their, *"We overordered: Last year's inventory must Go!"* Their dentist-whitened teeth. Their shoes (*tassels?*). My wife and I both feared that the American Ford dealer, or even an American Hyundai dealer, would find some sharpie way while we were vulnerably off in Germany to expropriate our ownership from us, some loophole, some righteous "entrepreneurship" in "doggie-dog" necessity. Jungle justification: a guy's gotta do, in this econ-wild, what a guy's gotta do. Conscience trimming-- even in Berkeley. Even if the sharpster is a churchgoer. So, in America, we honker down and rent a car. Hang the expense. Paranoia perhaps.[*] Hysteria maybe. But at least we sleep.

CHART FIVE

ENTREPRENEURS IN ADVANCED NATIONS

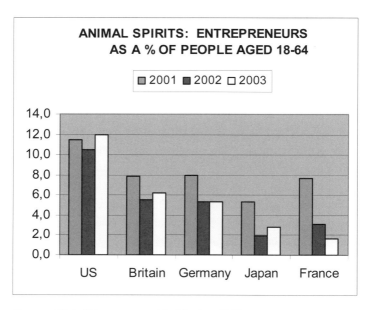

Source: Global Entrepreneurship Monitor 2003

---

[*] In contrast to the great pitcher Satchel Paige's aphorism, "Never look back, as somebody just might be gaining"-- I have seen, on CNN, the CEO of IBM pontificate that The key to Success in Business IS paranoia.

Actually, Europeans are rather startled when they visit here; they are awestricken by the paradox of our quality of life being so at odds with our accumulated wealth. Leaving aside our excusable history-gap-- the castles and Roman ruins and walled cities and cathedrals-- which is not our fault, and anyway we do have southwest native-American architecture, Europeans are amazed by our transitional, throwaway society: Firstoff, worstoff, those people, chins in palms, elbows on thighs, lolligagging (wasting) away on downtown stoops and curbs; then the castoff platoons bivouacking under bridges and viaducts, as if these are choice sites in Yellowstone. Did these Euro-tourists book Lufthansa by mistake to Karachi?

Europeans are even bemused at our Starbuckization of coffee, which should be a pleasure to idle and muse over in attractive surroundings-- as in Vienna, Paris, Berlin, Rome-- but which we pour into tooth-mush soap-tasting Styrofoam. Disposable, unpleasant, Get-da-job-done-no-wash-low-overhead Styrofoam. Drinking Starbucketed coffee is drinking an oxymoron, and whoever invented Styrofoam ought to be condemned to drink every beverage he drinks, always, out-of-STYROFOAM-- forever. Insert *that* rule into the Purgatory of a remake, Starbucketed, *Divine Comedy.* No waiters or waitresses in our American Starbuckization either. Right? Jiffysville. Hang there in assembly line at the counter. Conveyor perfunction as Perfection? Good ole QC: That's Quality Control, which, by the way, America invented too-- along with the QC acronym shorthand concept; and along with CBA: cost-benefit-analysis. Okay, QC: you *control* quality; you damp it down: you do not aim exactly to produce a "better" product, but an acceptable one, a widget (or coffee-delivery-system-- CDS-- that is tolerable: a cheaper bargain gizmajig that most people will use, or suffer but not suffer *too* much -- in excess of what most people will *not* use or not purchase; or reject, after use. Such becomes your New Improved, "fine-tuned" definition of Better. Ie, Imperfection is "Better", and real Better is suspect, and therefore it is Not Better, and maybe even stupid.[*] Tolerable tops pleasure: the earth is comfy, but it did not move. QC. The life and blood atomizing field of time and motion study (TMS) was also invented here in the U.S. In the thirties, by Frank and Lilian Gilbreth, who rearranged their last name to create-- hold

---

[*] Detroit has put on "hold" (or is that "H"?) the mass production of hybrid autos. Leave unQC to Honda or VW. And it is rather amazing that no corporate people in America refer to "BL", for Bottom Line. Or do they?

onto those reversed baseball caps!-- *Therbligs*, their "Pasteurized" unit of study: Fifty therbligs for a European cafe to deliver a cappuccino to a customer at their table; five therbligs for a Starbucks counter pickup? Therblig crunching as definite dollar enhancing. Nuff said? Sorry, but no: Then came in the U.S. inventory pricing methods-- LIFO, FIFO, NIFO, for Last in first out, first in first out, next in first out. Then came the brilliant industrial mathematicization worthy of E=MC2, by which I mean PU+D, which is pickup *and* delivery. Jesus have we ludicrously taken the fun out! Or ridiculously scientificized the commonplace. Europeans have not come up with *Plaisire* units (French), so far as I know, or a *genuss* measure (Germany). They just don't seem to crave such bloodless gauging. Yes, well Germany does have its Tchibo, and France their Columbo (not Peter Faulk, although they do enjoy him dubbed on television), but even these Euro-speed coffee oases use-- wouldncha-know?-- REAL CUPS. Flash: they're rewashable.

Then again there's that eensy matter of our, perish the word, poverty. Europeans are numbstruck and stupefied by our poor and decrepit and primitive, even backward-- here comes that awful military-industrialesquery -- infrastructure. Visitors from across the Atlantic just about slap their foreheads at our INFRASTRUCTURE-- or they grin with barely concealed *schadenfreude*. Our houses, not of stone, brick and concrete, but mostly of wood and stucco, meant to last perhaps two generations-- if we even think of "lasting" (In Baltimore, I grew up in the forties near the center of town, Druid Hill Park. "Droodlepark" in Balamorese. That ghetto-- for it was then a Jewish ghetto-- has by now Judeo-flown north to in some cases beyond the Pennsylvania state line, the good old Mason-Dixon, and they're getting pretty close to Three Mile Island. Thus, by suburbanization, the South is becoming the North); our houses' windows, usually, almost always, single-pained, unlike Europe's double; our primitive heating equipment (Oh those pathetic ducts!), unlike Europe's recent, and frequent, heating built goddamn right into houses' floors-- tile floors; even our light switches, those thin-cheesy-flimsy chippable, breakoffable, fillipers, compared to the cozy palm-sized pads today on European house walls, solid, less breakoffable, less ugly, like the, well, *Toilets*. Europeans are just dumbstruck by the prevalence of our substandard facilities, our disinclination towards beauty, the important aesthetics of life: Dresses, skirts, slacks, suits, crazy hair, bellies, masonry, cornices, wainscotting, boulevards, unornamented facades and entranceways, our enamelled plains of truckstops, our grim, boring quadrangularity, our "diners"-- even the off expressions that buff and paper over our faces. It is not the lowclass strivey (LS) that has Euro-women dressing up with colorful skirts and outfits even to go shopping, still embracing unabashedly the old feminine mystique; it is a desire to look beautiful, or attractive, a galvanizing force of all cultures, even the veiled Middle Eastern. While we unfathomably praise-up our "casual", and, well, sloppy, Come-as-you-are Greatness-- as unpretentious; which we do do with great pretention. Basically America is a land that just does not care how it looks, personally or architecturally; although, amazingly, "awesomely", it believes it looks-- personally and architecturally-- quite Great. And cares! To hark back to my toilet lead-in, I recollect my first foray into a cafe "bath"room in the fairly nowhere German city of Karlsruhe: the men's "bath"room's fixtures were shiney, brass, its floors a polished tile, its mirrors long and clean, its walls fresh-painted, its general feel not just comfortable but relaxing, clean-- homey. And my reaction: quite simply, Duh?-- where's the crap? Crud, I need crud. I wouldn't have been much surprised if there had been initialed designer guest towels hanging in that cafe "bath"room: Choose your own!-- and dainty toilet-top grammy Terricloth. You mean a public toilet doesn't have to be what in America has often become so awful it is a synonym for disgusting, an Archie Bunkerism, "a public *ter*-lit"? A redoubt so off-putting you, unhealthily, well, "hold it in", until you manage yourself to home. You mean in a cafe *Toilet* you could drop your Danish on the floor and still consider munching it?

Consider, I said. Consider. Hyperbole as lowperbole.

Our American "Greatness". Well, from pioneer times this country has always been prone to The Overlarge in speech, to the self-superlative. Not a bad urging, necessarily, all optimism and brightness, like governor Arnold Schwarzenegger's now patented, ubiquitous, "fabulous" ("De spider just clamped its pincers on my big testacles: *Fab*ulous!"). The most telling illustrative of our happy bluster is certainly America baptizing itself "America", and thus ingathering blithely, like a winner of all the chips at a gaming table, the honorific of the entire two continents of its hemisphere: A-*mer*-ica. A linguistic Monroe Doctrine. American Entitlement. In a less offensive, and more comic-parochial vein, I once heard one of those familiar barking child-man sportscasters refer to Joe Montana as, "The Greatest

Quarterback who ever played the game; almost as Great as The Greats--
Unitas, Staubach, Bradshaw."

Double Duh?

In Hollywood, when I was a screenwriter I once overheard a producer
comment, "This is Great. It's just not good. Let's change it and make it
great."

Also, once, with a wink: "Don't make that Great script too, you know,
'good'."

Equally as amazing, our adolescent, pervasive brandishings of certain
callowisms: "amazing", "awesome", "unbelievable", "incredible" and "take it
up a notch"-- for just about anything a "notch" above sheer nonentityhood.
Equally as "amazing": that so many Americans have visited Europe, seen the
sights of The Old World, snapped these gems on their Japanese and German
digital cameras, and certainly not any Kodaks-- Rochester-made-- as they
would have back in the fifties-- if we had gone to Europe back then-- and yet
we have failed to come away from our Europe-sightseeing with any sense,
by contrast, of America's jalopification. Europe is just Sights-- it does not
qualify for Real. The Real Deal. Except, that is, as a movie reel. Europe is
just a movie; and The Greatest, Us, We, are The Greatest because The
Greatest is The Greatest is The Greatest and cannot be anything but The
Greatest even if The Greatest really means, by code, it is second, or third,
rate, and all Quality Controlled to the gills. Europe as reality is either not
registered with us or it is squirreled away, repressed, the mental soil
shoveled over it, body, land, tram, toilet and casket. Or, and this is
frightening, it, Europe, is turned into a kind of contempt respository: *We* are
the muscular individualists, we Americans. We are rawboned, not fine-
boned fairies. Our flag is The Best, because, Why?-- because, uh, It *is*--
Didn't you HEAR me, Pierre!?-- our flag is The Best. *Why?!* Because, uh,
it's got stars'n'stripes, man, lots of 'em, and most other countries' flags are a
few lousy bars, tricolors'n'shit. We Americans, we play football and knock
heads. *Heads*, man. Okay, we knock helmets, like war, like *soldiers*'n'shit.
Like GIs. "Them" Europeans, they play *fuß*ball-- which sounds pussyish
anyway, what with that "fuß" crap, where they kick like goddamn pansies.
Their players aren't even Big; hell, they look pretty much like you and me,
like bookkeepers, and that's pathetic. We hire their *fuß*ball losers to kick our
football field goals. Some of those foreign losers can't even speak *English*
(of which, as a governor of Texas, not Dubya but a perfect precursor, once

declared: "If the English language was good enough for Jesus H. Christ then it's good enough for me!"). Those Euro-player-pansies, hell, they don't even get that many concussions. Europeans are fancydans, supercilious boulevardiers and beaux who know their wine and when to drink it, and have good high-assed postures and low cholesterol, and in the bargain they are, damn, only high class welfare mothers and dole dudes. Legalized fey unmuscular-- and Godless-- chiselers who speak a shitload of languages, secondhand languages (Can't they Get-it-Together!?), and they like talky-talk Art films (at least they act like they do, although they probably can't stand them "films" either and wont admit it.). Except, okay, those films often do have the real deal uncut pneumatic SEX where people go up and down and . . .

The reader will note that I have exaggerated. Definitely. How can I not admit the obvious? My intention here is certainly not to derogate my country (This is evident as the praise-theme of Chapter 7); my aim-- hidden so far-- is to help improve America through awareness of where America stands. So hyperbole does become the better part of lowperbole. But then again there is not *that* much exaggeration here. Because richness, wealth, really is not just the most swollen GDP-- or whatever they'll call it next decade (used to be GNP). Richness, wealth, is about participation in the full spread-out of public life; of public interest. Europe enjoys this by and large: in education, in industry, in health care, in news access, in public meetings, in public monetary support. They may gripe some over taxes, but their taxes do support a societal Europe. They're even genius enough to hold voting on *Sundays*, which certainly assists the turnout no little (What is with our *Tuesdays*!?). America, as one observer cleverly put it, "bowls alone". America's TV News is, as you know, violence and human interest. What intelligent value is served, I ask you, by those endless and somber inter-viewings of the families of victims? Various Victims. Endless Victims (like the woman whose ChowChow was heaved ten yards like a football by an irate driver whose car hers hit); all this until We become the victims of the victims of the victims. Did faux-empathetic-faced (and voiced) Diane Sawyer once, long ago, possess all the ripples of her cortical lobes? Perhaps she is happier the inauthentic way she is now. Our TV News, so solipsistically infected, tells us zilchsquat of the world. Watch the German news, the French, the British, you'll see that things are happening in Africa and Asia-- those continents haven't slipped into suspended animation, or off the spinning globe. We really have self-blindered ourselves. Walk the streets of the best neighborhoods in America and you'll see no one strolling outside. You know that-- you're probably right now inside your house. In America only the occasional oblivious mower is outside in the sun, or the insensate, lunatic leaf blower. You'd think every town had warnings posted: *Do Not Venture Out of Doors: Boston Strangler (Seattle Strangler; New York Strangler; Philadelphia Strangler)*. Walk a wealthy European street, not to mention an unwealthy one, and you will see them-- human beings!-- the French, the Germans, whoever, on their verandas and their balconies and their decks. Walking the avenues, quite healthily. Old Euro-people, caning their ways if need be, if even the eighty year-olds are not pumping away on bicycles. Paradoxically it looks like an old geezer society sometimes, of limping Walter Brennans; but that is because their octogenarians are Out There, not embedded with a roommate in a "home" with a few scalloped, gilt-edged photo remnants on their institutional dressers, as in our nation. People in Europe are talking outside, even in the opulent hillside lanes of Munich, the lakeside villas of Berlin. And I'm not even speaking here of the "warm" countries, Italy, Spain, Portugal, where you just know they are out in the streets-- enjoying dinner at ten PM. Apropos: I remember my mis-diagnosis when my wife and I received our first end-of-year report from a family in Düsseldorf on their annual family doings, from January until New Year's Eve (Sylvester, they call it, like the mischievous-hapless cat). "What arrogant maniacs," I commented to my wife. "What super-narcissistic delusions of grandeur to think *we* should care about the events of *their* twelve months." "Oh," my wife advised, "it's just European. Normal. We'll get many more annual reports. Friends tell their friends what has happened." And we did get more life-reports in the mail. I guess those people figured that we cared. And this is richness too. This is the antithesis of "bowling alone".

The unfortunate, and dangerous, undercoating of our delusions of grandeur is that they are inevitably held by, as they are caused by, the denying inadequate. Delusions of grandeur mean that You Are Not Grand. You are grandiose. And you are clinging hard to that false vision by your fingernails. Digging in too deep. In the economy of the psyche this can make you mean and angry. A guy in a corner staving off critique, or even contact, by flailing. Violent.

Even if he doesn't know it.

Especially if he doesn't know it.

THE YOUNG MODERNS
AND THEIR VERY DIFFERENT MALL

The Young Moderns wheel their babies and walk their children along the cobblestone streets of smalltown Ettlingen, and over the cobblestone bridges arching the river Alb, which runs its slow gait to the Rhine. Wheeling, walking, The Young Moderns, to the cafes along the river of this town that is now a suburb of Karlsruhe, to the stores occupying the first floors of the medieval and Renaissance houses with their slanted half-timber beams. The old castle spreads its grounds and towers and dome before them, as they wheel and walk about the central fountain. It is a pleasure to walk alongside The Young Moderns as you rewalk history.

The Young Moderns wheel their babies and walk their children along the plastified, reinforced concrete and metallified paint jobs of Hilltop Mall, outside Berkeley, California. They stop, The Young Moderns, for paper cup coffee-- To Go-- as they shop the stores lined along the plastic corridor smelling of generic perfume and peanuts. It is an annoying, enervating pain to be escorted by the dismal, moribund energy of The Young Moderns of the Mall.

Even to just buy dental floss is agreeable in a medieval town of slanted roof, of different slanting roofs, the corollary, the sister spot of which across the Atlantic is a sharp quadrangle. Walking the Medieval Mall you also tend to want to dress better. Perhaps not in cloak or cowl, but at least in, you know, *long pants*!

To quote from Robert Putnam's *Bowling Alone*: "Mall culture is not about overcoming isolation and connecting with others, but about privately surfing from store to store-- in the presence of others, but not in their company."

In that clenched economy of the "average" American psyche I fear there is coming to develop a warren where each man and woman wearing Old Glory on his or her lapel or flying Old Glory from their house flagpole, or hugging it in their hearts, harbors some fancy, not of patriotism quite, but of tying some "not-normal" adversary to his pickup's rear bumper, some fellow-citizen chiseler "beneath him", who is dragging the country down; they'll drag that abominable chiseler off, who is dragging the country down.

Just an aggressive setting in our individualist psyches. We wont act on it. Not all of us. Not much.

Anyway, we sublimate it. We damp The Thing down down down.

It only pops up now and then.

And then, maybe, we vote for politicians who trigger it. Pious syrup-smarties.

At institutions of higher learning, like Bob Jones University.

They trigger it, and pander to it, by hucksterizing how Good and Great and The Best we are.

And how Democratic.

Now it's no little discomfitting to punch holes in American democracy-- it's guiltifying; especially when I am Swiss-cheesing us vis-a-vis the French, who swerve to relishing authoritarianism (De Gaulle, Napoleon), and the Germans, who can gravitate comradely, doggedly, to obedience-- when they don't, obediently, comradely, doggedly, watch themselves. Truth's nature is unsettling, even in the service of setting things straight, wrestling with our Grand American Delusion. Once you have denied The Truth, all actions that you take must be flawed, and all your grand opinions.

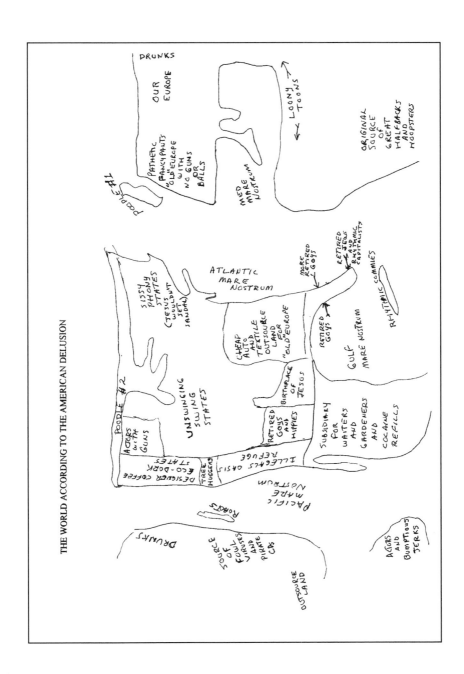

THE WORLD ACCORDING TO THE AMERICAN DELUSION

THE WORLD ACCORDING TO „OLD" EUROPE

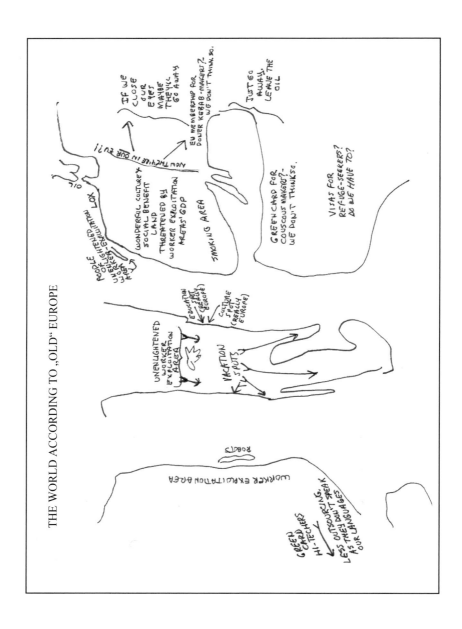

2

YOU CAN GET THERE FROM HERE; BUT IT WON'T BE ANY PICNIC

We had landed at Frankfurt. In the distance, the bunched-up skyscrapers of "Der Big Apple East", Europe's only architecturally American city-- downtown only of course-- rebuilt after the war with supertowers and office building spires, and what Germans therefore but absurdly also call "Bagdad am Main", after New York's "Baghdad on Hudson" (a label that has now become ironically true for the rather ugly reasons of delapidation). From the Frankfurt "flughafen" we had to travel south one hundred miles to Karlsruhe, where my wife teaches at the university.

Problem?

No problem: The frequent-arriving train stops across the airport entry lane from the sliding airport doors. Thirty yards, tops. One hour to the Karlsruhe Hauptbahnhof, the main train station. Coincidentally, Karlsruhe is Germany's twenty-second largest city, while my birthplace and growing-up metropolis of Baltimore is America's twenty-second largest-- although it was a proud eighth when I was Bar Mitzvah; yet while Karlsruhe's *Hauptbahnhof* is a soaring, vaulting, spreading, dynamic, people-bustling, store-loaded Grand Central, Baltimore's Penn Station remains today as it always was: a shabby thin closet of a depot. Karlsruhe's *Hauptbahnhof* announces Come on in, look around, dodge humans, have fun; Baltimore's Penn says hic town, Gateway to Palookaville, next stop Appalachia-- Why am I here?

By the way, it is even less than a one hour commute to the Karlsruhe station from the Frankfurt airport if one is fortunate enough to board the ICE, the InterCity Express, which may race at upwards of one hundred sixty miles per hour. Yes, they employ English names, although there is not one officially English-speaking nation on the continent. Except England, which is Europe tectonically speaking, but otherwise not, and which interestingly does not have the ICE-- and thus our colinguistic British Railways has the worst train service in the developed world. Outside, of course, of our USA with our average train speed of seventy miles per hour. And, the French supertrain, the TGV (*Très Grande Vitesse*: Very Great Speed) operates at 180 mph, at a profit (unlike AMTRAK) and is capable of an astonishing-- to us-- 320 kph-- if the passengers can handle it. The TGV has now been extended to Belgium, Germany, Switzerland and Italy, and to some small stations even-- one thousand in all-- in contrast to AMTRAK's meagre network. And Germany has recently built an even faster levitrain (top speed 360 kph) for the Chinese, from Shanghai eventually to Beijing. But all is not Shangrila in Shanghai: to catch a gander of the shuddery face of Germany's Chancellor Gerhard Schroeder as he "celebrated" its inauguration, as a passenger, one might wonder at its repose potentiality. Also, they have yet to iron out the kink of its tracks sinking slowly into the spongy north Chinese terrain. I make fun of the German engineering projections, yes, but in fairness WE are not even in the super-train ballgame.

Now, getting back to my wife and myself: From the Karlsruhe Hauptbahnhof we hop the local area tram to our village of Bad Herrenalb in The Black Forest. The tram can speed at up to 75 mph, as fast as an American train. A scenic cruise then through hill, river and sheep-and-horsy dale, the Alb Valley. All in all a pleasant trip that would in America require the gymnast-tumble logistics of Chevy Chase in one of those disaster-happy National Lampoon sojourns.

Here a comparison; to the travel-difficulties in America: Picture a European coming to our country. Not the most difficult visualization, although we are hardly the world's leading tourist destination (France is)-- even counting in Hawaii. Now, said sightseer could come of course from anywhere, but for simple comparison purposes I'll make him German. The visitor wishes to stay in-- well, let me choose a spot of comparable, albeit different, beauty to our Black Forest German town; and of similar distance from the airport: Big Sur. These magnificent cliffs and hills and sea are approximately one hundred miles south of the San Francisco Airport. The European would land there at SFO, and he might choose to fly then south to the small Monterey Airport; but of course that would entail three to six hours of waiting for a flight-- and probably longer-- plus baggage handling and retrieval (American customs and conveyors take about quadruple European time), all for a flyoff that is half climb and half descent. This is the same reason my wife and I decided not to go by plane from Frankfurt to the small Black Forest airport at Baden-Baden ("Germany's Monte Carlo"). So, there is our European Chevy Chase at SFO, weary hand-to-stubbled-chin, disoriented and figuring: Train? Well, there is the proud new extension of BART (Bay Area Rapid Transit) to "The City". It is slow, because after all it is not a line-dedicated airport to urban center (as most European cities posess now; even Asian cities do); rather BART is a continuation of the many-stop-start-and-rattle subway. You may be clustered up with commuters if you hit rush hour, or really, any daytime hour. And, being a subway, it certainly has no "bath"rooms. Anyway, this Euro-man was not intending to head north to San Francisco. Had he been on the way north to, say, an oasis of comparable beauty, Stinson Beach, Bodega Bay, or, forget it, far Mendocino, the problems I'm about to relate here would be far worse. But, southward from San Francisco *there just is no BART* (Funding issues, getting the "rapid transit" the thirty miles down to San Jose: Alas, tax insufficiency again). There is however CalTrain. But that is, wouldn't you know, a slow-rocking commuter lumberer; and its final distination is *only* San Jose. Seventy more miles to go from there to Big Sur. Taxi? Van? Well, Euro-man here is not so rich as the mythical rich American. And anyway, he would find the taxi-- or van-- to be a rattletrap Checker or Chevvie or Ford, not a smooth Mercedes or Volvo as in Europe; or even in the Middle East (I mean, *even in The Middle East* the taxis are Mercedes! One of the world's great mysteries.). And what about that ominous *bulletproof glass* smackdab there between him and the driver? Is America Afghanistan? And what about the taxi's name?-- Not merely "taxi", as in Europe, but The Free Kashmir Taxi Company. Or the Free Tibet. Or Chechniya. Euro-man here may well be pro all of those worthy causes, but isn't it incumbent that he at least venture an assessment whether his driver is a fanatic suicide crackpot about to make a point. Okay then, Greyhound? Leave the driving to them-- that sounds good, a relaxing spacious bus. But how does he find the station? And if he does manage to locate it, let's fess up, America's Greyhound depots are not the clean bright-colored European terminals; they hardly provide a Norman Rockwell tableau howdy of this country. He'd be furtively eyeballing his fellow Greyhound travelers to detect whether these funksters with the passé ponytails-- who all look like Jeff Bridges fluxed to Kurt Russell melded to Nick Nolte-- were just released from San Quentin, he clutching his bags hard to his chest by now, a wimpy, cautious, fraught, Euronurd. And you know, at the risk of fairness (or unfairness) I must say I am not in the habit of badmouthing Germans as cowards: these are tough strong people. They can take it-- in spades (I sometimes imagine that you could noggin-clobber a German, sledge-hammer him--or, yes, her-- and they would just stare back at you, neither plussed nor nonplussed: 'Uh, is what you did just hitting me?' Call it insensitivity or call it strength, but, let's face it, despite their science and music genius, any peoples who would evolve to onomatopoeticising a precious gem not to the pretty "jewel" or "*bijou*", but to the adenoidal "schmuck"? Oh well.). Anyway, back to my point: I almost forgot, CalTrain *does not stop* at the San Francisco airport. Poor Euro-dude would have to make his exhausted way first northward to San Francisco, approximately twenty miles of the slow and clutter-clustered BART, with all his baggage. *Then* board the Greyhound that he wont relish boarding. Or the mopey CalTrain train he wont fancy riding. So: Limo? Airport bus? And only then would he proceed back again south-- a detour of forty miles!-- he dreaming by now of a distant, unachievable Monterey. Had my wife and I left the Frankfurt Airport at precisely the same moment that Euro-man had departed the San Francisco Airport, we'd have been home in Bad Herrenalb schmoozing* over weissbeers while Euro-man was just passing south again, parallel to the airport he had just arrived at from which he had had to go *north*. Zero sum vacation.

And now, *from* Monterey, to Big Sur? Once he did eventually figure out, that is, how to deploy himself there, to Monterey-- and we really still have not accomplished *that* task; and we are resourceful, innovative, entre-preneurial Americans! He really would be stuck. In old Monterey. Not that Monterey isn't ocean-picturesque and Steinbeck nostalgic, but this foreign tourist is scratching his head contemplating Henry Miller, ultimate nirvana Big Sur. Taxi *then*-- at Monterey? For thirty more miles? Spend those big new dollar-dwarfing euros. Brave the ominous bulletproof glass unheardof in Europe (well, okay, it has been *heard-of*) as there is no Euro Rifle Association promoting bizarrely sublimated, what?-- individualism? Self-reliance? Self-defense from other equally self-reliant self-defenders? Hey--

---

* Original (German) meaning: necking.

brainstorm!-- rent a car? But he will steam and phumpher over the inevitable automatic transmission in his American rental, as if it is more difficult than clutchwork-- which, firstoff, it actually is for a European, especially after an eleven hour flight to another world. Hitchhike?

Are you kidding? On European television he has seen enough dubbed Grade B American movies where the hitcher gets dissected by a guy whose neighbors say, "Well, Isaiah Johnson sure *seemed* like a nice normal fellow. A little reclusive and shy, maybe-- but very good with our children." And anyway, Europeans oft-times use the middle finger for hitching, not the thumb. And you know where *that* will get you.

Hey, it's all a part of the trip, we might tell Euro-man. Safari. Adventure.

And how come there are no bizarro nice-guy-neighbor dissector-cannibals operating in Europe anyway? (Okay, precious few). Weird oversight in perversion distribution?-- of the non-sex variety. Same reason, I suppose, there are no alien landings in Strasbourg or Nuremberg or even Minsk. Just in Carswell, New Mexico. Why *is* that?

Aliens aren't partial to Europeans?

Apparently we Americans do not like things too easy, on a silver platter. No, that's not it. You know my theme here: Actually it seems we delude ourselves into believing that with a now tin platter we still possess the silver platter. Or: If you already have a silver platter, though your silver platter be seriously tarnished, bent, broken, lost, you do not have to buy yourself a new silver platter; you merely delude yourself that eyesores are rugged charm, and inconvenience is, what?-- *earned* convenience. Things are more satisfying that way, when you have *worked* for them. Struggled with them and their poor operation and their shabby presentation. It's kind of godly-blessed this way. Loaves and fishes, and shredded sheets for clothes. You don't even realize *you* don't seem to like to use your tarnished silver platter. Or your tin. It's guest-repulsing. If your guests are not your fella'murkins.

Worthwhile note: In 1849, commuters from Bridgeport, Connecticut could reach New York City in one hour. The same time as today. Now that's before Abraham Lincoln's presidency! That's sixteen years before The Civil War.

Supplement: I'm acquainted with a scandalized German who told me that he attempted recently to endure a middle American train ride from Memphis to Lexington, Kentucky, a distance of approximately 350 miles. It took eight hours. He didn't think he'd ever get there. He couldn't believe that he was in America. Take a stab at how long a comparable expedition, a simple provincial ride, would have required in France or Germany. Even in middle France: say from obscure tangential Reims to nowheresville Nancy. Hint: Forget the second wine glass after lunch. So why can't we have AMTRAK go super? Or just an improved better? Well, we would need *money*: For electrified, high-speed tracks, and a huge investment in rolling stock. No, it isn't so much that we would *need* money. Rather, we would need to *spend* money. We *have* money. But we would need to spend our money *publicly*. Some of it. More than we do.

Repeat: We *have* money.

But, *we're America!*

3

A WONDERFUL DRIVE

Dazed and choiceless, Euro-man cannot stand around at the San Francisco airport forever in droop-induced vacillation. Yet that is precisely what he does. Darn. He finds himself stricken now by this eery, what?-- shmushiness; by what seems to be the pan-vaguery of these American faces: this strange pulpy, unfocused, what?-- diffidence. It's quite incredible really: they are human certainly, certainly-- Leave us not be cruel. But this zombie aspect seems out of a different genetic mode. Maybe not chimp and bonobo, but-- well, maybe chimp and bonobo. He hears people muttering "Dudn't" for "doesn't", and "wadn't" for "wasn't", as if it constitutes far too much exertion to poise mouth and lip and jaw and *enunciate*, as he was taught "Oxford English" in his German school (in Schlemeremmerhausen). Maybe these Americanly dudn'ted-up faces are a consequence of a failure at incision-- or vice-versa. Is this "offness", this so, well, *non-Europeanness*, from the meat they consume, and the vegetables? Or is it psyche stuff? Or is it catching, like a virus? Or is it just, simply, Otherness from his precious Europe?-- once evil, sure once Neanderthal, but no longer-- Europe. But he does want to give these Americans here the benefit of the doubt-- he is no mean-eyed Euro-trash radical. It's merely that-- Gott!-- there is just this allover-seeming peculiar non-caring aspect, this fleshy pod mien; these galoomphy-lumpy aimless feet-splayed walks, as if Americans are being drifted off into two directions at once, so different from the direct, speed-scissors Euro-gaits of Germans, of French, of even those *frondeur* Italianos. God it looks as if the Americans are not the World's Superpower but the world's lackadaisical superschlumps (He is not acquainted with the Mister Magoo cartoons; but had he been, Magoo is who would have sprung to mind: Veritable thousands of Misters and Misses Magoos!-- dum-dedumdum-dumming along). And, lord, these *stomachs*!-- they're *fußballs*!-- one oblivious-obese waddle waddling after another after another. Land Penguins. Unbelievable. He'd heard rumors, but he assumed these were lies-- anti-American libels. The American movie stars don't look like this. Brad Pitt could be a European-- if he didn't speak. But these *real* Americans just seem so undisciplined, and unstudious, and unserious, as if they have never gone to schools, never read, never thought, never *what?* Never *lived?* . . .

> Don'know hist'ry or biology. . .
> Don'know much about the French ah took.

Eventually Euro-man does manage to shake off the ugly ambiguities, and he rents a car. A corpulent Chevrolet, its inertia makes it lead like a bad dancer, by its overample rump; and the cheesy-shiney plastic interior is a bit nauseating, like that emetic chintzed-up whorehouse he once visited in Cairo. But, he muses, isn't the Chevrolet the same as the Opel, made in Europe, but nonetheless made by GM? Apparently no-- not. The Opel is GM, yes, but it is manufactured by "we Europeans". Well, he would sell his soul now for an Opel. Or a Volvo. Or a VW. Or even a Spanish SEAT. Or anything from his home hemisphere. Like the inexpensive two-seater Smart, the high-up sitting Swatchcar made by Daimler and non-existent in the states-- although it does topple over once in a blue moon. Or twice. He still cannot believe that Daimler, having taken over Chrysler, has devolved to Daimler-*Chrysler*. Boy was that some mistake. "We" sure lost some serious prestige on that baby, and at least we've finally dumped their hanger-on Mitsubishi-- distinguished as the only econ-failure of Japanese vehicles. Must have been *some* reason "we" took on Chrysler. In his rental he stays alert by counting the rhythmic plip-plops of the cheap American tires on the freeway's cheaply, slovenly-sectioned road. Don't these people care! He longs for the smooth, obsessively well-kept-up highways of the autobahn. Or even France's pay *autoroute* system, with their pretentious "*cedez le passage*" signs. Or Switzerland's great scenic roadways. Well, at least he can relax, kick back, due to the slow pace, incredibly slow, even in the far left lane. Incredible. Unthinkable. Strange, he finds it, that hurried, overworked Americans, who labor far more hours than any other employees in any other Western nation, Americans becoming like browsweating, browbeaten characters in some Dickens novel or Upton Sinclair (He has read these in German, or French, if not in English, unlike a plain American's not having read Stendhal or Flaubert or Mann-- in French or German or even in, you know, *English*), those Americans *employed*, that is, or underemployed at WalMart, McDonald's, KFC, or ex-programmers doing handyman work, these Yank-rushers always boasting, "I'm busy, I'm so busy-busy-busy", they drive so lumbery, edgy tortoises. Why is that? He suspects that the slow driving by European standards reflects, again, some deep-dragging torpor in America, some meta fear-sloth. Like their regarding cigarettes in the ward-off way Dracula winced at the silver cross (Hey, take a smoke!-- the constricting anxiety of total Non-Puff will probably kill you anyway). The American Puritan-- the totalitarian clinical-- where McDonald's is required to pay three million to a woman for her having spilled her own coffee on her own self, and then label their cups with anti-spill warnings-- *Hot! Hot! Do Not Spill!*-- and where the same poor firm is being sued for "making people fat".

CHART SIX
RISK AVERSION

Amount a Citizen will Accept
To Compensate for Dying Risk
On a Job*

Japan--10
U.S.------------------------------------7
Switzerland-------------------------6
Australia----------------------4
Britain----------------------3.8
Canada----------------------3.8
India-------------1

* As a multiple of average income

Source: *The Economist* 1/2/04

At any rate, Euro-man really does doubt that the slow driving here is only true judiciousness, pure caution; and it surely cannot be Maturity. In Germany, *mein Gott*, the life-riskers would be racing in that speed lane, Mercedes, Porsches, Jaguars, BMWs, at upwards past two hundred kilometers per hour, one hundred thirty mph. While smoking. While demandingly devil-may-care flush on the bumper of the sluggard ahead, which loafer is worm-crawling at one-eighty. Just to get to the sauna. To relax.

But even at this American caterpillar crawl here (of ninety kilometers per) he cannot relax: Oh this awful poor road upkeep, thumpety-thump--shocking! scandal!-- as if the San Francisco peninsula is Bangladesh. He keeps having to swerve to miss highway canyons, fizzures, riverbeds. He thinks, *America*!? Land of Franklin, Washington, Jefferson, Roosevelt, Kennedy, and Potholes! (He hasn't confronted the occasional moon-crater sinkhole, yet.). Are these roads here just inexpensive temp-tar and asphalt, and not, as in Europe, the thick macadam composition like airport landing strips? Oh these Americans, they must need new auto shocks every year. Don't they complain!? Does Midas Muffler lobby state legislatures against road repairs? Must be bigtime baksheesh-kickback going on. Well, Euro-man has read his Euro Consumer Reports and knows that, sure, our American tire standards are quite surprisingly low. Dangerously low (Michelin, of France, spends 4.2 percent of its sales on R&D-- and it is used by five of the eleven Formula One teams; Goodyear spends 2.9 on R&D. Michelin thus came to invent the radial, and its latest contribution is the PAX, a tire that can function even when punctured. While Goodyear sits around and creates tires that *can* puncture, that is when they function.). Indeed, how can Americans be so health conscious, no, health-haughty, no, health-preachy, about cigarettes and lactose and sugar and cholesterol, these people gobbling yoghurt every time they have to swallow an antibiotic ("the cultures! the good *cultures*!") and yet be so benighted about roads and tires? A health-conscious unhealthy, unsafe (unconscious?) people? Weirdos. Maybe it really is best to just hang it all and smoke, like we Europeans do-- Even no few Euro-doctors!-- and knock back espresso after cappucino after espresso like "we" do; and even pull the reins on too many skin-shedding showers, even at the risk of BO; even though "our" shower-heads are better, being mounted on long flexible cable, so we may dusche our backs' centerpoints, our thoraxes, if we are so inclined. Eurofellow will soon discover how much more nicely appointed, a million times more, European cafes are than our American ones, not to mention that staple American crossbreed, the coffee shoppe, like Monk's on *Seinfeld*, which is shown all over Euro-TV (bedubbed). Strange kitchenlike compound thing, that American dishpan mongrel, the coffee shoppe.

And Whoah!-- Hey!—Euro-man is ploughing past Silicon Valley, and what are all those *wires* paralleling the freeway, as if they are preparing to hang bulbs and stars from them and celebrate an early Christmas? Electric wires? Telephone? Cable? Lord, is America some frail and vulnerable animal with its spinal cord fluttering outside its protective spine? And this is the world headquarters of hi-tech, the "Peninsula", San Jose. Then he recollects something like what Thomas Friedman has written (*The Lexus and the Olive Tree*-- German version): You go bankrupt in Germany, and your great grandchildren are looked down on, shamed like lepers, while they are reaching out for you-- Hey, come here!-- in the Valley of the Shadow of Silicon.

VOLTAGE STILL POSES A THREAT IN NEW YORK

It's a map of hidden danger. Three weeks after Jodie Lane, 30, a doctoral student, was killed by an electrified metal plate while walking her dogs in the East Village section of Manhattan, Consolidated Edison, the local utility, has found more than *280* (my italics) service-box lids, manhole covers and lampposts around the five boroughs and West-chester County with stray current passing through them.

The amount of voltage in each, the utility said Thursday, ranged from the single digits-- which would produce a mild shock-- to 140 at a lamppost in Queens, which could be fatal. The electrified spots were discovered during emergency inspections prompted by Lane's death.

A map created by the New York Times shows that the so-called hot spots were found in fairly equal numbers around Manhattan, Queens, Brooklyn and the Bronx... Potentially deadly steel service-box lids, man-hole covers and lampposts existed for unknown lengths of time at some of the city's busiest intersections.

Visits...to lampposts...revealed that two of them... still had electrical current passing through them.

The utility spokesman said the utility had fixed problems at that location and said he was not sure why there might still be stray voltage.

In Europe the wires are all underground; well, most of them; so the scenery is not marred, patchy, stringy, even way out in the European boondocks, what they insist on calling the "pampa". All these wires strung and drooping make America look like such a temporary, sagged-out place. Catch-as-catch-can. Sure, life itself is temporary; but must these Americans magnify by pantomime that Truth?

GERMAN EFFICIENCY
THE VIEW FROM THE STREET

Recently our street in Berkeley was repaired: new pipes laid, drainage berms built up. It took two weeks. Two weeks of the inconvenience of parking one block away, schlepping groceries uphill. More recently our German town of Bad Herrenalb commenced work on our street, *Lindenweg*: repairing, new pipes, drainage. Having learned from my California experience I parked one block away. Two weeks Berkeley, I figured, will translate to a breezily efficient three days of being put out here in the muscle land of Siemens and Daimler.

"I do not think so," our neighbor Herr Zoller told me. A man who ought to know. He'd lived here thirty years. He owns the best local cafe. His daughter wrote a history of our village: eleventh century monastery, Charlemagne rumored to have come through (although the Charlemagne-Came-Through story is like America's George Washington Slept Here). "My guess," ventured wise man Herr Zoller, "the *Lindenweg* road repair will take nine months."

Nine months!?

But Berkeley was *two weeks!*

First of course the composition paving was torn up. In Berkeley some five shoveled worker "persons" (Berkeley is ever "correct") augmented the two CAT loadlifters. Well, here in Germany, I reckoned, we'll get *twenty* worker-men. Forget it, we got three-- and one lonely CAT. The Three seemed to show up by occasional motif, as if this job were a hobby, something they dropped by for on breaks from other jobs. *Die Drei Strasseketeers*, I named them. Unlike in America, German workers are not friendly: You look at them, The Three look away. No schmoozing with civilians. Why?-- I have no idea. *Strasseketeers* just perform their jobs.

They shut down our water pipes. In Berkeley, one half day. Here, two weeks. Ignoring my jaw-drop astonishment, they drafted into action these narrow garden-type hoses to redirect water from a neighboring street pipe. Our Black Forest lane of evergreens, apple trees, lilies, rose bushes, reamined and remained a dug up canyon. With serious-focused eyes a *Strasseketeer* maneuvered the CAT like a puma, bouncing and grinding accomplishedly, and thus *appearing* to be accomplishing Something, which to my eyes bore a striking resemblance to Nothing-- except maybe fun. . . But I did guess he was doing Something.

More fun?-- they went ribboning off our driveway as if it were a crime scene, so I could not violate the now forbidden driving here on this street of sorrows, my VW straddling perhaps the various canyons and *Strasseketeer* ravines that seemed more like the Germany of 1946 than the Economic Miracle of more recent years.

"Wellsir, we are using better materials here than you do in America," opined the City Employee when I bumptiously-but-bravely called to complain. "We are using longer lasting materials. We are sinking the power lines and cable two meters beneath your street level. We are laying four levels of paving, the top of macadam. How many do you lay in California?"

I did not respond. My Berkeley guess was we used, what?-- tar pudding, soft stuff, one level, zero macadam, as my Berkeley street was already rumpling after six months, sloping and yielding like the La Brea Tar Pits. "Many layers," I proudly lied. "In California we lay *many* layers."

The *Bad Herrenalb* city worker did not even trouble himself to express an incredulous Harrumph. "Once completed," he told me, "your street here will not need repairing until 2020."

As best I could I pictured 2020. In Berkeley my beloved Sterling Avenue would be impassable, car tires snapping fizzure to fizzure.

Except, this German *Lindenweg* repair had taken, as my savvy neighbor predicted, *nine months!* And in Berkeley, two weeks. A (as the Germans who can speak English say, being proud they learned quote *Oxford* English) fortnite.

"Has anyone else complained?" I asked, naively expecting the City Employee to reply, "Yes, fifty of your fellow *Lindenweg* dwellers. They too are infuriated." I really was possessed of the delusional fantasy that I could meet with my neighbors and we might join forces into a resistance and fight the moping-earnest local German officialdom. Had I not lugubriously observed my neighbors lugubriously wheeling their garbage and recycling containers (and each domicile is possessed of many bins: glass, plastic, organic, paper-- which must be meticulously placed, centimeter-sharp, on the marks provided on your sidewalk for them), my neighbors schlepping their many containers the one full block to the only remote spot where the requisite pickup trucks could circumnavigate the eternal repair trucks and reach our obediently delivered garbage? Had I not fraternally watched, and joined, my neighbors in The Long March each morning to our distant cars?-- on the next street, the *Hauptstrasse.*

"No. No complaints," the City Employee said. "No neighbors of yours have complained." Boy was he seriously, yet casually, yet triumphantly, blasé.

> The coup de grâce, I must admit, was cute. As icing-- a very important, functional, decorous topping-- the diligent city workers had installed down along our *Lindenweg's* center, like a spine, like an armature, a banked triple-line of wide red bricks, for beauty and for drainage-- and for pride... No overhead telephone wires, no electric lines, no hanging cable. All deeply underground. As if Alexander Graham Bell and Ben Franklin and Thomas Edison were still alive and observing, and "fine-tuning". But in Germany: Land of "The Berlin Edison": von Humboldt.

There comes now a sudden pause, a lurch-hitch in our Euro-driver's rented American auto, like a soccer player making a feint, as if his hired Chevrolet has forgotten something and wants to go back to its garage; this when he presses quickly, sharply on the gas pedal. Ah yes: Regular American petrol is below standard in Europe. American Super is equivalent roughly to Euro-regular. European Consumer Reports again. These Americans, they let their oil companies get away with refinery murder. Don't these Americans know *anything*? Don't they read the papers? Is information like this *in* the American papers? Don't Americans, these deep carers about smoking and viruses, Care? Strange, goofy people.

Come on, relax. At least there are not those hurried German nuts all believing they are Michael Schumacher tailing your bumper by one inch at their two-miles-per-minute velocity. Relax! But *no*-- he cannot relax: There are just all these, well, *Chinese* driving, well, Orientally. Moping, yet zig-zagging, to a-- I've got to say it-- a different tune. At least they *look* Chinese. Never have accidents, these characters, just *cause* accidents. He does not know-- and he never will know-- that training by driver school is not compulsory in America for a license, as it is in Europe. He has never visited the back ward Bedlam of an American Department of Motor Vehicles with its intransigent-depressed "flack-catcher" adjuncts and its blathering "flack-thrower" facilitator helpers, and the unfacilitated-unhelped getting crazier as they are long-waitingly unfacilitated and unhelped. So different from their European correlatives, with their clean rugs and new furniture and all around calmness-- like the anteroom of a barrister. If Euroguy did find himself besotted in an American DMV he probably would forego ever driving again in this nation. After all, our DMVs are not much different in MO from our DPWs and our DESes and DSSes. Tone is tone is tone. Is stone.

*   *   *

By contrast: Before my wife and I purchased our VW Lupo in Germany, that sweet mini-model unavailable in America, as is the sweet Euro Ford Ka and the sweet Daimler "Swatch" (although this one had been known to concussionly loop-de-loop-- before they fixed it), I rented at EuroCar--a, you guessed it, VW Lupo. Handleable as a bike. Well, almost. In the city, true I was a bit frustrated: In opposition to the furiously-calm-racing autobahn where, save a *stau* (traffic jam), you might soar the one hundred (miles) to Frankfurt in little over an hour, in the cities the traffic is as languid and obedient and cowtowing as forties' Hollywood Germans (and sixties' *Hogan's Heroes* Germans [most popular sitcom ever in *Deutschland*]) all of them snap-clicking their heels to attention. Why the sudden shift?-- this vehicular schizophrenia. Mittel-Europe characteristic?-- that ultimate puppet-lurch to rules and regulations? Perhaps, but also those pesky automated radar photo installations posted alongside the major "alleys" and *strassen*. You go more than five kilometers-per over the legal limit-- usually sixty or seventy in urban areas (40 mph)-- and you are snapped: Gotcha. I did once, and a speed ticket came to my wife, the car being registered in her name, as she is the German citizen in the family. The picture of course showed Me-- no registered female: Ute was not docked speeding points. But, once alerted to these snapshot-radar posts, I became subdued-- Me an urban German. Me awed: Those instruments are costly; they cost bucks (okay, euros), to be planted all round the town. What can I say?-- You need Taxation for stuff like this: Redistribution to society. Very civilized, they certainly have effect.

And the "unruly" French have them too. And the British.

But Americans. Are we too freewheeling to go for such safety equipment? We certainly have enough accidents to warrant them. We Americans are historically the pragmatists and inductivizers, while the French have been unrealistic over-rationalizers and the Germans trapped in romanticist illusion with foggy dream-hopes of Lohengrins. Americans are the realists. Well, we were: *we* should be the ones with those "pragmatic" photo-posts; at best they would keep neophyte teenage wheelers in check. And us too. Law enforcement people would be happy. Sure, again, we might have to raise those pesky taxes; or divert a trickle of some of our other spending, as on defense. Okay, offense. Our corporate tax contributions are ridiculously low, but that isn't the whole picture: Our CEOs earn far more than French and

German CEOs. And I mean *far* more. Might the phrase *twenty times more* mean anything to you?-- sometimes it achieves that super multiple. To stay here within the world of autos and roads, successful, respected Michelin pays its CEO a tiny fraction of what less-successful (yet respected) Goodyear pays its CEO. And a good portion of even our untaxed, unCEO'd corporate earnings still does not work its way into the social community: it goes to stockholders. Far far less true in Europe. Forget paying for infra-structure-- that bloodless word (the word itself helping cause disinterest in itself); just pay for those auto accidents in other ways. Insurance rates. Hospital costs. Sorrow.

TABLE ONE

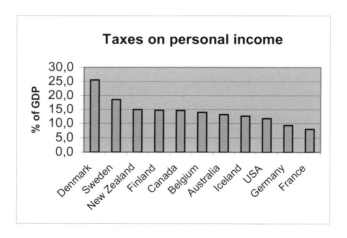

Source: OECD[*]

---

[*] Despite a recent tax cut, the German and French percentages here are misleadingly underpresented, as in these countries the tax rates are more sharply progressive, aimed at the rich-- in France especially-- and a great number of indirect taxes are not included, such as employee payroll taxes that total forty percent of gross earnings, and employer social security contributions far in excess of ours (which our employees tend to pay anyway); and higher property property taxes, and the dreaded, tremendous VAT, the "value-added" amounts on car purchase, gasoline, air tickets, cigarettes-- nearly eighty percent of the $5.30 price of a quality pack now in France; taxes on staples, like salt, and on luxuries like champagne and stereos and TVs, and on most forms of insurance; and dogs.

TABLE TWO

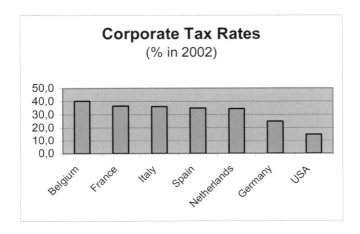

Source: OECD

Not only, by the way, are there planted radar-photo installations in Europe, but at some intersections a recorded voice tells you when to cross the street. I have seen and heard them in Paris and Berlin, and I suspect the average American might regard them as subliminally totalitarian: First a pedestrian dictator; next thing you know it's a state-sponsored Big Mac ration schedule for each individual fatso and fatette. And then there is in Europe the amber traffic light advising the driver not only when to soon stop, but when to start up again, a more expensive traffic fixture than in America-- where, by the way, the traffic light was invented (by an African-American name of Garett Morgan). And the European fixtures are firm-pole-planted to the left and right as well as overhead, not merely strung up and suspended, fragile piñatas as so often in America, treacherous dangler jump-ropes, pendulums swaying in gusty wind. And the street Walk request buttons aren't puny things, that usually don't work, but big wide pads-- like the neat easy toilet flush switch-- they even *light up*! And they do work!

On my first drive into Karlsruhe from our small town, as I approached the city I went through a tunnel, under the beautiful, handsome medieval castle city of Ettlingen. Sleek passage, dream thing, that tunnel, long and smooth and efficient. There are in fact many such subterranean underways in Germany, speeding traffic beneath bergs, burgs and villages and into and around and under big city downtowns-- like in Munich, Hamburg, Frankfurt, Berlin-- and midsize city downtowns, like Nuremberg, with even parking offshoot areas. Same in Paris, Vienna, even funky Marseilles (a Frenchwoman told me there are rumors that there are worker cafes down there). Few hideous-- and dangerous-- viaduct overpasses and skyways, as we have in America. These concealed under-routes can be quite extenuated, two, three miles even. Such modern funnels. Subdued lighting, like, indeed, in a chic bistro. Perfect up-to-date paving, unshattered wall tiles. Emergency exits. Have you driven through the warpy Holland or Lincoln tunnels lately?-- rumpled corrugational caves of Hades. Cheap materials? Make-work repair in two years providing employment overtime? Unlikely rationale. I envied the Germans so much their wealth-- or seeming wealth-- their, well, what other word is there for this but civilization?-- You know, as in 'Making life easier'-- although I knew that they complain endlessly about their "poverty". Their low growth rate. My envy had me hating them, in a way. When I exited the great long Ettlingen tunnel I then came upon a sign with computerized changing numerals: *Friedrichstrasse*-- 27; *Kaufhof*-- 32; *Rathaus*-- 43. What in the world were these lit-up changing numbers?-- some sort of official driver-tout off-track-betting? Nope: these numbers were telling us how many park spaces were available at the various city-- computerized-- park houses. Ever see such in America?

Nah: costs money.

I had come to Europe from the richest, best, nation-- right? Envied the world over-- right? A gazillion dollar defense budget to protect our pearly wealth from Evildoer Enviers, Freedom Haters, as we spend more on our armed forces-- 43 percent of *worldwide* defense spending is ours, more than the next two dozen countries combined!-- although the European Union does have many more soldiers under arms and receiving pay than we do. Only *our* vaunted wealth is not exactly "our". It is of course very private wealth-- *theirs* wealth-- and thus very mythical wealth, perhaps as storied as the foreign Have-Not "envy". As *We* seem to have become the Have-Nots (And did you know that the money raised by the breast cancer postage stamp goes not to the American Cancer Society, nor to any other cancer-research organization, but to the Defense Department?). American wealth really is a kind of Disney wealth, sequestered off in the distant towers and yellow brick roads of Oz. I mean, I'm driving in Karlsruhe, which is Nowheresville urban-wise, really (as I said, twenty-second largest city in Germany, official sister *stadt*, not of Moscow nor Rome nor London, but of drab Nottingham, tangential Nancy and obscure Halle. Hell, I shouldn't even be comparing Karlsruhe to San Francisco or New York, but to middle-rate Baltimore or Cincinnatti-- or maybe even Steubenville, Ohio), and there's no spooky-mystery-steam swooshing up out of the street manholes, as in America, or some ghoulish anti-world where maybe slaves are sweating away down in embedded pipes in shredded T-shirts; and there are these indented pull-in areas for street parking, which renders it easier to slip into a spot without being sideswiped by rearcoming traffic; and there are ubiquitous bike and walk paths, and bike racks all over town, and the bikes aren't stolen, so you never see some walking turkey hauling his front tire like a nut in Beckett or Sophocles, and the women oft-times ride their bikes while dressed up, their skirts flaring, flouncing to the viewer (I am admitting nothing here). And the houses, they aren't predominantly wood or stucco, as again I've already said but bears repeating: the houses are solid-- brick, stone; and the architecture, well, that playful scallop jugendstil, that intricate baroque. And then, at junctures the multicolored neat recycling bins. No, not bins. Pretty tombs and caskets. Not dumps. Even if they do happen to be regimented into lineup.

But gazillions to protect *our* American democracy, huh? Only, democracy is "of the people", No?-- I mean, That's what the word *means*!-- and the American people certainly do not now have much share in its giant GDP (the obscenity of which you may catch a whiff of in Table 4). What was, is, our wealth then? It surely doesn't shine in our quote infrastructure, that modular techno-erector set word (and I'll say again that that tiresome brickbat rigidity alyric itself may be doing real, usable, enjoyable "infrastructure" creation a great disservice, by putting people off-- or to sleep: Mel Brooks has observed that a "staircase" is hard and cold and says, Don't you *dare* come up me," and should be called a "tickletibumtiboo".). Anyway: infrastructure is "for the people". Demo. Should be, anyway. But "the people" seem to vote against the people, often just by not voting. Taxes!-- *No!* Government spending-- *Nosiree!* Government: problem. "Freedom": solution. Whatever that "freedom" is. (Push button: out pops brain.). I pictured most urban American parking lots: Tarmac postage stamps, temporary redoubt crannies where a building might soon rise up, or a bodega, with a few temporary parker guys-- suspicious tattoed non-shavers you give your *key* to-- they shunting your car to some nook in the total cranny. The parking "attendant" has to move three cars to fit yours in, and five to let you out. How many dinks-per-annum does that tote up to?-- assuming your car is even there when you return. I had come to Old Europe from New America, which turned out to be *Old*, worn, prehistory America, I'm afraid-- or premodern America (The tedious label "postmodern" is actually quite funny regarding our nation, as while the phrase postmodern is passé, its inventor, its progenitor, its origin and home, America, is really not quite yet even up to *modern*.). A prehistory, ours, that yet believes it is The New, The Leader, Post-History. I had come to the ancient world where architecture mattered, and comfort mattered, and so there were sleek-tiled tunnels under and around beautiful inner cities, with large cobblestone pedestrian zones in the centers of towns, square miles of them, not those intruding, overwhelming freeway skyways, those ugly American road ribbons over your-- urbanized, American-- head, no skyscrapers (except for Frankfurt and outskirt Paris), so one's eye is not forever Up, even if the Up has its adolescent immature allure; but the eye in Europe is ahead, around, and one's being is not showered in building-shadow-power, or submerged and drowned in it, but in architecture-power: Magnificence is not proclaimed by over-hammering, in a sense protesting too much, because underneath that weight of ours, behind it, within our concrete colonnades (and aren't they so unkempt, so dirty?-- but why bother washing them?), as hidden under a fourposter bed in a cheap motel, reside no few of America's antecedents (and an*ti*-cedents) and its enablers-- forced enablers-- its wretched. As if our overpasses were distinctly designed by our "city planners", discreetly devised for just such tent city "refuge"-- if they even achieve "tent" status. Divison of labor, of a perverse sort. Or, division of labor and non-labor. Oh America of dinosaurs. Oh America of Division. Oh holy crêpepaper "social net". Oh tolerant American passivity, which doth passeth all understanding. Doesn't it seem, somehow, somehow, as if we *want* the broken, and the decayed, to be present? Not *too* present, of course. Not in the Botox neighborhoods where we reside. But present, mind you. Object lesson. Cautionary tale.

A strange identity exists in America: You are A Good 'murkin if you vote The Big Tent (Republican). Why? Incredibly, *Why!?* Because The Big Tent is Good because it's A Big Tent. But a Big Tent stands for nothing except Y'all Come and be a Good 'murkin and vote for The Big Tent because it's Big *because* Y'all vote for it-- and so it is Go-ood. And Godly. Strange Big Tautology.

Insidious.

Thoughtless.

Exasperating.

And... vote winning.

Amazing.

TABLE THREE

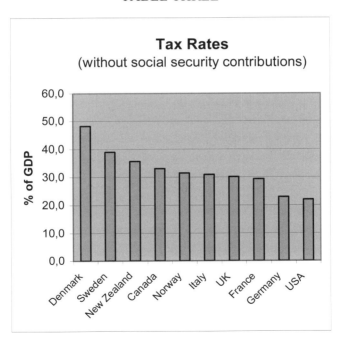

Source: OECD

TABLE FOUR[*]

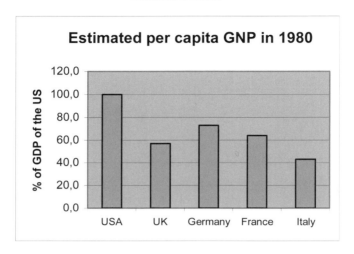

Source: OECD

Big serious note: Germany has embarked on a crash program to reduce acid rain pollution from power plants by ninety percent in six years, compared to the grudging, wanly conceived US air-pollution laws that give some industrial polluters *twenty to thirty years* to reform. America is the world champion not just in GDP and defense spending, but also in toxic waste dumping; it remains the only industrialized country without a policy on carbon dioxide. And as I write I see in the *New York Times* that George Bush's Environmental Protection Agency rescinded a Clinton era proposal to reduce mercury emissions from coal-fired power plants at up to ninety percent: a payoff to Bush's big contributors in the utility industry? Now emissions will be reduced, not ninety percent but thirty percent. If that. Airborne mercury is a toxic pollutant that threatens human health after it enters the food chain, usually through fish. We like fish-- lower cholesterol, brain food. An estimated 300 tons of mercury will now be allowed to poison us.

And then there is media pollution: Our Euro-man-- remember him? He finally surrenders himself to a motel, in Carmel. Exhausted, he couldn't quite make it down to Big Sur. He flops onto the bed. He remotes the

---

[*] There have been recent suggestions by economists that our figures are somewhat inflated by about 2 percent; perhaps that GDP should indeed be called, not Gross Domestic Product, but Gross Distorted Product.

television. Unlike in Europe, the ads scream and holler as if he's a deaf dude. "We have TV ads in Europe," he considers, "but they are so much more subtle and calm. *Mein Gott*, they are screaming loud here about these Fords and these Chevrolets and no money down and clear the lot for next season and Rebate and Rebate and Rebate. Cheesy (Actually, he mumbles *kwatch: Horseshit.*). Are these Americans tone deaf too?"

Picture an Orwell Land where the word Rich really means Poor.

Perhaps a good civics course should be required-- for every American citizen. A new community-savvy test for voting.

And driving.

And newspaper reading.

And speaking?

And listening?

And so, comprehending.

Jesus Christ was not an American citizen. Face it, Jesus the Christ looked not like Jeffrey Hunter nor Jeremy Irons nor Brad Pitt, nor whoever that Euro-handsome American-actor-Jesus was in Mel Gibson's "realistic Bible-bloody-faithful" *Passion.* Rather, face it, Jesus Christ looked like Yassir Arafat.

Picture that; meditate on it. I know you know it intellectually-- you'd get it right on a test. But intellect is barely our iceberg's tip.

The comic irony of our nation: With our golden doctrine of Progress, our loud banner of GoGo, our ludicrous, even ugly, applauding at the podium at each morning's opening of the New York Stock Exchange-- zealous (embarrassing?) kudos to money[*] -- we have dropped way behind Progress. Because real progress, decent progress, is a social thing. Not private. Example: *L'état Providence.* The French concept which ensures the wellbeing of its citizens-- or hopes to anyway-- whether those French citizens wish to be so conceptually ensured or not. Whether the aim is pie-in-the-sky and even succeeds or not. This idea was a brainstorm long before the modern notion of The Welfare State appeared. Under other names, like The Commonwealth, or *Gemeinde,* it also existed in England and Germany. Compared to ours, Old Europe's streets are now paved in gold.

---

[*] One wonders if at the major business schools-- Wharton, Harvard, Yale, Stanford, Haas-- the students are not obliged to watch videos of those charmingly amoral corporate rakes on old *Dynasty* and *Dallas*. Role models.

And Old Europe's streets are Not *paved in gold.*

CHART 7

WHAT'S BETTER HERE --- WHAT'S BETTER THERE	
HERE (Partial Listing) THERE	
Credit Card Use (still more prevalent)	Toilets
Supermarket bagging	Trams
(by the bagger,not by you)	
Bandaids (less clutchier)	Trains
Milk Cartons (less leaky; easier open)	Radiators
Store Hours (longer; including Sundays)	Public Schools
Number of Channels— on Cable	Health Insurance
Chinese Food	Drug Prices
Mexican Food	Appliances[*]
Potato Chips	Roads
Friendliness and acceptance	Cars
Coffee (Believe it or not)	Vacation Time
	Public TV
	Door knobs: real handles
	Traffic lights
	Post Offices: speedy service
	House materials
	Downtown environment
	Architecture
	Bus and train stations
	Commercials on TV
	Sex on TV: Redemptive,
	(or not)
	Cafes
	Parking meters (all work)
	Public telephones
	(neat cute huts)
	DMV offices (not jungles)
	Movie theatres
	(alcohol; seats)
	Auto Club offices (luxurious)
	Tire pumps in gas stations
	Yoghurts

[*] Washing machines; dryers: look sleeker, function near silently

4

THE GIGGLE OF THE MYTH

I could go on and on with the snapshots of our comparison-suffering -- some might label them easy potshots (like our share of *our own* domestic car market having dropped from 80 percent two decades ago to today's sixty percent)-- but I would like to insert here another smidgeon of analysis about the American delusion, our national denial in the face of reality: A Super Denial, as the reality to be denied is considerably strong. I am hardly revealing any confidences here, any secrets known but to a few hush-hush poverty-cognoscenti, a select society of satraps of international economics at Harvard and Stanford and the writers for *Harper's* and *The Nation*. Come on: so many Americans have been to Europe, if only for the tourist whirlwind week to ten days. And not just Euro-leaning New Yorkers, New Englanders and Californians. No, these have also been our fellow Americans from Kansas and Nebraska and Oklahoma, and Mississippi too (and Crawford in west Texas), who have been these days to Amsterdam, Berlin, London, Paris (and Podunkingenbergburg), who have witnessed the truth. And the con-comitant, well, lie of American Chosenness (Although I did once encounter a fellow countryman-- in a Baden-Baden bank-- who actually was rather flabbergasted that George Washington's portrait was not to be found on the euro [No Europeans have expressed astonishment to me however that the euro insignia-- the map of Europe-- is not imprinted on the dollar]). Sure, our flatout total wealth cannot be denied. There is good old Table 4 staring us in the face. Our Gross Domestic Product is thirty times larger than Russia's, twenty times weightier than India's, eight times that of China, more than two and a half times Japan's and twenty-two percent greater than the entire combined European Union's. And now it may be even heftier, by an estimated four billion dollars, as the EU has finally accepted the importation of our (Monsanto's) "Frankenfoods", our genetically modified grains, like "Roundup Ready" corn-- which can tolerate our "Roundup Ready" pesticides (Well, our agri-tech biz may be richer at any rate from "transgenics"-- although some unroundup ready French farmers recently ripped up a field of transgenic corn, as French police stood by, appreciative fans). Being so opulent, we have Beverly Hills, Rodeo Drive, the Hamptons, Palm Beach, Palm Springs, Fifth Avenue, etcetera. Though the truth is most nations also have their redoubts of magnificence; even sweltering Third World nations have skyscrapers.

Our capable CEOs' remuneration is certainly further boldface proof of our great wealth too, isn't it? As I've said, these Captains of Industry often pull down five times what a German CEO earns of a comparable-sized corporation. And sometimes *ten* times. And sometimes *twenty* times. Yes, even in Germany, not just less rich France or Italy or Spain (The average remuneration of a German blue-chip manager currently amounts to $1 million, compared to $3.1 million for France, $2.3 million for the UK and-- here we go-- *$6.2 million for the U.S.*). When for example German Daimler Benz took over the floundering Chrysler, which although it was hardly kept a secret, remained a reality few Americans seem *even yet* fully aware of, as that is some bitter pill to swallow (dissimilar only in magnitude to the charity recently sent by a German village to the "middle class poor" of a town in Wisconsin), the CEO of the successful premier takeover company, Jürgen Schrempp, made barely one fourth the yearly salary-- plus options, plus bonuses-- of Robert Eaton, the CEO of the ever-failing American company now taken under the "poorer" Germans' wing. And, while Volkswagen's CEO is paid less than one million dollars per year, Ford's is paid *thirty-two* million, and General Motors' top gun, twenty-two million. But to be fair and non-hyperbolic, I must include here that, while Nokia's CEO-- in Finland-- pulls down a cool one and one quarter million, competing Motorola's takes in just two and a half million, barely whooping him by a measly half. In fact, while the income received by the highest twenty percent of Germany's population is six times that of what is brought in by the lowest twenty percent, in America the ratio is *nine* times! While the American CEO makes on average *531* times what his hourly worker makes, the European CEO makes only eighty times what his European regular Joachim makes-- true partly because the Joachim makes a higher wage than the American Joe! But even the infamous-- and famous-- nineteenth century financier J.P. Morgan once suggested that executives earn no greater than just twenty times his poor slob worker's pay. J.P., no exploiting slouch himself, would be flabbergasted by his countryman descendants' unbridled temerity and *chutzpah*. Self-justifying *chutzpah* too. So, yes, we Americans are flush and well-heeled *in total*, unarguably that, but our wealth is like a few gorillas, paunchy ones, preening ones, squatting on a bevvy of bewildered, semi-suffocated gerbels. . . Gerbels who don't (can't?) realize their lungs are half-squashed, and who aspire to be, not happy gerberls, but gorillas. You need precious air to think clear.

TABLE FIVE

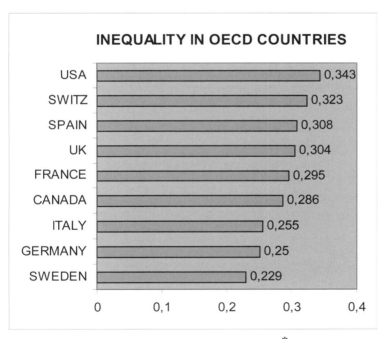

Coefficient for Disposable Personal Income,* Range 0 to 1

Source: Luxembourg Income Studies

---

* Even considerung our monster GDP, the gap between rich and poor is greater in the US than in most European nations.

Notwithstanding: this blatant evidence of our failure, when it plays here in the U.S. it just does not play well. It sounds subversive, like that oldtimey godless commie agit-prattle. No imprint on our collective cortex. Or if it does register it is a piccolo in an orchestra. It is as if American visitors to other developed nations feel they have happened upon a movie as imaginary as *Showboat*. A fancy-laced vacation show, the fascinating architectural endowments, the effervescent pedestrian zone cobblestone streets of shops and department stores crowded with shoppers in the city centers, with Life, as existed in America in the twenties through the fifties (look at the occasional documentary on PBS), so unlike the mostly deserted American downtowns now; deserted, that is, except for social workers and lawyers and homeless. Abandoned for the plastified American mall non-vista vistas with their smells of peanuts and lame dishwater coffee. No sudden eureka of an ancient alleyway in your mall, with old dusty bookstore and shoemaker and florid curiosity courtyard.

CHART EIGHT

QUALITY OF LIFE (U. N. Index)

Rank	Country
1	Norway
2	Sweden
3	Canada
4	Belgium
5	Australia
6	Germany
7	Switzerland
8	Denmark
9	France
10	United States

Why does all this not sink in to an American? The original reason was our oceanic distance-- distance makes the heart grow mythic-- but farawayness is of course no longer far. A more muscular reason is that we indirectly, and habitually, *see* nothing. It is as if we "pragmatists" have-- for pragmatic economic reasons?-- pragmatised ourselves out of pragmatism into an idealized romance, of Fundamentalism and Freedom and Goodness, while the romantic woolly-*penseur* Europeans have finally idealized themselves into some pretty good ideas that have become, presto-changeo, pragmatic-- and more just. Art is supported in Western Europe on a far greater scale than in the U.S., sometimes with rent-free leases for studios for promising sculptors and painters and film-makers, and often with plain checks. The funds usually come from government, so an artist is not compelled to subject himself to the long-tedious process of applying for a miniscule number of grants, as in America. A dwindling number of grants, in America. As one fledgling conductor says, "People here care a lot more about whether they like something than whether it's going to make any money."

We Americans are now trained for Non-Seeing. Our TV news, controlled by three mega corporations-- GE, Viacom, Disney-- tells us little of the world, beyond the "human interest" of fires and doggies and abductions, unlike Europe's variegated, broad spectrum TV news. Due to declining readership (due to crummy schooling; okay, inferior, unfinanced schooling?) our good newspapers are dwindling in size and number-- in addition to being owned, as with TV networks, by fewer and fewer local operations (Now it's mostly Gannett, NewsCorp [Fox] and The Tribune Company-- all unlike the active opinionated European print you see people devouring in Europe in cafes. Overseas national broadcasting licenses are limited (Except in Italy, where Berlusconi owns everything). If one individual or group owns more than thirty percent of a broadcaster (France), fifty percent (Germany), no license. Brain candy is kaibashed. Well, partially-- as brain candy, being brain *candy*, will get chewed. Networks like TFI, Canal Plus, France 1 and TV Cinq (France), ARTE (Germany and France) and ARD, ZDF and SAT (Germany; all of which control 40 percent of the TV market), and in Britain the BBC, the corollaries to our PBS, receive almost total government support, in contrast to America's fifteen percent. This underpinning is financed largely through monthly fees of about $40 per household: no drop-in-the-bucket, but worth it to not be set upon by the insipid humiliating filibuster, that guilt-saccharine torment-sermon Pledge Week, while you wait and wait for "Old Blue Eyes Returns from Retirement". Air time then to broaden the viewer spectrum, for the horizon beyond the provincial, even on commercial stations: Documentaries and foreign films-- though mostly dubbed, true, a bigtime profession in Europe

(You would believe Peter Faulk's "Columbo" spoke perfect French and fluent Hanoverian German, and with a well-nailed simulacrum of Faulk's ironic throat-rasp). French film in Germany; English; Italian; Spanish; even Israeli. Even some African. Same with France. Good luck finding foreign films on American TV. Of course fiction is fiction, storytelling is story-telling; but the backdrop of even the most amateurish movie is still the Real Foreign Background: you peek over the parochial and you see foreign things, foreign expression and motion and attitude. These life-aspects cannot be hidden, even with dubbing. Even in movietime falsity is discernable *some* real truth. And paradoxically these government-supported networks seem, not less independent, but *more*-- as the people expect serious reporting as their raison d'être (Viz: the BBC's stalwart investigation and pursuit of the Blair government's "sexing-up" terpsichore on Iraq's "weapons of mass destruction".

Here, two what I find charming examples of Europe's lack of overt plutocracy and oligopoly in their media; i.e., monochromaticism at a mini-mum: Television shows on different channels (*kanals* and *canals*) neither begin nor break for commercial at the in-sync same precise moment, as if it is God's will-- that surfing-forestall maneuver perfected by American media collusion. Delightfully (to a culture anarchist), now and then you will even discover *the same movie* being presented on two different networks in different stages of progress: I tuned in late once to see Tom Hanks, deserted on a desert island in *Cast Away*, and then I surfed to witness Tom Hanks' plane crash earlier in the film. Some may find this discombobulation primitive, annoying; but I was refreshed. It also ain't bad for film-analysis-- by the lazy man.

More reasons for The American Delusion: We can go anywhere with our English in the developed world, and to a considerable extent in the "developing" world, and be looked up to despite our not speaking French or German or Swedish or Chinese-- and despite these people's not particularly wishing to look up to us. English to us is a metaphysic, not a tongue. English as Earth's center. Pretty soon we'll even believe The Buddha spoke a sage and quiet Cockney-- when he spoke. Obviously such solipsism allows us to feel superior; but it is such a false and jingo superiority. An Unearned Superior, like a touchdown from an unforced fumble. We didn't struggle to *learn* the language. I don't know about you, but I inevitably take on more than a twinge of the inadequate in another country when a foreigner deigns to speak to me in "my" English because I haven't invested the time and headache he has in *learning-a-foreign-tongue* (Yes, I know, some Americans just feel, again, superior, as the foreigner may utter something mistaken like, "I will become a taxi".). The famous French observer Alexis de Tocqueville smiled at this American lacuna in its early stages in the mid-nineteenth century-- an amusing immaturity. The comic callow. But oh what will we do if Cantonese becomes the world-speak of the next century?-- as it well might. Then we'll be the ones relegated to mumbling like embarrassed, mortified clowns, as the Germans and the Dutch and the Swedes, you name them, struggle in earnest to learn that oriental dialect. But if by language we are "Superior" today, so our subliminal logic goes, so our infrastructure, and so our media, and so our colleges, and so our sports, and so our democracy. That's just QED. That's why we cannot suspend our disbelief as we visit Europe (or, rather, suspend our self-belief). Europe's superior foundations are there, before us-- road and car and house and shop and leisure-- but somehow they are Not There. Not touchable. Not to us. On a personal, clinical, level, such unseeing comportment would cry out for serious psychotherapy-- Freudian and behavioral combined (Maybe medication too). Alas, on an international plane our blindered, blinkered demeanor is just All-American, that's all, and therefore nice: Normalcy.

What we Americans display is what some psychotherapists call "noisy brains". Others, I've already written, call it our "halo effect". We are not calm and reflective enough to see the obvious.

There is a famous book published some thirty years ago called *The Denial of Death* (Woody Allen had his character obsess with it in *Manhattan*). An unpleasant subject, Serious Death-- our absolute brushoff-wipeout from Earth's face, we poor death-conscious, end-awaiting critters-- as if we are smudges on a window EasyWhiped, gone gone gone. Hell, this is worse than having to deliver a big talk your first time in Speech 101. So with our behemoth (but frail) consciousnesses we human animals "enrich ourselves" in a Houdini attempt to deny the undeniable. Business, invention, religion, movies, newspapers, history, Love. Not bad; but all still denials of The Big D. But we Americans have an additional labor. We must also deny our national impoverishment. Our unfairness. Our relative non-richness. We wear Old Glory on our lapels.

OUR CREDO:
THIS WE BELIEVE

We tell ourselves we're The Greatest, Richest, Free-est, until it's a psycho-given just about impossible to not-believe (Some 19 % of Americans believe that they belong to the exclusive richest 1 % of Americans). We do this deluded globalized endzone wiggle-waggle as if we just scored a touchdown. *In yo'face!*-- Jacques, Wilhelm, Fritz, whoever. Nearly three hundred million Neon Deons-- many poor as hell.

We tell ourselves the average American has more money in the bank than your average European. Though, ohboy, we don't. Most of us have *no* money: Debt doesn't count as money, Charlie. And Europeans don't owe. That's not their Thing. They *save*.

We tell ourselves, even if we don't have more money in the bank than the average European, we are *still* nonetheless richer, because, because, uh, because, uh . . . well, SOMETHING: We're *American!*

We buy ugly muscle cars (Cadillac now actually advertises overseas-- on conspicuous consuming Persian Gulf TV). Okay, we don't actually *buy* our "fatass" Grand Prixes and Eldorados, we "finance". Finance equals buy, to us (We believe that's good for the economy). And we could-care-less that our cars' gas emissions are so egregious to this planet that they would cost Ford and GM five times as much to curb as would those lesser global-warmers of Toyota and Honda; they'd cost much more to improve than would even the German muscle cars.

We believe that Europe can never match up with us because it is atomized, a continent (sort of) off the shoulder of Asia. But with the new EU you may, for one thing, drive unimpaired, uncustomed, unhalted, from the Baltic to Spain, as if you were going from Boston to Baltimore (Albeit not always at continental hyper-speeds).

We don't believe Singapore has (oops, "had") The World's Tallest Building (even before 9/11). We pretty much still believe "Singapore" is shacks and dinghies and Clark Gable and Ava Gardner. But

Singapore had the tallest building. Until Dubai edged them. DUBAI!?... Now we're third (as this book goes to press).

We cannot believe that *Air France* is now the world's largest airline.

We cannot fathom that little Norway's Oslo Corp and Germany's SAP are chasing at Bill Gates and Microsoft. *Huh?!*

We believe Moses spoke English in the Sinai (Sinai is itself an American name, right?-- proof positive being all the hospitals named Sinai), and that Moses Heston read the Ten Commandments in stentorian bigtime drama school English. Thus too with Jesus Christ, Caesar, Columbus, Galileo, Mephistopheles, Leonardo, van Gogh and whoever's residing way out beyond the borders of the universe. It is truly impossible for us to imagine those Greats communicating in any of those throaty or gutty or nasally babbles. Nothing other than our adenoidal English babble. That's sheer sacrilege. And we really do deep down believe it. Gut. No joke.

We don't believe Europeans yet have super-markets-- much less Asians-- or range-fed beef or avocadoes or fat-free milk or pineapples or pumpkins or the species of soft two-ply Charmin toilet "tissue" upon which Mister Whipple couldn't resist adminis-tering his creepy pervert-furtive squeeze.

We believe Bayer Aspirin is an American product, haha: Bayer derives from Bayrische. I.e., Bavaria. As in, you know, our "Beamer".

We believe Nivea is an American product.

We believe Danone is an American product-- because in America the smart ad boys extracted the Frenchy "e".

We believe Canon is an American product. And Shell; and Lever Brothers. And British Petroleum-- well, some of us anyway. . . And The United Colors of Benetton. Nope: Italian.

We don't, *can't*, believe Chrysler *belongs* to Daimler, lock, stock and barrell. It wasn't a merger. They are not partners. They are not equals. It was a takeover. And whatever happened to Lee Iacocca anyway?

We can't believe that Toyota's profit (for '04) was more than the combined profits of Ford and GM. That's perverse. That's sick. Ford and GM make their profits of late as "financial institutions": banking, making loans, not by making the cars they make.

We don't believe Westinghouse belongs to Siemens. It did; then it didn't. And now American Columbia studios and American TriStar Studios belong to Japanese SONY. You know how those conglomerationers conglomerate and unconglomerate. Read the business pages: it will drive you cross-eyed.

We don't believe Random House (remember Bennett Cerf?) belongs to German Bertelsmann (It did, then it didn't), which is now the largest book publisher in the world; and that a French consortium (okay, France, the state-- everything in France is a consortium) owned MGM. (It did, then it didn't.). Now it looks like Japan's SONY will own Frank and Clark and Rita and Bogey and John, "Pilgrim".

We hold our noses that L'Oréal is the world's biggest cosmetic firm-- even though it may be a product of a French consortium. Nobody's sure.

We refuse to accept that GE (*America's General Electric!*) outsources to, you know, India. And IBM. And New York securities outfits (I mean, *Wall *+#*$ing Street!*). And radiologists reading our homegrown MRIs. And that Corning, maker of our TV screens and auto windshields is leaving Pennsylvania, The Keystone State, for China, The People's Republic. And that our technology *executives* (some) are crib-learning Hindi-as-a-second-language in prep to head on out to India, for work where they might have lunch with the Indian processors-- and *decision-makers?*-- on our US Income Tax refunds, who then go home and do their India Income Tax refunds. And that Cognizant Technology Systems has 70 percent of its development operations in India; and that Mphasis (spelling theirs?), an American software call center company is now located in Bombay and Bangalore and Pune (where all the spirit gurus are sitting twisted knee-to nape) and Shanghai and-- hold onto your sombrero-- *Tijuana*.

We find it hard to comprehend that while America's major airlines are tottering on bankruptcy's edge-- with United already bankrupt (and welching on pensions) and Delta and American atotter-- Europe's big airlines remain financially healthy. Why?

We believe our poor and homeless are better, happier, than European poor and homeless. Somehow. They just Are (Well, they do smile-- okay, leer-- a lot).

We cannot believe that, percentagewise, there are far less European poor and homeless. Did somebody cook the stats?

We believe foreign politicians to be effete and probably closet homosexuals, if they are not closet (or open) bisexuals, or closet (or open) pedophiles and philanderers of every inclination imaginable. We are assisted in this dogma by the acute observation that even French socialists often are witnessed in the wearing of Armani suits-- and fancy-François scarves in hot TV studios when they are interviewed (by similarly dressed interviewers).

We scratch our heads when we read that the rate of households owning digital TV in France and Germany is rising at almost double our own rate.

We double-take when we learn that, with all our opulence of cellphones, only fifty percent of American adults own them, whereas *eighty* percent of Europeans walk the streets psychotically jabbering into those gizmos they call "handies"-- erroneously convinced it's an American term. But this cellphone abundance in Europe is certainly not due to personal disposable income alone, but also to conspicuous consumption, No? The Europeans' marginal propensity for flash and filigree, No?-- as with those fine suits and dresses and shoes. But, couldn't the "handies"-proliferation come from that Euro-super-propensity towards friendship too?

We believe that Europeans are damned godless, as evidenced by the French, big peacock lovers, recently converting their old church confessionals into neat roomy birdcages.

We believe that other nations do not front on beautiful oceans or seas, or have majestic mountain lakes-- or mountains for that matter (Well, sure, they have a few, but these are not God's mountains); or canyons.

We believe that foreign jocks are effete and unathletic for not indulging in American football or baseball; and we giggle (rightly) at their dorky winter sport of curling.

We believe that Europeans are basically wimps (and we pronounce this, "*wee*umps") for not having in their pathetic excuses for woods, bears, wolves, pumas, buffalo, and skunks (The Germans have imported "waschbears" [raccoons], and way-east Romania does have shootable bears).

We believe Melitta is as American as apple pie (which is of course also German). And we like American-made Black Forest Ham much better than Black Forest made Black Forest Ham.

We believe Levis manufacture is not out-sourced.

We believe that Radio Flyer, that icon of American sleds and wagons of our youth and our nostalgia are not manufactured in China.

We brag that we don't read "smart" books. I mean, we *brag* it. This is very weird. Take yourself a gander at the Best Seller List. Fiction and Non-Fiction (of course you will have to *read* to do even this).

We believe that Mount Rushmore is a natural phenomenon. Repeat: *We believe that Mount Rushmore is a natural phenomenon.* Somehow, those Dakota cliffs and ridges *formed themselves* into the inspiring busts of-- well, whoever those early Sainted presidents were. So much GREATER they were too than our Great presidents; although, amazingly, Mount Rushmore-- which proves AMERICA IS GOD'S COUNTRY-- has not as yet been declared a WONDER-OF-THE-WORLD, or a miracle by any extant pope. Perhaps if Ronald Reagan's silhouette manifests there some soon overnight. It probably will.

We believe hamburgers are better than filet mignon-- whatever filet mignon is. We believe that raw steak tartar is for dogs.

We believe that our homegrown fruits and vegetables have pumped us bigger and healthier than Europeans, although we are neither bigger nor healthier-- and we rank 28th in longevity (but a reverse respectable *8th* in shortgevity). Only, alas, are we *fatter*, hands down-- and our poor health care sure doesn't help here. On average we are smaller-- even counting in Greece and Italy and Albania, and *Japan!*, once the shortest folks on earth; and this is allowing for our monster football and basketball players. And our fatness. In Holland and Germany ceilings have had to be raised in recent years. *Lowered* in America perhaps?

CHART NINE

MALE HEIGHT* in centimeters

Mid 18th Century		1990		2000	
1. USA	174.1	Norway	178.9	Holland	180
2. Norway	168.6	Sweden	177.9	Norway	179
3. Sweden	168.6	Denmark	177.1	Sweden	178
4. Germany	167.3	USA	175.5	Germany	178
5. Denmark	165.3	Germany	175.4	Denmark	178
				USA	172

* Only American males of European origin were considered in this study at Ludwig Maximilian University in Munich. Had a sample of the entire US male population been included the American rating would be considerably down-metered. And down-inched.

We believe that Starbuck's styrofoam coffee is a neat speedo ADVANCEMENT.

We refuse to accept that our jazz ("The only true American art form"), well, the word "jazz" anyway, came from "*jaser*", old French for "to chatter". And we don't seem to be bright enough to realize that jazz cannot possibly be "The only true American art form"-- as *jazz is not an art form.* MUSIC is the art form. God we can be such proud turkeys.

We believe American Mad Cow Disease, with the victim so miserably out of his own control, will not be so bad as European Mad Cow Disease. And that it's okay if we are so "independent" as to not knuckle under to Euro-softies and sign onto: The Kyoto Protocol on the world environment; the Geneva-agreed International Court of Justice; the Anti-Ballistic Missile Treaty; "inhuman" death penalty abandonment-- which even the Turks have finally done.

We believe our Rich are nicer and Just Like Us, unlike those effete double-breast Euro-suit rich gambling in fancy-shmancy Monaco and Baden-Baden and not beautiful, tasteful Las Vegas. Our Rich deserve their richness.

We cannot believe that the real Disney castle -- the model for it-- is in Bavaria. And that Disney-Land France is a money-loser.

We believe that our FCC granting of still greater concentration of media ownership (news-papers, magazines, TV, radio, satellite) in one mega-firm, will make for bigger-better-faster News over the air waves and print sheets without a whole lot of annoying distracting dissent, like as over the FEA's rolling back clean air legislation-- such as that troubled even the REPUBLICAN Christy Todd Whit-man to quit as its appointed head.

We believe that the FCC's kaibashing Janet Jackson's right tit and Howard Stern's godless bad words is Good. Far better than would be not allowing some Australian to own damn media everything.

We are amused that the Sorbonne, for example, does not field a football team. And they call themselves a *University*?! The Sorbonne doesn't even have a goddamn stadium. Or cheerleaders. Or batons. Pathetic. Notre Dame would kick Sorbonne ass on the gridiron. And the coeds in cheer-uniform are neater at Ol'Miss.

We believe our universities are intellectually better too, as they are infinitely costlier and have great campuses in Gothic and Federal and Colonial and LA Romanesque; and it's a damn lie and racist heresy that the best, most serious students at our universities are, you know, from Vietnam and India... And, by the way, IIT-- The Indian Institute of Technology-- rates higher now than our MIT. No fable.

We believe that *Larry King,* CNN's absurd pride, is some smart man, just super-intelligent, hands down, and reads maybe fifty newspapers a day and so knows just about everything, except how incredibly dorky he looks-- like he just went to the bathroom (Number 2) in his braced-up *alte-kocker* pants. And how softball-smarm his interviews are. He's just trying to be nice to everyone. Hey, compare Larry to the *Hardtalk* (but fair talk) Tim Sebastian of the BBC.

We laugh our asses off at Euro-boxers, as they don't Ali-shuffle and rope-a-dope. Even when they beat our guys we laugh at them, these straight-aheaders, because we know in our hearts our guys are far better. Boy, I mean, just the chest-thumpy way our guys do their victory shimmies when they win-- just like our football touchdown scorers in the end zone. Why, I bet if a Euro-*fußball* player (soccer) played OUR football and scored a touchdown he'd just celebrate it quietly with false plain stoic dignity, like our football players used to do way back in the forties and fifties when we didn't know how rich we were.

We believe that despite the constitutional ability of our sparse-populated states to lean down with astronomically more weight in the Senate (New York-- 2 votes; North Dakota-- 2 votes), *and* in the presidential-deciding Electoral College, that we are not the world's greatest undemocratic democracy, but its leading best democracy-democracy (Uh: six million men, one vote, verses *half* a million, one vote. Duh?). No other government on the planet is set up so egregiously, flagrantly, inequitably-- crafty-STUPID.

We believe that the broad European thoroughfares and architecture and store appointments are the fiddlefaddle of the non-industrious, like they're into ART.

We believe our cellphones are the best, despite their being the worst: Try calling London from New York on your Verizon cell. Lotsaluck. Then watch a European breeze it on his Nokia or his Siemens.

We watch with blissful indifference as Germany (and now Denmark) accounts for 6 percent of their fuel energy through renewable sources: sun and wind. We account for less than .05 percent. They have the Green Party in their governments; or at least with clout even when it's out. Coalition politics: Subversive phraseology here.

We believe our sky high fees for bank checking accounts and ATMs are just-the-way-it-is. Like taxes. Like gravity. Like the universe. Like it ain't pure usury-- thus Medieval.

We cannot believe that German movie theatres are more luxurious than ours, with wider seats and thicker walls (and booze) and no ability to hear the dialogue from the adjoining cineplex.

We believe a quart and gallon whallops a liter as a measure any day, for although it is not standard metric it is NATURE'S way. GOD was into quarts and gallons, man. Christ was into quarts and gallons and dollars. Those stupid Euroers don't even know what six-foot tall is. (Try explaining it to them). What dimwits.

Ditto miles verses kilometers. I mean, you drive in Old Europe you believe with their km signs places are so Very Far Away. They probably use those tiny kilometers to make Europe seem bigger-- like America. Don't you think?

Ditto pounds verses kilograms. Pounds kicks kilos' ass-- although with opposite reasoning, as kilos are bigger. Look, I weigh seventy kilos and I haven't a clue as to what I weigh.

We believe that to dress up too nice-- like *Just to Shop?!*-- is Phoney Baloney. Maybe a hooker would do that; but not a nice normal American woman.

We *do* believe-- but find it repugnant-- that
the French (according to, well, a poll) have inter-
course more often per cap than we do. As do (another
poll) Porsche drivers. And Audi (for some in-
explicable reason).

We *know* BUD, "The King of Beers" is, like,
The King of Beers.

We believe (deludedly) that America, not
Europe, holds the greatest, profoundest commitment
to the notion that all-citizens-should-have-an-equal-
right-to-participate-in-economic-and-social-life.   We
believe that. Really. In our, American, way.

We believe, insanely, incredibly (even for us)
in Preemptive War. Be-- what's that hot new word?--
PROACTIVE. Like with flossing.

A strong, direct answer to why we do not recognize our new
inferiority-- for, face up, we have to recognize it, as that is what it is, our
New Inferiority (or, to be generous, our New Possible Inferiority, or New
Imminent Inferiority)-- is surely that this denial is a sine-qua-non. It has
become our oxygen. We cannot live and breathe without denying. This is not
the greatest state to be in: Warren Buffett, the billionaire investor-advisor
(who still lives in a shack in Nebraska-- or maybe it's a bungalow), calls us
"Squanderville". But how could we accept that, say, German Life, or
Swedish, or French, is prettier, better, street-safer, that one's home there
might even remain unlocked in the average town, even when no one is at
home? I recollect when I arrived in LA as a fledgling screenwriter how
shocked I was that so many of the super houses in the Hollywood Hills, and
Beverly Hills, had formidable *bars* crisscrossing the windows, as if these
plush residences were veritable prisons: it looked like the wealthy neighborhoods of Karachi or Bombay, with the wretched teeming down below in
plain view; and actually was this not so far from the truth? Central L.A. was
not so far off; from some barred windows you might look down on decrepit
Riotland. Though millions of refugees and poor *would* like to come to
America, still, for even menial work, like cleaning Wal Mart aisles from
midnight till dawn, off the books, no benefits, as billions in the world are
starving, most Europeans nowadays gaggle at the idea of immigration to our

country; or they merely smirk: crude, ugly America?-- where you could get yourself *killed*? Are you kidding? *Merci* and *danke*, but *nein* and *non*. Polls do not of course show the laughter, but they do consistently register Europeans' disdain for the hypothetical notion of their living in our nation. And in the bargain the Europeans are burdened with their own refuge-seekers from around the world, working for "black money"—i.e., off the books: Britain and Germany now receive more refugees than does our land of "Give me your tired, your poor, your wretched humble yearning..." If we accepted all this evidence, as plaincut out-there as our broken infrastructures, if we *looked*, we would by definition have to admit that We Are Not The Greatest. That we, The New Nation, so long proud of its innovation, its adaptability, its know-how, we have lost our long-taught identity, our historical identity, and it will be super hard work now to re-up and change both our image and our self-image, revamp it, and then our environment.

It might even require-- here comes the required redundancy-- the Read my lips. Yup, New Taxes (And again, Tables 1 through 3 show that our taxes are not particularly high.). In any case, these New Taxes should be levied on those who have so far quite escaped the *old* taxes, those who can afford it. For as it stands congress now literally takes money from those bringing in from $30,000 to $60,000 per year and funnels about $4000 of these monies-- in ways subtle and unsubtle-- to the Super-Rich, the top one-one-hundredth of one percent of Americans (America now possesses one-third of the earth's millionaires). Often these people, America's Super-Rich, pay nothing-- even no taxes on their private Learjets. The unruly French would storm the Palais Royale (as there stands no longer an unstormed Bastille) if this thievery continued to obviate over there; the reserved Germans would march *lichterketten* (with candles), as they now do in mourning and regret of the Holocaust. But neither the French nor the Germans possess the all out numbers of bloated Super-Rich that we boast, and that we carry. So a decent equitability on taxation would as much constitute "soak the rich" as would truth characterize the Bush declaration, "America possesses no weapons of mass destruction, and has never used them."

Is this disclosure a revelation? It is staggering that it seems to be precisely that-- revelation: So I can't repeat the revelation enough, as even billionaires, gonzo-beneficiaries of our system like Warren Buffett and George Soros, reaffirm such inequity and inveigh against its deleterious effects. The maldistribution now hovers like some thick ominously lethal smog we breathe but cannot see, a hole in the economic ozone. We in individualist America have just been tattoed head to toe, not with MOTHER, but with the indelible myth of our Individualism, and ironically the wedding of such dazzling filament to Business-- which pursuit by now is about as distant from hearty yeoman Individualism as a "Massachusetts liberal" is from a seventeenth century Massachusetts Puritan. And, by the way, if you are the object of such indoctrination, and reindoctrination, *you cannot be individualist*. Even if the indoctrination messsage *is* Individualism. Even the heady oppositionalism of Hegel's dialectic-- with Marx as its point guard-- could not achieve that ridiculous synthesis. One need only compare an American professional basketball game to a European one to see in sweet moving cameo the difference. The American teams shake'n'bake terrifically, gracefully, wondrously, each individual player a sailing, dribbling ballet virtuoso, while in Europe *plays* are worked on, by a *team*. It looks stiff, linear, undramatic, even tedious (Jack Nicholson probably wouldn't attend any of Berlin's "roundball" games, as he does nightly with the LA Lakers), but plays do work. The Americans, while they are not really a *team* but an assortment of the best maestros and soloists money can buy, are still the best "team"-- it is after all, Our Game-- though I suspect we wont be the best for much longer. The distance is definitely narrowing, because total no-holds-barred individualism has its strong drawbacks. Like ego, and like how about blindness? Or, okay, myopia? In basketball the fancy flamingo who has the crowd on its feet, and the ticket sales, and therefore millions from endorsements, this hoops Merlin cannot so easily see the open man, the easy scorer (much less the semi-open man who *can* see the *fully* open man), not while this dramatic Merlin is in fullout-fly-drive shake'n'bake.

One of the saddest symptomatic examples of all this is the case of Yao Ming, the Chinese seven foot-six center, the first player to come to our NBA from that country. Poor Yao is not scoring anywhere near what the coach (and owner) believe he should score; Yao is not dominating the boards like Shaquille O'Neill, who is only a pathetic seven foot one or two. So, the pros are trying to teach unindividualist Yao not to be so selfless, not to pass off so much to his shrimpy teammates-- little people who wallow under the rim at six foot five to six foot eleven. They are trying to teach Yao to not be so concerned about humiliating his opponents: *Hey, Chrissakes, throw a wicked elbow to somebody's jaw, Yao!* Poor Yao, he gets it sports-intellectually of course, but in his sports-heart he doesn't get it: Yao is just a sorry old non-individualist who may have read too much Mao. A team guy. A basketball humanist (Too bad, bemoan the ad boys: with a whoopdedoo monniker like YAO! we could have a field day and go great promo guns). Same story in our American foot-ball, with the scrambling "individualist" quarterback. This one-guyishness despite football's disconcerting (and ever increasing) factorial division of labor, its planning, its platooning, its military cellphone headgear "coordination", as if football were blackboarded at Harvard Business School or at IBM. This despite (or because of?) our football's *un*democracy (like our basketball's): you must be a mammoth to play college or pro. You must be, normally, abnormal. Beyond normal (The blocking specialist mammoth cannot run or scramble; the scrambler does not mammothly block; whereas in "the old days" players "went both ways"-- which has an altogether unassociated meaning today). Our today's American football is so unlike Europe's *fußball* (Soccer), where the guys resemble, you know, plain *guys*... And, by the way, what is *up* with our silly callow naming of our teams Cowboys and Indians and Bears and Tigers?-- as if to appeal to the eight year old cohort, as if our teams are breakfast cereal. At least soccer's Manchester United sounds adult, like maybe a union. Real Madrid doesn't call itself the Madrid Matadors for godsakes, as cute and Madison Ave as the Matadors might ring. Hey, grow up! In what our iconic historian Frederick Jackson Turner often called "the technology of haste", we whip up an easy, instant, hurried mythology of Individualism. The Business of America is Individualism is Business. I.e. is profit. Even the religion of America, while it is mostly Christianity-- and statistics indicate us to be the most churchgoing nation in the West-- the religion of America is Individualism is *Business*. A Polish friend of mine visiting here was agape at the double-figure abundance of preachers on American TV. "They pound the Bible, hard, like angry butchers," he said, quizzically critical, "and they order everybody to make money like Bible pounding. They *shame* them." And my shocked-bemused Polish friend was from what is probably the most religious nation in Europe's Christendom-- even after it was communist for forty odd years.

We are a competitive Action Society-- which certainly is good. Who wants to be an uncompetitive passive society? Even guru-heavy India doesn't nowadays want that-- if it ever did. It is over eighty years now since the perceptive sociologist Max Weber pointed out the connection between "the Protestant ethic and the spirit of capitalism", as did R.H. Tawney in *Religion and the Rise of Capitalism*: that rewarding rush of Salvation as evidenced by commercial diligence and success. And now global data have supported those old observers-- surveys from Gallup and the World Bank. Success, our pulpit, from the Success-Persona hawkers on TV and in books, the smiley aim-jawed Peter Principler hyperbolites to the flavor-of-the-month money-maker mavins popping up on (of all sources) PBS, often in the next time slot after PBS shows pushing "Eastern" serenity (I've seen none of such numbskull credulous hoopla on European TV). Except, the new research seems also to show that there is a point of diminishing returns to Big Religion: faith eventually, and not surprisingly, Islamicizes; a pillow, a comforter, it *depresses* economic growth. It shouldn't come as a one-two whallop to realize that competitive action, by its own inertia, round and round and round untempered, can become empty Action, as narrow and unrelated as riding a stationary bicycle, empty-eyed, sweat-logged. A bunch of absurd, perplexed Sisyphusers-- and unknowingly perplexed. Paradox-ically, deeply *in*active activity. Innovation ascends, then overwhelms (buttons! keys! screens! beeps! warnings! guidebooks! viruses!)-- then it dulls. This curious-- and not-so-curious-- phenomenon is given a name in *Shadow Syndromes*, a psychoanalytic view into "American Noise", our over-robust proclamation of Robustness (while we become fat and unrobust), such that even the word "businessman" has come to transform its meaning in America: A businessman was originally in England a man of public affairs (In France, an "*homme d'affaires*"). Ralph Nader, our premier business watchdog, might once have been described as a true "businessman" par excellence. The above does of course sound funny to our modern ears, but in Europe, where a man-of-affairs is not by identity a Businessman, a German company, for example, could not so easily funk up the Rhine as if it were the Hudson or the Alleghany or the Ohio, because, one, the company's constituent body, of "businessmen"-- men of affairs-- wouldn't allow that: Its board has union representation, what they call *Mitbestimmung* (making things right together; or, cooperative management), the funding vigilant banks are fundamentally society-protective; the towns affected have sentry-like oversight, with political muscle; the corporation's labor would have say; and there is a fifty percent chance that the company is, at least in small part, government-owned.[*] Such organized grouping, allowing for "patient capital", has come to be known as the Stakeholder Company. And yet, shackled as American business might feel by these "unfair constraints", German firms seem to do better: Germany boasts the highest share of world trade in goods requiring high skills-- 20 percent, with the U.S. lagging at 14 percent; the best machine tools, like pistons and valves, metal punching and laser cutting equipment, are produced in Germany (and *exported* to China; not the reverse, imported *from* China, as with us); autos, trucks, chemicals and engineering hardware ship *out*, not *in*, as the respective German companies compete more over quality and excellence, than by slicing price (*Leistungswettbewerb*).

So in Western Europe the corporation is accountable in about five different ways. UnAmerican ways. Man-of-affairs ways, in the old-fashioned sense, where even the lowly union man is not so very lowly, not an unmanlified cog, but can experience himself to be integral, a person of worth, of connection and value. Through his worker association he becomes one part of the participatory assemblages in each mercantile endeavor: *verbände*, like the Federation of German Industry; the German Chambers of Industry and Commerce; the Federation of Employers' Associations; employee associations; town councils; church assemblies. Over 1200 are represented in the city of Berlin alone, combining an energetic competition with an industrious cooperation-- a guided tempering-- even if the main entrepreneur does not wholly fancy such "cooperative restraints". Simply, the values that underpin a social contract, fairness, reciprocity and opportunity-- the values that from the Enlightenment did begin to hint of underpinning civilized society-- are precisely those values that across the Atlantic go to supporting a successful company... In France, there are national councils for just about every endeavor, every organized action (and most there *are*), and there is a great deal too much controlling nationalization (the "championing" of large-scale companies-- Air France, Renault, Crédit Lyonnais, France Telecom, almost all TV)-- so jobs are assured, in commerce as well as in civil service (as there often is in effect no difference, and unions will even strike *against* privatization-- as recently happened with *Electricité de France* and *Gaz de France*); train rates are consequently low, and post offices are, amazingly, efficient-- while, yes, innovation may be

---

[*] This last is diminishing-- moderately. Even *Deutsche Post* has undergone a successful IPO (public offering) of a portion of its stock.

stunted. And certain influential journals, like *Le Figaro*, are-- as everyone knows and finds amusing-- tantamount to being government organs, and-- as everyone knows and finds amusing-- unions, and even non-union people, will strike and demonstrate (and remonstrate) at the-- suspiciously joyous-- drop of a hat: wages, hours, layoffs-- you name it, they wont hear of it. When Michelin announced layoffs, due to the price of rubber rising a bowl-over twenty percent, unions weighed in: layoffs "adjusted" downward to no-rehiring for those employees retiring; this concession from an advanced company that (unlike any in America) has already taken the initiative to set up development funds in locales where it has plants-- in Germany, France and England-- to offer technical advice and low interest loans (unsecured) to growing small companies. Still, those French shoutey "*grèves*" and "*manifs*" do happen; and they can be damned annoying and inconveniencing when you want to cross a street or study or hail a taxi, or take a train (or just think); but to adjust and accommodate to them "les bizzynessmen" must become righteous, consultational, "*hommes d'affaires*", as are the managers of Michelin. Even when these French street events descend to habit, or even addiction, or even delirious perverse French fun-- in The Stalemate Society.

Here, from Adam Gopnik's skewer-charming *Paris to the Moon*:

> The "generalized" stike... has shut down Paris. The commuter and intercity trains haven't run for two weeks... The Métro is closed down... There are no buses, and the post office has stopped delivering the mail... The Ritz has had a dropoff in occupancy of 25 percent... The Louvre, like a city under siege, has been struggling to stay open and can guarantee only a narrow access corridor, leading directly to the *Mona Lisa*. The government has even commandeered the *bateaux-mouches*-- those ugly, flat-bottomed open-air tourist boats... and has turned them into ferryboats to get commuters up and down the Seine... the chickens stopped rotating at the outdoor market in my neighborhood.

And there's little need for manipulative corporate contributions to political campaigns in Europe (usually such weighted distributions are illegal anyway), as the campaigns are short and inexpensive: not TV-ad inundated.

Sounds kinda like, uh, Democracy?

Or at least a more serious attempt at it. Through a sense of Community to at least balance out the harsher Business individualisms.

Is the Euro-way adult? Our leaders would certainly call it naive. And slow.

Well, "community", if it does not come about naturally is far more difficult to appreciate in moving-van no-community America. Despite that *Air France* and *France Télécom* have become more privatized, the state is easily the largest employer in France, no nook or cranny is beyond its extensive reach; not fully. The French legislature can influence lower prices, as on CocaCola and Danone-- to reduce inflation while increasing demand (and employment); and a full one-quarter of the French workforce is in some aspect of the "civil service" (they tend to hate that Angloism with its servant-sycophant overtones and innuendoes; they prefer *fonctionnaire*); as one-seventh in Britain and Germany is in government employ. Whereas in America less than a mere one-twelfth of us are state bureaucrats supposedly -- in one way or another-- watching out for the exploitation of our fellow citizens. But, I must say, our less-than-one-twelfth would be fine, if that one-thirteenth or so actually *were* social sentries. Ombudsmen teammates of a sort. Even fractionally.

Item: The world's largest group of labor unions, The International Confederation of Free Trade Unions, pointed to the United States, along with China, Burma, Colombia and Belarus, as a serious violator of worker rights (See WalMart, Chapter 7). In the other four nations union people are jailed, and killed, but we do not work that way. We only fire, lay off, and threaten plant closure. Most Americans are not aware of this, but when workers in the U.S. attempt to organize, employers typically hire anti-union consultants (in *75 percent of cases*) who: advise employers on how to attract workers to anti-union meetings (97 percent of cases); threaten those plant-closures if a union wins a vote (71 percent); evilly call in federal immigra-tion agents (52 percent); illegally discharge workers for pro-union activity. After five decades of union slippage in America, only 13.5 percent of all workers belong (8.5 percent in the private sector); but if workers did not face such a war against organizing, surveys say upwards of 44 percent would choose to belong to a union. Admittedly these worker groups can be rather regimenting themselves, and peer-pressure coercive; but when the cruel alternative is considered throughout modern industrial history, the somewhat tasteless and numbing indoctrination of worker alliance, often inevitable for worker power, is certainly a necessary tactic. As you may surmise by now, the average union membership in Europe is not our Lilliputian 8.5 percent but approximately 45 percent.

Items: Our government erects tariff walls for Big Biz, as recently it did to save US Steel, with its inefficient capacity; the government helps support Boeing, in Daddy Warbucks mode, with lucrative defense contracts, as with its own ineffiencies Boeing had to "downsize" by 40,000 workers (assisting in the extension of the nation's Rust Belt from Pittsburgh and Detroit and Wheeling to Seattle and Tacoma). Boeing recently lost to Europe's Airbus a coveted $2 billion Chinese order for twenty planes, and a more coveted Abu Dhabi deal of $7 billion (as well as a defeat in Turkey by $1.5 billion). So Boeing now lags far behind rival Airbus, a cross-nation consolidation[*] which is today the world's leading commercial aviation manufacturer. You know, like *passenger planes*? The new Airbus 380 super-jumbo doubledecker, built in Toulouse, will carry up to 880 passengers. This, by putting the interests of plane-building, consortium compromise, order-seeking and customer-pleasing, before those of stockholder-dividend-demanding. Similarly, Renault and Peugeot cooperate by pooling the purchase of components for lower price; and *Deutsche Telekom* and *France Télécom* are cooperating on research and development. And then there is our bolstered-up Motorola lagging with less than half the mobile phone market of little Finland's unbolstered Nokia. Nokia, and Swedish Ericsson, had benefited when the cooperative Scandinavian mobile telephone network was set up way back in '83, paving the way for the European standard band width, which is now the global standard (being employed, ironically, by Samsung and Sony in Asia, to take market share away now from Nokia).

Again, by cooperation and planning, the EU has brought together an annual $7 billion for investment in the new nanotechnology of chip making, one of the "key drivers" in the knowledge industry. The aim here is to lead the world in that industry by 2010. America is certainly not sleeping on nanotechnology, but with our individualist atomization of R&D, even in Silicon Valley, we are dropping behind. Once more.

---

[*] Thus, subsidized itself, but not surreptitiously: not counter to its nations' outspoken ideology; rather, in conformity with their principles of consolidation.

So why our bolstering-boosting-- and yet ideologically denied—Government Welfare? Our government as Business Community's community, not *our* community-- which, yes, even the French do-- and the Germans do-- albeit not in the distorted name of Individualism; thus not against the Community of people, but ultimately for it. Simply, when you establish a government policy that supports big business, yes, across the board, not specific lobby-potent business, a government policy that also supports people-in-general, as a matter of principle, then you have neither "corporate welfare" nor dole-dolloping, not hypocrisy but canon. Why then do we surreptitiously Atlas-up poorly performing big business, as we laud it as Big Business?-- which can obviously beget a vicious distorted circle. Because-- The Shadow Syndrome-- our unindividualist Indvidualism, which is in the long-run as blind as it is counterproductive. In Europe, as I've said, there does thrive a stronger identification with town, with one's land (in the general sense), with one's own people. And although this sort of "particularism"-- once labelled "amoral familism"-- can at times be borish and petty, it is not idealist romantic hokum. Its consequence: In Europe production technique, factory efficiency, *product*, remain paramount; company profits aren't sine qua non, not immediately anyway: profits are reinvested for long-term prospects, rather than showered out as dividends to the distant stockholder (America, 80%; Europe, 20% to 33%). Volkswagen, for example, pays only 16 percent of its post-tax earnings as dividends, retaining the rest as investment in research and development, which, at 4.8 percent of turnover tops Ford's 4 percent and GM's 3.6 percent. Again, in Europe management even consults the-- hold onto to your portfolios!-- *workers*, laborers who are on the factory floor and therefore might just know a specific thing or two about tools and parts and process: i.e., what will work, out on the street. This "dynamic conservatism" is surely one reason why American productivity-- of Boeing, GM, Ford, US Steel-- is lower in output per man hour than in France, Germany, Belgium or Holland. Not in total output, no-- we are too populous a nation for that indignity. Yet, we are just creeping along in individual worker productivity. With one-quarter of our population, France outstrips us in steel production. But why should the unconsulted, unpartnered laborers here care? They're often not even well-equipped with up-to-date machinery; while in good Old Europe they don't "sweat the assets" wearing them out for quick old-fashioned (new fashioned?) Protestant ethic profit. Well, not as much as we do anyway, as most shareholders there (25 to 35 percent) are conservative banks—Deutsche Bank, Commerzbank, Dresdner Bank, and the *Banque Nationale de France* (a.k.a. the French government)-- all interested in long term success; and all today under the watchful aegis of the EU Central Bank (vigilant, but admittedly not yet with so much controlling armor). For good or ill, private stockholders are far fewer than in the U.S. People simply save their money, in banks-- maybe even in their mattresses (I would not be surprised). In Western Europe average people don't go into debt (Germany, 10 percent of earnings is saved; France, 12 percent; Italy, 15 percent; the U.S., just *2 percent*-- so far less is available here for bank investment in the economy). Sure there are corporate takeovers in Germany and in France (which has recently bailed-out Alstom, its turbine-to-train conglomerate, which built the famous speed-train TGV, but also overextended itself in worldwide investments), but these events do not go on our hayride-carnival scale (Again, read the business pages: even with a scorecard you wont be able to keep up on who or what owns what. And that is dismaying, more than it is hyperbolically comical.). Sure, Europe indulges in "synergy"-- another word for cutting employment-- but not in the same ballpark as the way we "synergize"—i.e. "downsize", i.e. "outsource". By the way, those steel tariffs we then had to back down from when Europe threatened to reciprocate against American Business. Fair is fair: They'd import no more Florida oranges, nor Carolina textiles, nor Detroit Harleys--a company we kindly subsidize anyway: for our (ambiguous) reputation.

Fact: The consequences of this American predilection for tight asset-squeezing has been obsolescence-- as in steel-- and a loss of our productivity to only sixteen percent of our economy. This compared to Germany's thirty-two percent-- double. Like a nervous trapeze artist, our economy is kept aloft, not by our mythological "individualist productive selves", but by foreign investment in our dollars (See our Trade Deficit with the European Union in Table 6. And with China, Table 7). No other major economy in the world accepts the insanity of perennial trade deficits-- some maintain huge surpluses. But we require-- hold onto your portfolios again-- *two billion dollars a day of foreign investment* in American dollars to stay afloat, thus accumulating by now $3 *trillion* in debt obligations abroad (and $5 *trillion* more projected for the next ten years); and we remain bragging that we are superior to the foreigners supporting us (Like France and Germany we run a budget deficit of about five percent; *unlike* them we also run that bonkers-pathetic trade deficit; also unlike those nations we don't seem to believe we run *either* deficit).[*] We could be called ingrates-- if we *knew* we were ingrates. But 90 percent of us don't know that the other, fortunate, ten percent (the super-rich) are ingrates. Something is awfully Kafkaesque here. Or, a wan Kafka welded onto a sourpussed ironic Camus onto a wryly satisfied grinning depressed Beckett. After all, if the steady foreign holder from his trapeze swing no longer grasps the suspended swaying showoff American trapeze artist who is looping and twisting happily egregious-- while yet shouting contemptuous put-downs to his (putative) catcher-holder -- the dude plummets: China's trade is now greater with the EU than with the U.S.; and if it (or Japan) suddenly decides to no longer hold dollars-- in effect to give us welfare beggars (Well, that *is* what we are!) money-- we can kiss that thing of ours that sits on our "Restroom" "Bathroom" seat that we invented but can't bring ourselves to call (except in comedians' jokes) a TOILET, goodbye.

TABLE 6

U.S. TRADE DEFICIT WITH THE E.U.

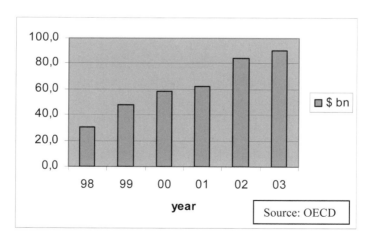

Source: OECD

---

[*] As the London *Financial Times* observed after George W. Bush's second round of tax cuts, this was not conservatism but madness. "On the management of fiscal policy, the lunatics are now in charge of the asylum... Reason cuts no ice; economic theory is dismissed; and contrary evidence is ignored... Watching the world's economic superpower slowly destroy perhaps the world's most enviable fiscal position is something to behold."

TABLE 7

THE US TRADE DEFICIT WITH CHINA

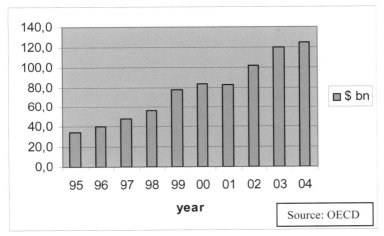

Source: OECD

Fact: With the considerable exception of WMD (You know, the evanescent Weapons of Mass Destruction we decided to stamp out in Iraq?), the U.S. has arrived at the ghost-haunted way station where it manufactures almost nothing, in relative world terms: We net import machinery, technology, autos, textiles, oil, and furniture-- and money. What we export are lumber, grains, fruit, fish, and raw cotton, the southern farmers of which crop we subsidize, thereby immiserating the cotton laborers of west Africa and Brazil-- while the EU has agreed to eliminate all of its export subsidies for farm goods. As William Greider writes, "In theory, wealthy countries are expected to ship investment capital to poorer countries to build factories and infrastructure. But at present, most of the world's capital is flowing in reverse: The net inflow of foreign capital to the United States represents a staggering 75 percent of the net outflows from the rest of the world." Now that's hogging. That's like some eccentric billionaire with a panhandler porkpie hat out, slump-for-fun, at the entrance to The Plaza. If countries had contempt for us they might call us a Lumber-Fish Republic (And countries do have contempt for us). And worse-boding: Due to the present Republican administration's fealty to Fundamentalism, we have fallen down a deep hole in stem cell research. Stem cells are those potent cells drawn from discarded embryos, unviable for life embryos; but they do have the unmatchable ability to create any type of tissue in the human body, and thus to help in the cure of Parkinson's Disease and Lou Gehrig's Disease and Alzheimer's and diabetes, and repair damage to spinal chords. Paralyzed Christopher Reeve's deep contempt for "Dubya" (I was witness to it on the BBC interview show *Hardtalk*) is nothing if not justifiable. The leading nations in stem cell work are now Sweden, Israel, Britain and Finland (Germany, though ripe to join in, is understandably hesitant: its Nazi eugenics illegacy holds it back. So, would it be incorrect and unfair to observe that Deutsche Third Reichism and American Fundamentalism are partners here, sharing mutual interests and hatreds?).

Fact: In our chaotic (okay, freewheeling; okay, "laissez-faire", okay "unstructured") economy, we recently lost 600,000 jobs, (although some statistics say the figure was more nearly 3 million). But although layoffs infected Detroit, no one lost his job in automotive Stuttgart or motor Munich. Anyway it was not wham-bam-boom job-loss, not that "horrible sucking sound" H. Ross Perot made dubiously infamous, but a net job loss: 31.7 million jobs were eliminated while 31.1 million jobs were created. Or just 28 million. Not so atrocious, you might say. It was just one of those Developed World Things, you might say. Downturn. Happened all over. Cyclical. The upturn is now rolling-- what's the humungus problem? Could have been lots worse, and it definitely has gotten better with this global upturn. A bit better, anyway. But it was not as if "just" 600,000 people lost their jobs (or three million people); it was rather tens of millions who went out of work, while sevens of millions, and not necessarily the same people, found work. There exists a great deal of unhealthy jitters and tremblings (and stunted growth: See Chapter 6) in those chaotic numbers, those musical job chairs, as *these are families*.

Item: It was not a U.S. firm like AT&T or SBC but a French one that has installed almost half of the new telephone lines in China. So the job losses aren't likely to be from *France Télécom* but from AT&T and SBC. True, sure, job loss happens in Europe too of course, but *low-skilled, middle-aged workers in the U.S. are seven to eight times more likely to lose their jobs than similar people in Germany or France*. And when the dreaded does happen in Western Europe it occurs over a far thicker safety net (see Chapters 5 and 6). Same with our recent scares and hullabaloo over outsourcing. The U.S. is the prime market for outsourcing: IBM; securities firms; engineering outfits; radiologists; technology executives. Amazon.com, Cisco Systems, Apple Computer, Boeing, GE, Kraft. Outsourcing certainly happens in Europe too, as does "downsizing" (proof being that the French do have a word for it: *dégraissage*). But the average Frenchman will fight *dégraissage* beak and claw, as will his government; and it is dampened down by your basic German community board overseeing corporations' behavior-- sometimes even getting together in *gasthäuser* over beers (*der stammtisch,* or stem table, as in medieval drinking rounds around the sawn-off burl stem of an oak). Or, if hobnobbing fails, the Germans can go the French route: the powerful trade union IG Metall has held nationwide protests against Siemens for its threatened outsourcing; then came meetings, compromise: the work week went up from 35 to 36 hours-- in some cases 40 hours (the American minimal-normal)-- but only during "boom periods" (Does the American metal industry even *have* "boom periods"?). Job-reduction was not merely reduced, but halted. A similar route is now in process with Daimler-Chrysler and Bosch, the top executives of the former agreeing to take a pay cut themselves of up to ten percent (And can you imagine our American executives pledging such?).* And then, when a diminished outsourcing still is allowed to be "employed" by European corporations, well, again, there is-- unlike here at home-- that appreciable worker safety net. . . Except, that is not all: outsourced work is skill lost, motivation and know-how drifted away. America's problem here is not only job loss, but character lost. Its Edison soul.

True awful ironic Joke: Our woodworking craftsmanship, once world-admired, might no longer be so hot: Since 2001 the US has lost 34,000 jobs in wooden furniture manufacturing-- about one-third of our entire workforce-- mostly to the boondock rice-paddie town of Lecong. That's in China. Lecong now promotes itself as the "furniture capital of the world", with its main street a long Vegas-like strip of gaudy showrooms (3500 stores, 6000 factories) and exhibition centers. Wasn't the furniture capital once Grand Rapids, Michigan? But, wait: how come *German* furniture exports *to* China have quintupled?-- from $16 million to $80

---

* Interestingly, the work weeks have recently been reduced to less than 35 hours at Deutsche Telekom and Opel.

million in two years. Good question. Quality? The Germans aren't demanding import tariffs, but *we* have just defensively imposed duties of up to 200 percent. Even though the Chinese raw materials-- like wood-- come mostly from the U.S.

TABLE EIGHT

INTERNATIONAL ACQUISITIONS OF FOREIGN FIRMS (2000)[*]	
BRITAIN:	337 billion
FRANCE:	157 billion
U.S.:	156 billion
GERMANY:	150 billion

Source: World Economic Forum

Sad fact: Increasingly, American environmental and public health advocates take their cases, not to our-- hopeless, circumscribed-- EPA, but to the European Union, hoping to use regulations there as a strong lever to push the United States-- in promoting air filtered from heat-trapping gasses, in chemical discharge, and electronic dangers-- even from (uhoh) computer screens. American lawmakers primarily look to our old Business-bottom-line friend Cost-Benefit-analysis-- which means nothing will be done here-- while Europeans look far more towards society's welfare in general. In Europe they have begun setting serious targets for conversion to renewable fuels, and taxing carbon emissions to accelerate that conversion. Once a law is passed in Brussels, environmentalists can lean on American congressmen to take a second stab. (And a third; and a fourth-- as many stabs will be needed here to ward off Cost-Benefit analysis). "We feel that Europe is a real opportunity," says Ned Helme, executive director for the Center for Clean Air Policy in Washington.

Another truth, another big irony: The United States was built, not on free-grab-for-all (cost-benefit-analysis, for example), but on a public interest principle, a watchdog community tradition designed especially by James Madison (*The Federalist Papers*) to protect the citizen from special interests

---

[*] This after years of America's having led in foreign acquisitions by leaps and bounds, and as European banks are preparing to take over many once sacrosanct American banks.

conspiring in a wide-open land: the sort of grab-bagism that had resulted in the South Seas stock meltdown swindles and busts of John Law in England, a premodel of our Enron disaster, and the misrepresentations and bankrupting scams of the *Crédit Mobilier* in France. In the eighteenth century our congress looked out suspiciously against special stock whipups and land grants to hoodwinkers. The citizen was represented: Community.

Another truth, another irony: Mass production, "The Uniformity System" (*actually called in Europe "The American System"*) as first developed by Eli Whitney, was not achieved by "individualist" Eli Whitney alone -- the self-made bold risk-taking entrepreneur. Rather with government boosting. Large American government support made possible what we call the Industrial Revolution. Every school child knows about Whitney's invention of the cotton gin-- or every American child did acknowledge that by rote, even in public school, before these schools became The American Disgrace. Now if school children hear the atavistic name Eli Whitney they are likely to chalk him up as some cool-gliding NFL halfback. But before the cotton gin, Whitney developed his system for the mass manufacture of muskets-- for export to European wars, mostly. American manufacturers then created standardized wheels, gears, pulleys, shafts and screws, for the world. Whitney himself, and the others who followed him, were only able to succeed however with great amounts of government financial aid, with leadership from men like Madison, Jefferson and John Adams. American economic greatness began then *with* American government subsidy-- but not handout (Whitney paid back)-- and without hypocritical, misleading cries of American laissez-faire independence for the industrialist. The government has always been there, only in early days it was out front, no subterfuge. No Myth to protect, then. None needed. The poor new nation couldn't have taken off without new-minted government dollars.

And: The courageous, hearty American Loner of American hero-fantasia did not open up the West, as intoxicating as such tall tales of him have been. No, the *caravan* joined our Atlantic to our Pacific: Mutual support, in effect the trading company group, as the English and the Dutch had done earlier in the East. Daniel Boone, of the coonskin cap and backwoods savvy, who barehanded "killed one bar", was also an organizer, a team player, of the Transylvania Company (no Dracula involved). Boone was even a county executive in Kentucky, and before that a member of the

Virginia legislature. A go-to-meetings guy-- a Discussion Dude, a Suit. Davy Crockett, by the way, king of the wild countryside that he was, served two terms seated in Congress-- with no air-conditioning then in brutal-humid longtailed jacket Washington. Oscar Wilde had once quipped, upon reading Marx and Engels and Robert Owen and Saint-Simon, that socialism would never work because it would entail too many meetings. Funny thing, capitalism worked *because* it entailed the same. It required launching: by meeting. Unheroic meeting; or heroic.

We just make heroes too easily in America; singular super-falsed-up-entities, from Washington to Lincoln to Kennedy to Michael Jordan, to Tiger Woods. To ridiculously unheroic men like John Wayne, and Ronald Reagan and George W. Bush, none who ever even fought in war one-- but who seem, psychotically, to believe they did-- none who ever did anything heroic and life-risking, entrepreneurs of myth, one might say. A not so unrecent TIME-CNN-Gallup poll (2003) actually had George W. Bush as The Most Admired American; and, undigestibly, as a man who performed better military service than did his Presidential opponent, war hero John Kerry. I mean, double duh? (even if Kerry's three wounds were all in truth "superficial", as the froth-mouthers of the Right woundingly maintain.). For godssakes, there are devoted surgeons who labor to save lives in sixteen hour operations, sometimes while they themselves are sick; there are selfless souls who have sacrificed family and risked disease to labor in AIDS lands; there are firemen and police who risk their lives every day; and America, knowing about such people (as who doesn't?), America *still* comes up with a cocky-smirky-bouncy-winky semi-literate (actually he doesn't even seem to be "semi" by any authentic scale of literacy) who has done NOTHING but be the easygoing landing pad of fortune. He, we admire the most!? Are we *that* off-the-walls!? In the "olden days", The Most Admired might have been Doctor Ralph Bunch, Martin Luther King, Mother Theresa, even the Polish Pope. And even in these now days you'd never catch a European being so naive (and media-manipulated?) as to Most Admire their own Chancellor Schröder or President Chirac-- for whom they held their noses as they voted, as the choice was down to Chirac and the super-racist Jean Marie le Pen. But we Americans, innocently at first, then hopeful, almost lovingly naive, as if The Fable is a factor of production as significant as any of the-factors-of-production taught in first year economics (land, labor, capital, entrepreneurship), we archly imagine lollapalooza tales wholesale of our

Great Individuals-- like Donald Trump?-- and thus *our* Individualism by trickle-down identity; *our* Know-How; *our* invincibility. This is sweet, but it is so childish, our relishing a gaudy chiaroscuro of our "progress"-- in Golden Arches and wide-winged Stealth bombers, in once-bewinged Cadillacs with Jayne Mansfield bumpers and country-singing self-described "Outlaws" who pull down ten million per-- "outlaw" perchance only in evading taxes (Our "heroes" aren't heroes, and our "outlaws" aren't outlaws). And our relishing the Babbitbubble "recreations" of Rome and ancient Egypt in Las Vegas.

In our land of great distances and migrations, steady crisscross and doubleback migrations, and short-lived neighborlinesses and ethnic vagueries of identity, we fear the steady and limited and controlled, and small, as foreign and unvisionary, as stodgy. A woodsman like Davy Crockett, in reality just a good Tennessee fellow, could be in legend-- printed out in the presses of distant, urban brickrow Boston and Beacon Hill --a giant. Bigger and bigger as farther and farther. An American Unifier. And No, Virginia, there was no Johnny Appleseed; only wideflung communities of plainfolk planters. *Teams.* Mythology: America itself The Hero, a substitute for Europe's Joan of Arc or Charlemagne. A substitute of much greater need and importance than Joan of Arc or Charlemagne. But in mythology's *down* side-- and drat, there always is that *down* side-- we have ended up desperately unable to see non-mythology, which is Reality. When we witness those aforementioned conveniences in France or Germany that do not exist in America we both see and appreciate them *and* we are impervious to seeing and appreciating. There and not-there, these new convenient well-tiled tunnels and sweet fast trams and trains and broad city boulevards that dip under intersections, and computerized parking lots; and so *we* have become the stodgy ones in our Big Denial. We have become the dull teacup Europeans we imagine Europeans are (And those talky-talk French flicks don't help). Dismissable, we say, all that Euro-stuff. No we don't even say it. Saying would be some admission: No, these advances just do not quite exist. Reality is not real if it is not an American Hero reality, like Rocky Balboa, one of the most unlikely, impossible phenomena to ever come down the pugilist pike-- boxing's Horatio Alger played out for the non-boxing (and non-black) Walter Mitty. So, isn't this why "we"-- okay, Californians-- voted The Terminator into its governorship? No *hero*, for godssakes, but a man who won-- the real life metaphor is almost too gnawingly beautiful, too awfully apt-- *Pose Downs*. A grinning croucher-flexer. Imagine a screenwriter, a desperate one, sweatingly smuggling in such a hokey idea to a producer in his office. Nathaniel West perhaps. Hear the laughter (the producer has his hands folded at his neck's nape) at what isn't even a B movie, but a D one. An F one. A societal delusion of grandeur.

We the People, The Credulous Incredulous Credible Credulans.

Like the reverent-religious way we pronounce "hero": *Hee!*-Row!

In Germany, my next door neighbor Fritz (that really is the guy's name), a Mercedes middle manager, *flies the Mercedes flag!* Yupski. On nice days Fritz ambles out in front of his Black Forest house, gingerbread shingle affair, then Fritz nonchalantly tugs on a knotbutton rope, and that tri-spoked blue-white Episcopalean-looking Daimler insignia waves and ripples at the top of a flagpole high enough to be a Bavarian Maypole-- about thirty feet. At first I thought Fritz was simply tasteless, low class, a German troglodgyte. I mean, this hoopla-loyalty was a tad Neanderthal, robot-goon, even for a gung-ho employee. It reminded me of the once-great IBM in the fifties and sixties, with its rote IBM corporate song and its rote-robot IBM corporate chorale in IBM tuxedoes (Women's lib hadn't hit paydirt yet), the IBM that went complacent and missed out on the PC Revolution, and so almost dissolved and perished. "Fritz," I ventured, "why do you fly the Mercedes flag?" And Fritz regarded me uncomprehendingly, fixedly, as if *I* were the trog. "I *work* there," he said, as if that were explanation enough for any idiot. "So?" I said, again conjuring IBM. And again Fritz regarded me uncomprehendingly, even ferociously. He was no complacent IBMer. "I *work* there," he repeated, slowly, grinding it in, as if I didn't quite ken his German-- or the word "*arbeit*", 'work' in its true strong devoted meaning. But I had put in three misery-laden years at The Goethe Institute, competing with Serbs, Croats, Turks and various Africans, so I understood his German (actually *Bad-ish*; no pun intended). Fritz then turned back to working in his yard-- a favorite German thing. And I tried to imagine him now as, say, a GM employee unfurling the Cadillac logo on high. Or a Ford worker sailing that historic insignia and saluting. Identity. Loyalty. Product Pride. In corporate community. Or, community *through* the corporation. Which translates, simply, any way you translate it, into plain Community... Fritz, the middle-manager goes off to work in a suit, but he had started out on the factory floor. He has no MBA; he believes that American managers of large companies are selfish, barely loyal short-termers. Diffident clock-watchers who don't see change coming, don't adapt. Fritz knows, and I suppose loves, not "bottom line" but craft. He knows, and is friendly with, factory floor workers beneath him. He listens to them-- because he *is* them. He will remain with Daimler until he retires. Such affiliations obviously make the dreaded Outsourcing less a likelihood, less even a possibility; though Fritz admits, sure, it does happen in Germany. Just not like it does in my country. Fritz, by the way, acknowledges no "Chrysler": To him the Daimler-Chrysler duet is really a Daimler-Benz solo. To everybody.

Look, I am hardly suggesting that Cadillac workers unfurl the Cadillac banner and daffily salute. For one thing, as you would expect, the Cadillac bears a very intricate, overdone coat of arms, worthy of Richard Coeur de Lion on a gaudy day. And we Americans *Don't do that sort of thing*-- except with Old Glory. My point-- sure, for the umpteenth time: While American cities today stagnate because of our folk-ethic of laissez-faire-- or folk tale-- Europe relies on community. Well, it doesn't so much rely on it as it *is* it. Or it manifests it. We have evolved one way, *from* Community, from the Mayflower Compact and the Puritan Covenant and the tight circular caravan, that group anti-redskin bulwark as we wagon-wheeled over Texas, Oregon and the Louisiana Purchase. Europe has evolved the other way, *from* the individual serf's land plot (or strip) and tithe to his landlord prince, then hamlet and farm. Europe has fallen away from the aforementioned "amoral familism" (jargon for 'Anyone outside your nuclear unit is *no* one: screw him'), and we have unfortunately drifted *towards* that Katie-bar-the-door mentality. One man's evo, the other's devo. We tend no longer to invest our faith-- or money for that matter-- in the group, or the city, because *there doesn't seem to be a group*, or a city; not for our varied nation of immigrants and migrants and suburbanites-- The American Bedouin. Less and less can we trace our families, mixed and manifold as they are, back to this village, this state, that country-- even though the effort (The American Family Tree) wouldn't even constitute such formidable spiderweb tracework. We are simply not interested. Cosetted (and closeted) in our exurban mall warrens, and tract warrens, we seldom even visit our cities. Screw *them*, say we amoral anomist familists. Now we identify with

Success, energetic Success or slovenly or casual-corrupt Success, and Success alone-- what the philosopher William James lamented (obviously long ago) as "our national disease," with its-- his words-- "moral flabbiness".[*] As Daniel Boorstin has written (in *The Americans*), Jamestown, the first permanent American settlement, became also the first American ghost town. But whether or not Romulus and Remus ever existed, Rome is still Rome. Paris is still Paris.

Still, from the Pilgrims at Plymouth in 1620, America once was communitarian. We were the super-communionists. Our hotels were residences, public in effect, not snooty private temp-places, as they were then in Europe. Our trains began as public carriages, with open seating, as opposed to the private, again snootyish, compartmentalization of European conveyances. Our railroads, which ran from "nowhere in particular to nowhere at all", as *The London Times* once amusedly mused, were built with government grants; land ownership was bestowed by government, as were oil well sites, and even some wells, in rugged self-reliant muscular Lone Star Texas. New York (or New Amsterdam) and Chicago, in fact, began by community provision-- no dei ex-machinas: water, streets, sidewalks, street lamps, bridges, stores, parks.   And it had to be this way. At the turn of the nineteenth into the twentieth century, it was our own domestic, group concern regathering that had the "improvitarian" Progressive Era follow upon The Gilded Age of freewheeling robber-barons, as we dealt with urban problems similar to today's: immigration, poverty, unemployment, urban ugliness. In those more simple days, however, The Great Delusion was not hovering over us like a regal dome. Black and white was black and white. We were not hampered by an overgrown credulity that we were The Biggest, The Greatest, The Richest, The Singularist-- as we weren't. We could humbly huddle-up and join up and try to fix things up: committees; unions; government support:

> Hull House (Settlement House)
> The Knights of Labor
> Boy Scouts/ Girl Scouts

---

[*] What could be more gauling than those ubiquitous American television ad-dramas that "realistically" show executives realistically solving corporate problems in their Dockers? I have never seen comparable easy-striver *publicités* or *werbung* on German or French TV. Perhaps next these American actor-"executives" will be solving corporate dilemnas in their pajamas.

4-H Clubs
The Playground Association
NAACP
Knights of Columbus
Modern Woodwork America
Rotary Clubs
Kiwanis Clubs
Jaycees
Salvation Army
Shriners
NRA
ABA (books, not basketball)
Loyal Order of Moose
Sierra Club
PTA
VFW
Goodwill Industries
Teamsters
YWCA/YMCA
Community Chest
American Legion
ACLU
etc.

Eras have more momentum than one might imagine: Slowly, then rapidly, snowballing, all those groups arrived way back then. Notes, chords, finding purposeful life. No, absolutely necessary life. And even two centuries before, on board the famous Puritan ship, before even setting anchor on The Rock, the "Roundheads", our forefathers (well, sort of), the first immigrants, had formed that old Mayflower Compact, which set up their government-to-be. Pretty communitarian birthright.

But now we "Bowl Alone", as the sociologist Robert Putnam has enjoyed putting it (Actually though, I've never even seen a European bowl--alone or otherwise). Individualist Dupes, one might say, we are plain born into some distinct species of the libertarian here these days. I say "some species" as, at the higher levels one does commonly come across country club golfers chipping and putting in chummy bucolic collectives (But no, not bowlers.[*]). Still, for the most part, you have to do some serious thinking, some steady observing and reflecting, and *reading*?-- and caring-- to up and rise out of the American Me Me Me Me Me.

Observation: When Novartis, the Swiss pharmaceutical firm, needed a new supercomputer for designing drugs, it harvested one by innovation: uniting the computer powers in the thousands of personal computers in its offices: Grid Computing, a new fastening-on method linked-up more and more in "Old" Europe, and barely fidgeted with in America-- even by the casual-capable comers in Dockers. Why? Because we MeMe shake'n'bake teamlessly, shamelessly, like the L.A. Lakers (Yes, it did provide great pleasure to see the *team*-- no monster stars-- Detroit Pistons whup Shaquille'n'Kobe in the 2004 NBA championships). We just tastelessly shimmy our V-dance between the goalposts and baskets. We hamstring ourselves by "competing computing" rather than uniting-computing; we shackle-up laissez-faire (phoney-baloney laissez-faire, that is) with our government's reluctance to orchestrate even a minor planned-out policy. Planning being, you know, the Devil's Due, the Devil's Discipline (for some reason), instinctive God-individualist anathema. But deployment of an advanced computer grid in the U.S. in many industries, it has been estimated, might add to our GDP upwards of fifty billion dollars, and two hundred thousand more jobs. Yup, it is done in "Old", ancient, newly-Godless Europe; sometimes next door to the remains of Caesar's Roman baths (which is not a modern niteclub). Why not?

By the way, our American, Hands-off *my* company (except when *my* company *needs* a government welfare outstretched hands-*on* for *my* company) "libertarianism" was in fact once Europe's liberalism-- which was the original Anglified monnicker for laissez-faire. You know, in French it means "leave to do", i.e. leave me alone to act as I please. Adam Smith, the biblical godfather of today's conservatism, was in fact then an "old European liberal". If History is anything it is the history of irony, of topsy-turvy twists and transformations (and interpretations of the transformations: the anthropological battle still goes on-- though it hardly now rages-- whether

---

[*] The late Stephen Jay Gould once wryly observed how American New-Agers, when describing that "sweet groove" achieved by meditation, often employ the metaphors of tennis volleys or golf drives, never "low class" bowling rolls-- which certainly rely as well on "the groove".

human society originated with "reciprocity and redistribution" or with primal-self-interest capitalism); so History is really a kind of non-history. Or history as *a*-history. Or self-justification of Your Now by Your (made up, spun-out) History. But there is no way out from denying that today's "communitarian" Europe was the land that began its economic takeoff to communitarianism by way of a self-styled, risk-taking individualism (of what economists call "self-sustained growth"), and that the original meaning of that label liberalism has now come to mean its opposite. Modern Europe was the land that began its development (or evolution, if you will) out of the stultifying medieval and mercantile ages by singular entrepreneurship, by risk-taking and inventiveness-- more than did America. More, because earlier. More, because it also took in and swallowed-up South America's gold-- what came to be called the price revolution of the sixteenth century, or its profit inflation for the Big Boys. Then, eventually (after a few wars and starvations and stuff), old capitalist Europe entrepreneured itself into group-entrepreneurship, out of "old" "American" single entrepreneurship. Europeans were the (if you will, and maybe you wont) entrepreneurs of entrepreneurianism. Clear? Partial list of old Europe's old capitalist innovations:

> Crédit Mobilier-- France: the original financing institution
>
> Crédit Lyonnais-- France: the first true deposit banks
>
> Bon Marché-- France: the first department stores.
>
> Félix Potin-- France: the first chain groceries
>   selling their own packaged products
>
> Hanseatic shippers-- Germany
>
> Ship building-- Germany
>
> Fulling mills-- England
>
> Steel smelting and rolling mills-- England. Josiah Wilkinson
>   (He of the razor blades)
>
> Scientific rotation agriculture-- England: Jethro Tull (Yes, there really was
>   an inventor-entrepreneur by that name before the sixties rock band)
>
> Banks: Fugger, and Rothschild, etc.
>
> Motion pictures and photography– Lumière brothers,
>   and Nicéphore Niepce-- France
>
> Soap invented-- France
>
> Toilet paper-- France

Pasteurization-- France

Steam power harnessed-- England. James Watt

Iron rails for railroads-- Germany. von Moltke; Liszt (Friedrich,
        not the composer Franz)

The *Junkers* (general all-round entrepreneurs)

Radio wave employment-- Germany. Hertz (not the auto rental guy);
        Roentgen (the X-ray)

Heavy machinery-- Germany: Alfred Krupp

Electrical development-- Germany. von Humboldt, a.k.a.,
"Germany's Edison",
        as Edison was dubbed, "America's Humboldt";
        as was Siemens

Chemical and electric: Germany-- Siemens: invented the first dynamo

Wilhelm Bunsen: the Bunsen Burner-- Germany.

Fine cutlery-- England. Josiah Wedgewood

All of the explorers

Aspirin-- Germany (Bayer)

Underpants – France (Wouldn't you know it)

Condoms – France (in town of Condom)

Rocket propulsion-- Germany

Saxophone-- Germany (Adolph Sax)

The sewing machine and pressure cooker-- France

Liposuction-- France

The veggie-mixer-- France

The IQ test-- France (Binet). Okay, with help from Stanford.

The classic CocaCola bottle (which you can still get in Europe,
        though not in the U.S.-- France

Teflon-- France

The original (snappy-but-minimal-snappy) Lucky Strike package-- France

Community and individual were always at odds historically--
economic, political and legal. That polarity, that tug of war, is humanly
inevitable-- until circumstance, or culture, or planning (call it what you will)
forced them to be at one. Grid computing. Servo-mechanisms. Sir Francis
Bacon and his crowd IPOing the Incas and the Aztecs precious metals.

So perhaps we need a New Individualism-- *here*, at home in The
Good Old: one that really does in, and take on, the "old" one.

JOE SHLUMPSKI, CEO

I have often wondered if a corporate Board of Directors, say of Disney, couldn't but lasso in some Joe Shlumpski off Wilshire Boulevard (or Ventura Boulevard in "The Valley") and dub him CEO-- not for a day, like the popular fifties TV show *Queen for a Day*, but for an official corporate term of leadership; and I suspect that Joe, providing he spoke English well-- with a confident, gabbable (Americanian) bonhommie, or with a snappy German or French accent-- would do as successfully as the previous traditionally "elected" CEO-- in this case, Michael Eisner. Joe would have a hunch that they produce a certain movie, or perhaps he would "study" the accountants' and script-assessors' data (all data are, after all, a mishmash of suppositions, ruled-in thises and ruled-out thats and algebraics with assumptions as questionable as they are traditional). I am aware that movies have been made pursuant to this theme; but these have been fanciful, comical (or demonic) vehicles for Danny Kaye and Tony Curtis and Kevin Kline and Steve Martin. They did not feature an anonymous "hero", plainfellow and tickless, unarrogant and ungaloomphy, and holding no wallable MA from Wharton or Yale or Harvard. But he would not be any anti-hero either. Just your Normal Guy: Joe Shlumpski might very well turn out as the best corporate bet. And I am not waxing facetious here!... Well, extremely.

CEO mystique KAPLOOHIE!.

5

AMERICA LOVES EVOLUTION
AMERICA HATES EVOLUTION

Another American joke is now making the rounds of Europe: How does an American live with those exorbitant pharmaceutical prices? With that pathetic unemployment compensation? With their inadequate to non-existent health care and disappearing pensions? With decrepit streets and bridges and railroads?-- and all those bullet-firing implements? With their corporate CEOs on infinitely greater Welfare than their poor American brothers begging in the streets, who receive no Welfare? How does an American live with all these? Well, how else?-- but *with those bullet-firing instruments!* Real Answer: He calls it Freedom, the American does, Freedom and Greatness, and Wealth, and then he feels just great. . . Then the Europeans chuckle, sadistically, like some Gerard Depardieu. Well, some do.

Just a joke, folks. Not unlike our Polish joke about The Polish Space Program going to the sun safe from its terrific furnace-fire by especially designing the journey for dark cold night.

By the way, ask a French speaker what the smarty American neo-logism NeoCon says to them. Clue: "Con", in the parlance, is glutimous maximus. Or jerk. Or schmuck.

Neo is Neo.

Whole lotta laughing going on.

But as the originator of social insurance (in 1883, that's Bismarck) observed: "A special Providence takes care of fools, drunkards, and the United States." With which statement, wrongly, we United Statesers seem to agree. Seem to believe. And Bismarck really didn't (As of course then we had *no* social insurance, he truly figured we'd come down tumbling; and he established national social insurance in Germany so *he* wouldn't come down tumbling-- by way of the rabble). How frightening to imagine, and accept, that while we are the land of most opportunity-- and we are (for yet some)-- we are also the land of least opportunity-- for many. A Have-Not nation, and a Have nation. Not all-things-to-all-people, but some-things-to-some-people, like the shenaniganeeers at those high-up corporate levels, where there is terrific opportunity.

THE DOC AIN'T GOT NO COATRACK

I have begun to notice that in doctors' and dentists' offices in America (or at least in Berkeley and San Francisco) there seem no longer to exist coatracks. One asks the assistant at the desk and she says, "Oh, please, take your coat with you." "To the doctor's *examining room*?" "Yes." Are they fearing theft?-- by some poor uninsured bastard reduced to selling insured patients' coats? Bands of unjacketed homeless so debased as to raid the coat-racks of American medical arts buildings? Will the physicians' liability insurance rates rise with unguarded hallway coat-racks?-- unless the doctors are advised to hang a (sleazy) sign: NOT RESPONSIBLE FOR ARTICLES OF CLOTHING LEFT WHILE PATIENT IS BEING EXAMINED FOR LIFE-THREATENING ILLNESS. In Germany, and France, benighted trusting doctors and dentists still have coatracks. Uninsured Americans on vacation might go to a continental physician and rip off a herringbone or cashmere or nice Harris tweed... Of course, American neurologists and orthopoedists, etc, might solve this American medical problem by hiring uniformed guards, as does WalMart. You know, guys just out of prison who cannot get any other job and who know how to use those guns they've got holstered-- on any brazen, tumorous cancer patient. Or, maybe just bouncers, like at a sports bar.

We Americans are kneejerk libertarians, as if we are borne from the womb bawling intractably, "Whaah!-- government is the *problem*!-- *Not* the solution!-- Whaah!-- burp-- I'm Self-*Reliant*! *Get* me out of this *hospital*!" More adultly (or pedestrianly) we believe, strong-and-stark, in the-survival-of-the-fittest. At least a majority of us swears by this, our unison, our axiom. A man or woman should pull his or her weight, or schlep and drag and sweat it along, if so necessary. Ultimately he will be all-the-better for the sweat-drenched schleppery. No life-caddies toting your clubs and baggage-- except maybe one's unconcealable nepotistic fathers and uncles. Recently in Berkeley a woman stood before The Cheese Board, a Berkeley communitarian institution established in the "Berzerkerley" sixties, with a loose alliance tying it to the now world famous Berkeley eatery Chez Panisse (an ample Clinton favorite). The woman held up a placard that read HELP ONLY THOSE WHO ARE NOT IDLE. Those who were idle-- like herself?-- ought not receive assistance, did not deserve it. Ought fade away. Sheer social Darwinism-- which Darwin himself despised, and disowned. And The Placard Lady is of course no American anomaly; though she certainly was a *Berkeley* aberration. Oh sure we do give charity-- the most in the West. But charity is a drop in the bucket. We are simply not a people who cares about its people as a People, a concept that has come to be known in Europe as *solidarität*, or *solidarité*, or *la providence*-- or, forgodssakes, *la fraternité*. Only twelve percent of high income Americans believe that the state, *any* state, should offer a basic income, a *survival* income, to all citizens; whereas in Britain forty-seven percent of high incomers believe in civilized survival for all; in Germany, forty-five percent (and a full one-third of their GDP is spent on it); 36 percent in France; in Italy, the rate of belief in a basic state support is fifty-three percent. And even among *low* income Americans just thirty-three percent believe in such humanitarian help, compared to seventy-one percent in Britain, sixty-six percent in Germany and a whopping *eighty* percent among Italians. Placard Ladyites, angry or smug bootstrappers or decent, we believe that our social and economic mobility, our great American caste escalator, will up and take care of things. Except, it wont, for the simple reason that we ain't got much of an escalator-- it's on-the-blink: We are not so upwardly mobile anymore, if we are upwardly mobile now *at all*, and not your basic rank-budgeless nation caught in a Hinduesque mud. In Germany, people ascend the social ladder at a relatively high rate: 20 percent of the population has moved up from lower to middle-class, or from middle to higher middle; in America the rates and direction are almost precisely opposite-- two ships passing in the night. College-- decent college, where you learn something-- costs too much in America for too many to attend and ascend the societal staircase (and so the old Mel Brooks etymological witticism has come true: " 'Staircase' " is hard; it says, 'Don't you *dare* climb up me'."); America is no longer a "tickletibumtiboo"; job training costs too much in America (only ten percent of our offspring now surpass their parents' economic rung-- about the same as in Europe in general, including its east, like Rumania, Bulgaria, Slovenia) and far less than in Germany and France. Apparently prisons cost way too much for us as well, and we have far more prisons per capita than any nation, not even just any developed nation. *Any* nation. So what have we done?-- we now have many *privatized*. For Profit prisons. Corporation prisons-- and you can imagine the corner-cost cuts on rehab *there*. Not to mention on food? Bottom line: cream-chipped beef on toast-- at best, like Christmas Eve. Cost cuts for which society will later pay the piper. *And then have to cut back more.* And then pay carpenters for more bars on our windows. And the taxi expense of visiting your husband at San Quentin in for life (California's Three Strikes Your Out Law) for stealing a nylon zip-up corduroy at his neurologist's office.

But implied also by the Placard Lady sign was that those who were not idle, unlike herself, did not, would not, *could* not, require help. Would never hear of help, would never ask for Help. Ever. And shouldn't. Here now social Darwinism as absolute paradox, for as a religious nation-- *the* religious church-cramming, pew-filling developed nation (even allowing for the politicians courting high regard on Sundays)-- America does not believe in any "hypothesis" so "damn unGodly" as Darwinism. Well, as scientific Darwinism in Nature, anyway. Only in the social and economic bailiwicks should there be natural selection and Survival of the Fittest. It's rueful, it's lamentable, and it's painful, that while natural Darwinism postulates evolution, in effect an ongoing elevation of the human race by adaptation, *social* Darwinism promotes-- and ferociously promotes-- an exclusivizing devo. The American Paradox. Well, one of the many: Down with natural evolution. Up with the social *de*volution based upon the original, "natural" idea of evo.

But come on: so many people remain "unfit". Or become it, and then remain it. We are just poor vulnerable breakable biological critters equipped with strengths-- and often capricious flimsy strengths that abandon us, flying south, and not just for the winter-- and we are mill-stoned by our fragile weaknesses: "The thousand natural shocks that," Shakespeare saw, "the flesh is heir to." Fitness is not a founders' constitutional right from 1776, nor is it a theological given. Fitness is neither self-evident nor other-evident. To be existential (France) fitness (or un-fitness) precedes essence. To be inductive (American/British), fitness is There-- look!-- in the winner person(s) interviewed on TV for their various-winnings, and un-fitness is There-- look!-- in the loser personas observed in the far-off-ground, on TV or in "real life"-- losing. While in Germany the incomes of the old and disabled average approximately 20 percent *above* the poverty line, in America these incomes have settled at about seventy percent *of* the poverty line, this dubious help-- but absolutely necessary help-- coming from pensions, Disability Insurance and SSI (Supplementary Security Income, a branch of Social Security); this help "gushing in" at a monumental 0.7 percent of GDP, or less than half of what comes to the old and disabled in Britain or Germany, and one-quarter of the Swedish "windfall to the worthless".[*] Envious personal note here: My wife's German mother, the widow of a *hausmeister* (not the master of a house, literally, but a janitor) in Rottweil, lives in an apartment twice as large and far better furnished than the flat that my mother, the widow of a taxi "fleet" owner (four taxicabs) in Baltimore lived in until her death. Didn't God decree it should be the other way around in America? Hold the phone-- this seems to be Against Nature.

Did Nature screw up? . . . Or did we?

One of the sad cameos I eventually honed in on while living in Europe is something that you do *not* notice, not immediately, and it may take time before you realize you are actively not-noticing something that in America you actively notice and then doubly-actively have to *not* notice: There are few hands out beggars in Europe--Western Europe. Some, but few. And no street "idlers" aggressively confronting you as if it's their franchise for a specifically assigned block (as the comedian [humorist?] Robert Klein once put it with fake irritation). Curiously, an American finds the center-city streets of "the Old World" rather devoid, missing some absent Something,

---

[*] State budgets are so broke that food deliveries to many of the helpless elderly will end. Nearly 1 million Americans are losing their Medicaid benefits.

hard to lay your finger on. Some, well, call it spice? Some active ingredient of a "normal" city spectrum. Ah yes, our panhandler! Where is our beloved and be-hated panhandler! You know, the "contrast gainer" (Saul Bellow) who makes us feel both smugly better and guiltily worse about ourselves. Well, I will say that Paris is the exception here; the gravitational pull of chestnuts and mulberries and ornate balconies and *les places* has Paris teeming with about twenty thousand homeless-- not usually French, but Gypsies, Russians, Croats, Serbs, Algerians, Moroccans, Senegalese, Ghanans, you name it. But populous, Eurocentric metropolitan Paris is still poverty-peanuts in comparison to the less populous San Francisco Bay Area's *ninety* thousand homeless and New York's monumental six figure triumph-- despite ex-mayor Rudy Giuliani's "zero tolerance", rubber-stamped by his billionaire successor, Michael Blumberg.

THEY don't much exist there across the seas?-- those bums.

Of course even counting in our homeless, we are not here talking about world poverty, but "developed poverty". World poverty means a person thriving on less than one dollar per day; that's Earth's global benchmark for about 1.3 billion people (1/3 of humanity). But what we are discussing here is rich poverty, the stratosphere of poverty, starting at about *three* dollars per day. Big bucks. And We win the Developed Poverty Olympics. The City-on-the-Hill Immiseration Champions-- that's us.

Some months ago on CBS *Sixty Minutes* it was reported that there are food lines all over America, as jobs are lost, or jobs are simply not providing substantial enough wages. Middle class citizens-- not dole recipients-- made up the bulk of the line shown and spot-interviewed in Wisconsin. According to *The Guardian*, two million of Ohio's eleven million people made use of food charities last year: A lot of normal not-unfit folks. With the exception of refugees from Africa and Eurasia, I have never seen or heard of a food line in Spain, or France, or Germany, not to mention the Scandinavian countries. Not in the last five decades.

How can this weirdness be happening? How can it be that America ranks lower than all the Western democracies in public outlays on pensions, health, and income maintenance? Did Nature really screw up? Warning: stats galore to follow. Unavoidable: France allotted 25.5% of GDP to public outlays on pensions, health and income maintenance; Germany allotted 19.3%; and we 11.5%. One-eighth of Americans live below the poverty line.

One *fiftieth* in Germany; one-twentieth in France, burdened as it is with its immigrant Algerians. How can it be that we stack up the highest proportion in the advanced west of elderly living in poverty? (U.S. 20%; Germany 7.7%; France, 4.8%; Italy, 4.4%), and more Americans over sixty-five working than anywhere in Western Europe. With the United States considered as 1, the ratios of public social spending were, U.K. 1.5; Germany, 1.4; Sweden 2.6. . . But hey: 8.6% of German children do live in poverty; and 7.4 in France; and a whopping 10.5 percent in Italy. Disgraceful, no? Sure, absolutely. But not near as miserable as the American Misery Gold Medal of *25%*. Yup, we possess the worst child-poverty rate of all the industrialized countries! It's not even a contest; it's a blowout. In the thirties, Franklin Roosevelt looked over America and saw us as one-third "ill-housed, ill-clad, ill-nourished". We did rise up out of that miasma; but now we've back fallen to, what?-- one-fifth?

Increase since 1999 in U.S. households in which there was hunger due to poverty during the year: 22 percent.

Ill-clad, ill-housed, ill-nourished.

Ohboy did Nature screw up.

TABLE NINE

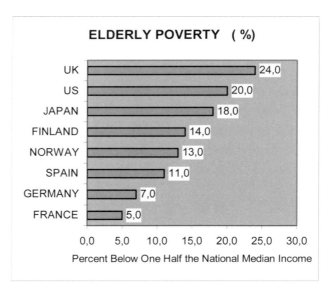

Source: Luxembourg Income Studies

TABLE TEN

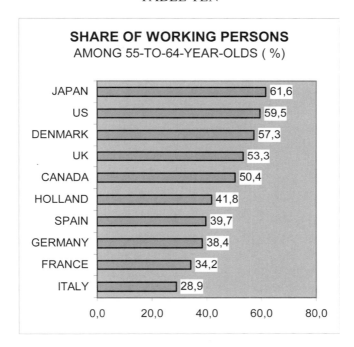

SHARE OF WORKING PERSONS
AMONG 55-TO-64-YEAR-OLDS (%)

JAPAN	61,6
US	59,5
DENMARK	57,3
UK	53,3
CANADA	50,4
HOLLAND	41,8
SPAIN	39,7
GERMANY	38,4
FRANCE	34,2
ITALY	28,9

Source: OECD

Obvious answer to these How-can-it-be's? To these injustices it is hardly obscene to call obscene: Our social net. Social spending throughout Europe runs a full *fifty percent* above that in the U.S., as property in that other world is not viewed as the polaric antagonist of "social", as an absolute personal Lockean right, to be done with only as the propertied may please: Instead, property is a privilege demanding quid pro quos, social obligations, like-- here's that word again-- *Community*: A true conception of The Public Welfare. But thickening our cobweb Net America-- with, say, more job training and placement?-- these would apparently be a betrayal, not only of our industrious selves, but of our industrious myth selves. From Maine to Montana, Oregon to Oklahoma, welfare payments crawl along at approxi-mately one eighth of the low average salary. That is, *if* you qualify That is, if with a disconsolate embarrassed monkey on your back you manage to guerrilla-crawl through the bureaucracy-- which is often as peremptory as it is perfunctory-- and, adopting the nation's contemptuous self-myth, you act out Oops, forgot to say, *May* I? And *that* is, if you can hang onto the pittance you qualified for-- beyond six months. And *that* is, if you are not critically deranged (mentally disturbed), even schizophrenic, and have been expelled by the state mental hospital (a mixed blessing-curse, as these are not the pleasantest of redoubts anyway: poor funding: tax insufficiencies), even if this state institution hasn't yet been *Privatized* (Bad privatized, not good privatized), thus for you to be "treated" on the streets by your vial of iffily-wounding anti-psychotic spansules (*if* you obediently swallow them, as the psychotic can be quite laissez-faire too), and without a clue as to negotiating the paperified rigamarole of cobweb welfare-- which is barely worth the rigamarole anyway. And horrifyingly, to save more money yet, astoundingly, we are now beginning to privatize agencies that *determine* if you are eligible for welfare; and isn't this like having a five-star general head up Conscientious Objectors? That private watch-dogging of public welfare would be on commission, I suppose? Cut'em and take your cut (Texas the pioneer here. And Florida.). And more appallingly, to save more money yet, our American Welfare processing-- some advance legions of it-- is now being "outsourced" to "call-centers" in places like-- the irony is as laughable as it is repugnant-- Bombay (So that poor, indigent Indians need not be relegated to the welfare dished out by New Delhi?). Pity the poor expedited "recipient" in Kansas City who has a problem suddenly-- evicted from his squalid indigent hotel (and by the way I haven't seen such worm pits of mite and chigger in Europe)-- and our "recipient" must complain quick now to a kindly (indifferent) non-idiomatic-American-English speaker at (get this dazzleglobaltechnism-- and it's authentic) *Spectramind*, in Bollywood:

Recipient: Hello, may I speak to my worker? I have the receipts she asked for. May I bring them in?

India-Processor: Certainly. You may. But the fare to Bombay is two thousand dollars, economy. Relax, take a Valium-- a generic one: Diazepam -- sounds like some goodly marmalade, no? They are dirt cheap, our diazepams, not like your rip-off American Valiums; as your generics are made here in India.

And they are (By Indians who are now contracting AIDS at geo-metric rates?).

Can you imagine German welfare being outsourced to Sri Lanka?-- as the Tamil Tigers come crashing through those swinging (barricaded) welfare office doors.[*]

Notwithstanding, we should be proud that Welfare in America has raised the income of the poor, reducing the proportion of adults in poverty from 26.7 % to 19.1%. . . Well, proud, that is, until we gander at Europe: Germany, 7.6% adults in poverty; France, 7.5%; Italy, 6.5%; Britain, 14.6%.

I mean, you really could experience an entirely nice day in urban west Europe without bumping into an impoverished, dirt-clothed, demanding, loser. And a whole *intentional* day I mean, hunting for your Euro-loser (And they usually aren't "demanding" anyway). While in America, Holey-moley it's bumper-bodies. It's musical derelicts. SRO. You got to have the real-good-moves to avoid somebody downtrodden once you get Downtown Downtrodden Downbeat Anywhere USA-- as if you'd want to go there, as Hey, we've got Malls. Not for the Uptrodden, our Malls, but for the Middle-Trodden (Our Uptrodden do not despise our Downtrodden-- no contact, thus no reason. Only our MiddleTrodden despise our Downtrodden-- and so vote, you know...). Yes, we should have a better welfare system. I mean, not just waterfall (trickle) paychecks, but training-- towards good jobs. Sorry to keep harping it, but: "old" Europe does have this.

Daunted (but faking undaunted) I go on: More stats galore. Unavoidable.

And our Unemployment Compensation, that other civilized aid, it stands now at an average of one half of the unemployed qualifier's employed wage before he lost his job. Pretty good, huh, as unemployment compensation lasts six months; with a congressionally voted ad hoc extension-- nine

---

[*] In fairness to the U.S., let's acknowledge that German is not as a rule spoken in Sri Lanka. Nor French. While the American CEO thrives with English as the gold standard, the American worker pays with his language as coin-of-the-globe (It is estimated that 14 million American jobs are at risk to outsourcing.). Thus, American VISA and Mastercard may outsource "customer assistance" departments to Bangalore-- where, for what they call "brain gain", the Bangalorian will be stringently trained to sideline his tonsorial Indian accent in favor of the midwest American Woody Guthrie twang-- the Bollywood type not being able to do Berlinish or Parisian or Roman. There are down sides to speaking in WorldSpeak, although of course the French might outsource to Senegal (French-speaking)-- once the Senegalese are organized for it, or interested-- and if ever self-protective, and alert, and above all vociferous, the French citizenry would accede to it.

months. Pretty great, no? Pretty damned empathetically civilized. . . . No, paltry. Here I go again: In Germany, social welfare, even for, say, some uncitizen Zambian somehow wending his weary way there, rests at one-half the average low salary; roughly what our Unemployment Compensation would be. And German unemployment payments level off at about seventy percent of salary (France, the same. Britain, sixty-four percent). And both maintain until the person finds work-- work that fits him, matches his skills or potential, work he *wants*!-- even if that takes years. And years. Until retirement-- *Shazam*! (They're shaving it a whisker, as this book goes to press: World-competing exigencies; i.e. an alternative to outsourcing). In Europe, tax and transfer policies still manage to lift about half the non-elderly poor out of poverty. In the U.S. this dynamic is reversed: like puppeteers releasing Howdy Doody's strings we drop the buggers down. This "reversal" might of course be reversed, somewhat anyway, if we *trained* our unemployed. But we don't. Not much. Who are you kidding? Training *costs,* fella. In Germany, where a training tradition goes back to the medieval guilds (as in England and France) the cost for retraining runs to 1.02 percent of their GDP. In America it hobbles at 0.25 percent. That's a multiple of over four. So where do our poor saps-- *whom we* (and ill luck?) *have made poor saps*-- go?

Good question.

Here's another question: Has this decent, soft-touch, "muddleheaded", "communitarian", "*un*entrepreneurial" assistance in Europe, in Germany, made Germans, say, slackers? Dumped their productivity down? (Some Germans worry so: CDU-- Christian Democrats-- center Right, e.g. Republicans). Well, among our considerable prejudices about Germans, our jaundices (and observations, some accurate too) "slackers" never even clambers to the long list. "Slackers" is pretty much the antithesis of every characterization embedded into our Germanic slanderboard.[*] By the way, the European "Welfare State"-- which of course it really isn't-- originated from the Right as much as from the Left. Hang onto your reversed baseball caps on this one: On the Right a conservative religious impulse led towards supporting workless family and community-- the same reason Welfarism is rejected by our Right. Tempering capitalism's less egalitarian consequences is where Europe's Right met its Left. Little wonder then that poverty in

---

[*] Roughly one-third of Americans and Russians still associate Germany with the Nazi country led by Hitler. Poll by *Deutsche Welle* TV.

Germany exists at barely one-third the American rate. . . But of course our unemployment is far lower than Europe's. So say our statistics-- and stats don't lie, right? They only spin and fib. Our winning unemployment numbers are frequently reported on television newscasts in the various anchor stylings: "We are superior"-- pomp-voiced imperturbable Jennings; "Everything's honky-dory"-- nice *maître de* Brokaw; "I'm dubious, I'm fearful"-- edgy, concernedish Rather. Except, these workless stats are as cooked and recooked as those guys' practiced anchor styles: Our unemployment rate as usually reported is at about five or six percent. In truth it is more like ten or eleven percent. Firstoff, *one American in eight has worked at McDonald's.* Can you fully comprehend that!? An incredible, stupefying proportion, especially when this number does not include Burger King and Wendy's and KFC.* So: fast food outlets have replaced-- okay, complemented-- the army (and prison) as the primary sources of American slack-jobtime "social-ismicization". As comical as sad. Second grounds for our unemployment-disguisement: you've got out of work Silicon Valleyish brains now doing handiwork building fences and painting houses, when they can scare up such gigs (thus displacing fulltime carpenters-- and handymen-- who also obviously need that work); and other white collar out-of-workers no longer even reporting in and registering after six months-- which they could do (should do/would do) in Europe, as the unemployment compensation there steamrolls on (Well, compared to us it still does). Then, you've got the considerable omitting of inmates-- yes, those prison folk: as we in The Land of the Free incarcerate a far far higher proportion of our citizenry than does any other Western nation (*two million* twiddle-away in jail here), as we seem to put "certain incorrigibles" in positions where they haven't much other choice-- except Iraq-- as the total employment potential of McDonald's et al. wont make much dent. Repeat: *Two million* of our working-age citizens incarcerated. And as I've said, one hundred fifty thousand of them are even locked up in private corporation prisons, for profit "enterprises"-- which constitutes the entire population of French jails. Our "budget crunch" (We're super-stinges on social support and *still* we suffer a budget crunch?!), that

---

* The KFC acronym apparently because blacks, the major customers, may be turned off by the "Kentucky", and white adults, health conscious, sent off by the "fried". Mightn't they then have gone with KF Chicken? No: A chicken surname sounds suspiciously like a comic coward who wishes to conceal some creepy prename.

"crunch" suggesting-- and our ideology *presenting*-- this particular private-lockup "solution" (California's jailing costs have risen from 200 million dollars in '75 to 4.8 billion in 2000), as some facilities, as in L.A., had no more bunk beds, or cots, to stack up-- and nowhere to stack them-- and they were serving lunches less nutritious than do some of our public schools: PBJ (peanut butter and jelly). Rationalization?-- On such low-pro diets the inmates can't gump up the muscle to taunt guards? Anyway, we are now constrained to set most jailees free after ten percent of their sentences are served. Misdemeanorwise. Here, stats: 78 per 100,000 of the workable are housed in European prisons; 519 per 100,000 are in our American prisons.

America:	greater than	500	per 100,000
Britain:	"	136	per 100,000
Italy:	"	57	per 100,000
Japan:	"	32	per 100,000

And even within this shocker numerology is the hidden fact-- though not surprising fact-- that the American incarceration rate is seven times more for blacks than whites, and five to ten times such incarceration rate of any developed country. And that, unlike in Europe we have no independent prison commissions to guard against, you know, torture, and other health-breaking conditions-- especially in the for-profit prison corporations. Incredibly, over forty percent of African-American men over the age of twenty have been out of the (non-prison) labor force *at all times* during the last two decades: twelve percent of blacks; one and a half percent of whites. As one French wag put it: "America's jails are its form of new urban housing." As many blacks have put it: "America's jails are its colleges for blacks." Or its employment solution (But that aforementioned French commentator: he should know that *half* of France's prison population is Muslim).

It ain't Ivy League tuition; but ultimately it does cost us more.

Not less.

Economic policy, and theory, resides in its own ethereal "ceteribus paribus" realm (justifiable, sort of), along with its mates (un-neat and messy), the social and political; so it is not my intention to judge moral rightness or wrongness. No, I lie: It *was* not my intention to assess our ethics; but *the stats have made me do it*. It *is* my intention, to take a full follow-through cut. After all, there are welfare chiselers in Europe and unemployment fineglers there: such behavior is as selfishly human as is our selfishly primitive chiseling-*off* or our needy's needs; there are obviously pensioners, semi-opulent characters in Europe, who go on and on Taking although they could still, surely, find a good job placement. Euro-slackers are not fooling anyone, capitalist or socialist or Green. But that is precisely my point: these people seem to be suffered across the Atlantic, as the price of a fair and modern--and humane-- civilization where only, say, one European in fifty is relegated to having fried his future at a fast McOutfit. And sure, suffering Euro-slackers may squealch some the entrepreneurial spirit (and the go-getter necessity?-- if not compulsion); indeed it does: American economic growth rates are more often faster and higher than in any competitive developed country. We usually own advanced world growth rates, so we may do the tasteless (uneducated man's) American end-zone wiggle-waggle on that one: *In yo'face, Euro-mother.* But Europe's GDP "lose-out" here seems to be the European community's price. Its acknowl-edged, argued-about, but then ultimately accepted and willing, price. Well, mostly willing anyway. Sure, they do squabble about affording their social programs; they do second-guess: One Euro-study guesstimated that if growth rates did not increase, the German pension system, if left generously unchanged, would move into deficit in 2018, with pension debt reaching fifty percent of GDP by 2032. And pension systems in France and Italy are in even shakier shape.[*] Still, ultimately, a community-care decision always seems to prevail. . . And in any case, as many of us here worry, the American system of Social Security-- by far less giving-- is also feared (by Alan Greenspan, et al.) to become even *more* speedily insolvent. As it stands though, I must admit to a more relaxed, less guilty clutching when walking the streets of any European city without being hounded as I am here, pleaded to, succored, demanded of, even threatened, by the sometimes dismal, sometimes leering, always degraded, and sometimes the unpredictably violent.

---

[*] Can you imagine American AMTRAK employees being able to retire at age *fifty*-- *on full salary*, as are *les cheminots*, the French railroad workers? As are those frilly members of *La Comédie Française*. And others... One significant easement in France however is that businesses have been able to draw on a public fund, *Les Fonds Nationals pour l'Emploi*, to assist in taking care of early retirement pay.

TABLE ELEVEN

PER CAPITA INCOME GROWTH IN ADVANCED COUNTRIES
AVERAGE ANNUAL GROWTH IN %[*]

Period	1960-1969	1979-1989	1989-1996
US	2.3	1.5	1.0
JAPAN	6.4	3.1	2.0
GERMANY (east & west)	3.3	1.9	1.3
FRANCE	3.7	1.6	1.3
ITALY	4.1	2.3	1.0
UK	2.2	2.2	1.0
CANADA	3.4	1.8	0.1

Source: Inequality and the Global Economy.
Jeff Faux and Larry Mishel

TABLE TWELVE

CHANGE IN INCOME INEQUALITY

Country	Change Period	Per-centage	Abso-lute
US	79-95	0.79	0.35
JAPAN	79-93	0.84	0.25
GERMANY (west)	79-95	0.50	0.13
FRANCE	79-89	0.40	0.12
ITALY	80-91	0.64	0.58
UK	79-95	1.80	0.22
CANADA	79-95	0.02	0.001

Source: Inequality and the Global Economy.
Jeff Faux and Larry Mishel

---

[*] Income inequality grew the greatest in the US. In only the US did changes in the tax and transfer system (welfare, etc.) exacerbate inequality.

> Because of the strong social net there has not been a
> sizeable increase in poverty in most advanced
> countries corresponding to the growth of market
> income inequality, with two exceptions: US and UK –
> where poverty has gone up 2.4 % and 5.4 %.

It is as if, after centuries of wars, revolutions, terrors and anti-terrors, and exterminations and subjugations, and the built-in injustices of monarchies thriving on (or off) peasantdom, Europe has at least (and at last) worked its way to the conclusion, Let humanity be human (We'll even relax and smoke, and observe naked bodies having sex in-- even-- good movies. As long as not involved is that fatty Depardieu). Let us at least try all this.

AN EXEMPLARY (AND CAUTIONARY) TRUE TALE

I am a writer who plays jazz saxophone, although I suppose a more accurate accounting of what I do on that (German invented) horn (Adolph Sax: and this is not a hip fake name) would require me to add the demeaning "at": I play "at" jazz saxophone. Aside: It is never-endingly "wondrous-strange" to me to hear a reserved *a*-ductile German jazz-lover-- and there are many German jazz-lovers-- wax all reverent-eyed about his "heroes": Coltrane; Parker; "Dexter"; "Sonny"; Lester Young; all dead black Americans who were-- well, what is the opposite of the non-ductile German?—super-melifluous. In any case (though with intention) I digress. A player, or a player-ater like myself sometimes needs his horn repaired: Corks, pads, keys, air loss, cleaning (And metal-stress, if you can *really* blow, like Hank Crawford on alto). I have had my horn worked on in inner city Oakland and in inner city Munich. In the latter town I drove to the parking lot nearby, lifted my horn (gig-bagged) from the car, walked the one block to Musik Beste. Nice street. Nice stores. Nice pedestrians, with their direct, purposive Germanic workhorse gaits; nice apartment buildings, post war bombing and pre. Nice walk. I brought in my horn. Done, while I waited. Half hour. In the former town, Oakland, I parked at a nearby lot. The ticket machine cackled and shimmied out its burdensome scroll as if the routine effort would shake it apart like a bulldog tormenting a ragdoll, whereas the park-ticket machine in the Munich lot, solid and large as a Whirlpool refrigerator (compared to the Oakland lot's puny toaster-oven) operated smooth and solid, its emanating ticket not, as in the Oakland lot (which was a *new* lot), an elongated Talmud paperwork corrugation also like an amusement park's series of ride admissions. No, the German ticket was simply a solid plastic card, more durable than a credit card. The Munich lot's attendant, by the way, sat behind a glass wall enclosure in a large computer-banked-up room that created the air of serious functional importance you see in decision chambers of bad sci-fi movies.

As I carried my saxophone to Best Repair in Oakland I passed the parking lot ticket booth lady. You know the kind of "music" rumbling from her little cubby office, PA broadcasting for all the world to absorb through pore and epiderm: The body-rupturing booty-beat. Ground grumbling stuff, cement pillar reverberations. I gathered up and walked to Oakland's Best Music, dodging, threading, by the assorted beggars, the beaten and the drunk and the conniving, the fatigued hustlers of downtown urban America; the junked mattresses and battered boxes. Thus I found myself clutching my gig bag against my chest like a bookworm milquetoast might his bookbag full of Henry Adams and Herman Melville, against its sudden appropriation by one of America's discarded, they feeling fully justified no doubt. A Selmer Mark II, a four thousand dollar potential loss. Oh the ugly despair of America, where ironically the jazz I love to play began. *Out of which* ugly despair it ironically began.

Now, musical instrument repair establishments tend to be located in low rent neighborhoods, as they require much space for equipment and storage-- as for tubas and bass clarinets and baritone saxes, which are big fellows. But the Munich neighborhood, as modest as it was, was just that-- modest. Not rundown, heels and mouth and saliva dribble. And Munich rents are not cheap, by Oakland standards. They're higher. And I should mention that the Oakland shop was in Oakland's new center city. The repair houses themselves were comparable: well-equipped; professional; diligent technicians. The American repair guy joked. The German repair guy was earnest, solemn, serious (Stereotypes become stereotypes for a reason), so one might have thought each worked in the other fellow's neighborhood (I did however have to wait a week in Oakland to pick up my fixed horn)... A nice pleasant walk back to my car at the *parkhaus* in Munich. But the ugly-fearful-misery-dodge in Oakland. The ticket lady's PA broadcast badass booty beat as I paid her-- whereas the German ticket machine also handled payment. Smoothly. Unshaking and unquaking.

Brainstorm. Light bulb: It isn't just that we pay low taxes, and so reap poor infrastructure. The expectation is by now so habitual for us to live in grunge, to wade through grime, indescribable discarded viral Things, as if we reside in an Everglades of nature-given GDP muck that we couldn't even *imagine* that more equitable spending (and distribution) would change anything. I'm not even sure we now know that anything *needs* changing. Most of us, anyway. We've gone crud-blind. As my Yiddish grandmother used to say, "*Oy gewalt!*" (*Gewalt* means violence). We forget the *gewalt*-- and forget our downtowns-- and just hop the freeway to Malls. What?-- twenty miles?

6

THE OTHER UNFORTUNATES

Now let's forget the poor in America verses the poor in Western Europe. Enough of that depressing scenery and casting. We'll leave all that stipulated. Granted. Pretty cold of us to forget, but let's just deal now with Normal.

"Normal" folk. Us.

Us?

Well, flash: 77 percent of American expatriot employees in Europe would prefer to *remain in Europe*, not repatriate; even if they lost their professional jobs. So reports a Cignet survey--2001. (A peripherally interesting aspect of this survey is that it was reported in *The International Herald Tribune* in 2004, as if three years had to go by before it was deemed that the English language readers of the paper, Americans, were ready to see such dismal news-- of themselves.).

Now repeat: Only ten percent of American adult men surpass their fathers economically, while in Germany it is twenty percent.

That's just not the way they taught us in school that life was for us in these United States.

That is surely not why anyone would come to America. To do worse than his father? Might as well understudy old Alexi in the family butcher shop in Minsk.

Put it this way: What we are is not the most powerful most rich nation, but the most powerful *un*rich nation.

Which, in a way, renders us *not-the-most-powerful nation*.

And we do know this.

Oh in the nooks, crannies and hollows of our brains where you can know something and still not know it-- there we do know it.

What we have here is a national corpus collusum problem (or "issue"). You know, that skinny central bridge in the cortex that communicates from left to right to right to left: "A bridge over troubled waters". A colossal corpus collosum problem-- if you will.

In our country you do see many cars, old ones, half moribund vehicles wending their weary, pleading, belching ways on life-support: bumped bumpers, slipped fenders, filliped grillwork, Ductape, exhaust tornadoes. It is as if many American autos are erupting out murky smokescreens to escape their crime scenes, or caning limpidly to rehab. It is not uncommon to witness tow trucks cruising the streets of Berkeley and Oakland, near frequent as taxis. More frequent. In (Yes I know I'm being borish but...) Germany, even in France, even in sporadically delapidated provincial France, the average car is fairly new, even when it is not a luxury-mobile. Even when, as in France, and in Italy, they also drive bumper car fashion-- more than we do-- hang the bourgeois dents and dings. *Epâter le bourgeoisie.*

But I do remember being astounded at the sheer abundance on German streets of Mercedes, big 700 series BMWs, even Jaguars and of course Porsches. In the speed-limitless far left lane of the *autobahnen* they soar by you at flabbergasting speeds up to two hundred fifty kilometers per hour (approximately one hundred seventy miles per hour), snazzy luxurious blurs; and the drivers relaxed yet, smoking: emblems of what was until recently called *Das Economic Miracle*-- which truth requires that I admit has been of late a piecemeal miracle, somewhat tarnished by the parental fostering of Germany's east. And the employee parking lot at the capacious Mercedes plant near Stuttgart is *all* Mercedes. Look at them, lined up like some beautificated and becalmed Panzer division. "How can there be so many?" I asked my German wife. "So many what?" she responded. It was out-and-out plain normalcy for her, these street-yacht armadas with all their highfallutin numeral labels which in America would exist in tight formation only in Beverly Hills and Palm Springs-- if even thereabouts. Even in our wealthiest counties, Marin, across the Golden Gate, just north of San Francisco, Montgomery in Maryland, just northwest of Washington, the roads are populated by Hondas, Toyotas and Volvos-- even economical inconspicuous-consumed Kias and Hundais. Good cars, and not much of the likes of Chevvies and Fords, mind you, but hardly ostentatious gonzo-carriages imported from Daimler and Bayrische Motorenwerke.

So many *what*? My wife, being German, had never noticed.

"How do they afford these megamobiles?" I asked.

"Rhineland capitalism," my wife said flatly. QED; as if observing that all tires are oval. She is an economics professor, my wife. "Social capitalism."

Was there some mockery smoothly carpeting Ute's voice? Social capitalism: Some heuristic (but nonetheless magical) lesson-taunting? You bet there was: An I told you so. And by the way, at the Peugeot plant outside Paris, although it's not quite standardized Peugeot City (lots of worker-bee Renaults parked there as well) it's still not like the GM Cadillac plant lots in our country where you will be hard-pressed to find Cadillac one. A new one. A relatively new one. On that native soil *worker* lot, I mean. What you will find, historically, *de rigueur*, are Toyota pickup trucks (Ford would be in *such* bad taste). Cadillac certainly could not resort to the automotive oxymoron of making pickups. A Cadillac *pickup*?!-- gimme a break. Cadillac has admirably resisted the American money-maker for a quite a while. But now, guess what: Uhoh, finally, *the Cadillac division of GM now makes a Cadillac pickup truck.* Profit is profit, baby. Lake Michigan Capitalism: Pickups are America's best-sellers; and so there *will* be worker Cadillacs now in the Cadillac lot at Dearborn. Pickup Cadillacs. In all fairness though: Mercedes does make a flatbed truck, and busses. And that dorky little Smart-- the "Swatch" car. Available only in Europe.

But mystery: As I've said, German CEOs rake in only at best the third of what American corporate leaders "earn". At best. Often German CEOs pull down, not the measly one third, but the microbial one-tenth what ours do, in comparable size corporations-- while our bigboys "earn" enough to feed and clothe the entire population of Hispaniola (Haiti and the Dominican Republic). And these German CEOs are managers who "husband" their firms, folks; they don't pull up stakes every four years or so and move on, loyalty-poor, as do our native homegrown CEOs: shake'n'bakin' from a hair care company to a shmata outfit; slamdunking from a razor manufacturer to athletic shoes: our mobility, albeit *horizontal* mobility, at the stratospheric thin air princedomite level. Job-jumper American CEOs in what?--giant getaway-guzzler Lincoln SUVs? Cadillac SUVs? No, likelihood is Mer-cedes. And German doctors, they rake in far less than our medical men do (and medical women); on average, one third. *One third!* Physicians are not gods in Germany or France, despite their having to compose MD dissertations at the end of medical school, unlike our-- wellpaid-- crowd of undissertators. Anyway, this sheer proliferation of XKEs and Kompressors (a great name, no?) and Roadsters and Corniches-- even the damn foreign *taxis* are Mercedes. It could not all be just doctors and CEOs. Who *are* they?

Guess what:

Normal folk. "Us".

And I'll repeat that identity again for you: Normal folk. Us.

True the conventional, "normal", Germanic-reserved German man (and some women) is as car-obsessed as Michael Schumacher, and super-bourgeois about his auto luxury (if, rather oppositionally, he is not one of those Euro-economizers-- usually old or spinsterish-- driving about in some puny-midget Euro-car like a Smart or a Ka (Ford-made; but only for Over There) in which no one in America would dare mortifiedly ferry himself, except my wife and I in our VW "Lupo"-- unavailable in God's Country); but I'll still have to grant that the German would be more inclined in any case to purchase a Mercedes than would his American counterpart. And this holds for Teutonic Germans from Prussian Berlin and Bavarian Germans in elegant Munich and Schwäbisch Germans from downhome "hillbilly" Stuttgart, and even the "Französisch" (Frenchish) Germans of Cologne and Düsseldorf-- though not the modest Hansa Germans up there devouring lox by the North and Baltic Seas: The Germans are, as Luigi Barzini famously put it, a "mutable people": French by the Rhine, Italian near the Alps, British in Hamburg and American in their general industry. But with shorter daily industrial working hours on average in Germany, at higher pay (those good unions again, like IG Metall, not regarded with contempt-- latent and blatant contempt-- as is the case in America) Germans wind up working an average *three hundred* less hours per year than Americans (one hundred hours less than us in Britain, two hundred fifty less in France-- with its swollen, mammoth civil service and its nutty-sounding chanson partner Association for the Respect of Individuals and Patrimony). The upshot: We Americans have one-third less paid holidays. That's right, one-third less paid days of celebration or memorium in America.

ILLUSTRATIVE

Source: Informationsdienst Wissenschaft

So, what's thence to celebrate? And aside from our still having to buy crummier cars-- okay, more prosaic to less reliable ones-- won't all this Amero-work wear and weigh on our American neuropsychologies?-- this *forty percent* more hours during Yannkee Doodle Dandy lifetimes (As the cliché goes, Europeans live to work, while Americans work to live). You bet our overwork will weigh down on us-- and it damn does! We got guns and we got anger! All this along with that higher hourly pay in Germany-- and you really didn't believe *that* one, did you?-- it is absolute sacrilege. But, well, in that mittel-Europe land, labor is garnering $25.56 per hour on average, and up to $35, compared to the American $16.79. Which is, I should say, why Mercedes opened a new plant in Tuscaloosa, Alabama, and

BMW in South Carolina (Yes, *they* "outsource" to *us*! We're Germany's India!). In both cases, however, the German auto firms did worry that our labor wasn't up to Euro-snuff, not trained well, not attitudinally regarding itself as a body of "paid professionals", as those German workers do, they with a shareholder stake in their company. As one German auto manager put it: "Training costs money, but *not* to train costs a great deal more money." Here then the wages-- of we dubiously trained-- were but one-half. Yes, *we're* Bombay and Bangalore. And then, with German service sector wages at eighty-five percent of those in manufacturing, compared to America's paltry sixty-seven percent (and this American figure is certainly inflated, as it does not count our considerable fount of illegals earning "black money"), with all this, this paid Euro-Normalcy, the German naturally enjoys more time-- therefore money-- therefore outlook-- for his indulgences, whether they be Mercedeses or *gasthaus* chatting-drinking. Or five-week holidays in perhaps his exurban *schrebergarten*; or in France in one's countryside *maison secondaire*. Or just sun-sea calmness (or wildness) on Majorca. Or having one's wife not work. Which is perhaps why you see so many "*schicki-micki*" (fancy-shmancy) ladies over there dressed to the tens, not nines-- in France even more of such-- even as they are navigating on those omnipresent bicycles. I mean, when they aren't shop-cruising or cafe-klatch-venturing, in the wife's canary sport coupe Kompressor, like a Hollywood producer's frau. Boy, a throwback, huh: Women so unliberated they're liberated-- or vice-versa. Stepfordburgville Wives. Well, let's employ our version of the U.S. Army's recruitment slogan: women free-to-be-whoever-it-is-they-be. They could work but they don't have to (One fifth more American women work than European women-- that's a considerable number). Not the best setup for womanly human-development, women's "evolution" necessarily across the seas, I agree on that: Self-potential-binding dressup schmoozing and no office routine cowtowing. Good and bad there. Devo as evo as devo, as retro (as happy?). As evo? Perhaps.

Nonetheless, even accounting for German conspicuous consumption, the If-you've-got-it-flaunt-it syndrome, even the fact that that behavior might be ugly and distasteful, the fact is-- *they can afford to conspicuously consume*. If they want to. To quote Tony Judt (director of the Remarque Institute at NYU), "Europe today is... richer than the United States."

America in total can only be considered richer than Europe-as-a-whole because we work, not smart, but long, but hard.

We've become the slump-shouldered Upton Sinclair and Dickens victims. Many of us.

And of course we're richer in total because-- well, I don't want to sound like a discredited commie bastard (I mean, The Second World *is* finished, perversely tottered on by what would be anathema to Marx and Lenin, hereditary monarchy: Cuba and North Korea)-- but still, we in America are richer in total because we in America are a bigger country, that's all. And because our big total GDP clutches to-- or is clutched onto by -- our super-rich. In any case, our GDP is often-inflated by the government's convenient emphasizing of consumption totals, not production: What we buy, not what we make; so our trade deficits become, falsely, misleadingly, year-after-year, "a sign of strength". And really our major stockholders are but a few. We citizens really don't own our own country.

SO WHO REALLY IS THE FAIREST OF THEM ALL?
An Amalgamated Surmisal[*]

In America the most commonly employed measure of productivity is output per hour in the non-farm business sector, while for the euro area *the entire economy* is considered, including the public sector, where productivity growth is always, inevitably, slower. In America, investment in computers and software are counted in GDP; in Europe they are expenses-- and so *not* counted in. In America we spend more on heating and air-conditioning, because of our more extreme climatology-- which boosts GDP. And America's ever-risingly-higher crime rate means we spend far more on security, for both home and business; and on prisons, which also inflate GDP -- but assuredly not as any indication of GDP as a measure of richness and luxury. Further, the convenience of Europe's considerable, efficient, modern public transport-- a justifiable measure of social wealth-- also does not show up in their GDP figures.

---

[*] *The Economist*-- 6/17/04: "The Economic Future of Europe". NBER Working Paper #10310."Euroland's Secret Success Story"-- Goldman Sachs, Global Economics Paper #102; Study by Robert Gordon, economist at Northwestern University. OECD.

Consequently, the EU growth rate is probably not slower than that of the U.S. but approximately equal to it. Or greater.

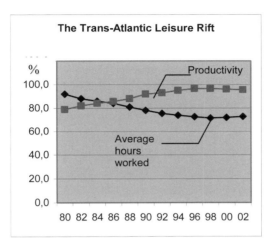

The Trans-Atlantic Leisure Rift

Source: Goldman Sachs, OECD

Productivity, average hours worked and gross domestic product per capita in the original 15 EU members, relative to the United States ... Productivity has risen faster in Europe than in the United States.

In addition, despite the U.S. figures of lower unemployment, (explained away earlier) since 1997 more jobs have been created in the euro area than in America (8% to 6%); same with total employment growth. And far more leisure time has been taken. Add in that Europe's budget deficits are one-third that of America's-- ie, Europe in general really enjoys a *budget surplus*. Add in even further that total household debt in America amounts to 84% of GDP, compared with only 50% in the euro zone; and American household savings are less than 2% of disposable income, compared to European households' 12%. Upshot: *Europe's living standards on average are at least as high as America's. Likely higher.*

Alright, wait, hold on-- the foreign norm is different, no? The foreign norm, or expectation, tends to not include a house-as-a-home, but an apartment straining to serve that home function. Europeans don't necessarily covet, or crave, or enjoy, the American roominess; their sense of space is at odds with ours, as any American will immediately be confronted with in a bodily-contact (sometimes bodily-stinky) European grocery line. Have you ever hosted a Euro-visitor? Germans and Brits and the French, come on, they rattle around in our expanses of Victorians and Bedfords and Carlyles-- suburban-mini as these "expanses" are; they often look more lost (and confused) than impressed. Picture a Prime Minister of England abandoning modest brick rowhouse Number 10 Downing Street for the mega White House: It just doesn't fit: the Prime Minister would lose dignity and respect rather than gain it in our Manse of Pale "Purity". So Europeans suffer less mortgages, less refinance obsession, less property taxes. And even (additionally) their incomes are taxed more on consumption (at the cash register-- the dreaded VAT [value added tax]) than on wage-deduction: which can mean choice-- if they wish such choice, whether to buy a product or not; which can mean less of a belly-punch below the belt, and therefore more savings-- and potentially more money for schools and/or health care. But of course I am talking about middle-class Americans; as you know we do have many apartment-dwellers stacked-up here too. Still, expectations really *are* other "over there". Undeniably Other: Germany's strong land-roots; France's great grandeur claims; Italy's *dolce far niente*; England's class status with ironic humor. Not to mention the out-of-reach, tolerating and laconic-- and unkennable-- Scandinavians. Whether it's a home and garage or "the vision thing", we are more idealist here. We have ultimate aim and *purpose*, woven with that Godly weave, as if a carport is inscripted in Gideon's Bible. We also have worldwide mission; or we think we do. So we think we must sacrifice.

What worldwide purpose do we have? What mission? What daily non-work time for more sacrifice? After late dinner? During *Doctor Phil*?

An "average" Honda'd American, or even a Chevroleted one, if he lives in an urban area, has to worry about public schools. And he really does have to worry there. He or she fears he sends off his child to a free local public elementary school-- or middle school, or high-- all at peril that his offspring, his scion, his treasure, will become not a nuclear physicist nor a neurologist, nor even a clever, reliable accountant, but one of those DJs bizarrely spinning record-discs up and back to transmute those basal buffs into a hip-hop beat, and the kid ridiculously squawking in ersatz Jamaican pidgin Rasta-English. They even teach DJ 101 now at the prestigious Berklee school of Music, as, being at the pinnacle of popularity-- and selling power-- DJ skills were demanded by the same students who were learning ancient Greek modal scales and oboes. Is there, I wonder, Beginner-Intermediate-Advanced DJing? Will Juilliard soon knuckle under and adopt the course? Needless to say-- so I'll say it-- this is not the way in schools in Europe; and I'll spell it out. But first let me demonstrate why it is what it is here at home. Everyone is familiar with the often-comicified Dumbing of America so parodied by Jay Leno in his *Tonight Show* on-the-street routines: Jay asks an average, random, mallgoer, a native speaker, "What are the two countries bordering America?" She replies, with a coy smile, embarrassed but beside herself to be on TV, "Uh, Spain?-- Uh, Europe?" Forget that not only is Europe neither smackdab nor remotely on our border, forget that it remains resting across the wide Atlantic, forget that it is a continent; she doesn't even know *Europe is not a nation*! And this nicely dressed normal (white) American woman cannot even come up with *Canada*?-- this normal midscale suburban American shopper who likely graduated high school, maybe had a touch of (American) college; and isn't it horrifying to conjecture that perhaps she even *graduated* from an American college-- which supposition is not so farfetched. The audience laughs: At her answer? At itself?-- by subliminal, embarrassed, unconscious identification? Or is it guffawing merely because the electronic laugh lights have flashed their Hilarious Crackup Order to everyone in the NBC studio seats? Or is the audience in stitches because most people comprising it *do* know the answer? Sad to say, I really do doubt this last. But certainly the entire Leno bit is not even of marginal wit (Jay is compelled to fill up an hour five nights per week; for which, with his writer staff aid, he pulls down triple the millions [or quintuple?] what his European colleagues earn on their talk shows [Thomas Gottschalk; Harold Schmidt], which "wit" we, the drowsily overworked audience, the badly educated-- yet imagining we *are* educated-- the undemandingly demanding, seem to crave: The Big Insipid). Of course one might speculatively Rolodex his way back through history's pages and wonder if some Roman empire shopper-lady, upon being asked, at The Forum, where, say, Naples was (210 miles south), might answer--with a shit-eating grin-- Uh, way over by-- whatsit?-- Babylon? The Tigris and Euphrates?

Yes, I know Naples-was-Neapolis-back-then (I also know that re- sounds like some old twenties ditty): Greek for New Town. You know, like Newton, in Massachusetts. But I went to public school back in the fifties, when the Dark Ages (like segregation, like McCarthy) were also-- oh the paradoxes of society-- the Bright Ages: In public school, Lordy, we learned Latin! Well, yes these were Bright Ages for *paleface* kids-- though not in egalitarian citizenship, I'm afraid. Oh the twists and turns of social history-- and I am certainly not advocating segregation. Which of course we still do "enjoy"-- defacto anyway. And which race-separation (sociological, sure, not legal) is the obvious causus belli of, not just our poor, and our middle, but especially of our athletes-- with media microphones-- to GorillaSpeak:

Ahs gone whup 'at fahn young mayin.

This by comparison with their colleagues, the jocks of Europe-- even if these latter are no poets lauriate either. When the Englishman Lennox Lewis hung up his boxing gloves as retired heaviweight champion of the WBC and WBA, he spoke articulately of his achievements and his gratefulness, his hoped for legacy (Arrogantly, but articulate). But have you ever heard, say Leon Spinks speak? That bronchiation will curdle your blood. Or even our beloved, humorous, self-deprecating George Foreman? It's like floundering under Santa Monica Bay, arduously blowing one's last bubbles. Same comparison with ex-heaviweight contender Axel Schultz of Germany-- a fluent talker in his own tongue. And the fighting ex-champ Klitchko brothers of Germany and the Ukraine hold-- Mamamia!-- PhDs! (Okay, maybe they are in Phys Ed, but *still...*). Compare an American football player's communicating "skills" to a European *fußball* player's. It is almost like two different species of mammal. The reason for our poverty of tongue?-- of disrespect for language: Of disinterest in language-- unless of course the words jangle in the kind of Neanderthal rhyme that O.J. Simpson's lawyer Johnny Cochran cleverly used in court to acquit his client (with an inner city L.A. jury):

If da glove dont fit, you must acquit.

The disinterest in the wiring, the word-current, the electricity of culture. That is POVERTY, bigtime. And this is no racist comment: Lennox Lewis is black.

This public school anxiety, this justified quiver and quake the American parent experiences about local American schooling, is a consequence of poor teaching of course (teachers often do not even possess a minor field in their subject), and poor teacher pay (starting salaries for teachers in elementary and secondary schools are at least one-third higher in Germany and France) and a leaden motivation for cultural learning (or almost *any* learning), where social studies are barely taught (social studies, mall-folks, are politics, sociology, civics, economics, history); this as programs are cut back, replaced by the empty-reform standardized dumb-dumb barebones testing of President Bush's cynically named No Child Left Behind Act-- which more accurately is the Most Children Left Behind Act (or the No Child Gets Ahead Act)-- with its unnuanced "drill and grill curricula" (which also requires all students in the program to be registered, with their vital statistics fully available: If the boy (or girl) does not do well, he may be visited by a convincing Army recruiter who knows "all about him", and so can tilt the stumbling school-kid towards military enlistment. Reason enough to torture an Iraqi?). You do of course remember ketchup being officially morphed into a nutritious vegetable-- which began with Reagan the Revered -- and potatoes now often being the only other veggie served; if there remains, that is, a school cafeteria serving *anything*. What is this?-- The American Veggie Famine? In France, *baguettes* are served to children with school meals (even when the French economy is in deficit), and teaching there is considered among the highest professions. . . Then there is the anxiety as well over the dangers in these our urban public schools, which are nowadays rogueishly referred to as "the prison gangsta pipeline". "Institutions of learning" are now forced into a "zero tolerance" ever-watchful zone of the trivial transgression: suspension for spitball (or possible arrest and record), which can near parallel The Patriot Act for its suppression of anything beyond the straight and narrow.

Unfair becomes fair, in an unfair world.

Our respect and grasp of just what education even may consist has become by now so diluted and bastardized that even when education is promoted, it is touted by embarrassingly lame, mush-literate slogans of our "Mayberry Machiavellis" like, "Getta-edjacayshun", as grammatically incorrect as it is sorry in its substance and comprehension (*By the edja-cayters!*), implying as it does: Go to school, suffer through some stupid math'n'stuff and pick up your diploma-- your edjacayshun ticket-- so's you can get your Good Job (and watch Jay Leno), then go on to state college (or community, or junior) and take them BUSINESS courses (or Bid'niss courses), gobble them suckers on up. Plato? Dante? Goethe? Shakespeare? Einstein?-- How much money did *them* turkeys make off the Big Board?-- where everybody claps maniacly (disgustingly) when Wall Street opens. Always leaning pragmatic in this country, we have now gone whole-hog and come to regard education as supreme-tool-Pragmatic, as a *means* to Business Success. No chump change for me. While Europeans by and large regard education as a means to, well, EDUCATION.

Boy are They weird!?

And I do wonder who will this "Mayberry Machiavelli-ism" hurt most when, finally-- as all our edjacayters (and our now edjacayted), annoyingly, love to say, "the-day-is-over"? "At-the-end-of-the-day".

Odd thing is, English happens to be the most creative language in the West. We HumVee along with 500,000 words, clever neologisms forming Darwinistically like hybrid plants and animals (like Ligers, for the rare offspring of a Lion and Tiger: no word for such offbeat feline in German or French-- no idea to even come up with one). We manage this fluid word-proliferation almost geometrically, while German lumbers along with but 300,000 words-- even with its modular erector set amalgams like, say, *wiedergutmachung* ("again-good-making"; as in "dealing with your past"); and French, so controlled and ever-eyeballed by council and committee, French *Deux Chevaux* of lexikonery turtle along at 200,000 vocables. When I (enjoyably-maliciously) informed a French friend of his nation's linguistic rear-pulling sloth, its word-caboose state, he eyed me, honestly with a moment's rage, a near homicidal fix, as if I were Carlos the Jackal and should be jailed.

But still, with our English language super-rabbiting away we in America trail with our education as edjacayshun. Now I am hardly against an enlightened native pragmatism for godssakes, and I'm certainly not a voice in the wilderness crying out that we ought to invest far more in our public schools-- at least triple what we are now spending. But what funds there are do just seem to magically cascade into National Defense (Got to keep Boeing afloat, as Europe's AirBus is leaving it in the dust; got to repork the porkbarrell naval ship construction down in Biloxi for Trent Lott; got to land some Texas Army installations for Tom "The Hammer" DeLay,

Republican Whip-man.). Well, these Defense boondoggles are Monster Culprits; that is, after our other Brobdingnagian Culprits: our tax-reductions-for-the-rich capers (or tax *eliminations* for the rich), habitual and routine and expected and "entitled" as these are, and so they don't even seem shenaniganey. The rest of us don't appear to greatly resent these economic loopdeloops, even if we know of them (Education might instruct us; edjacayshun surely wont), this financial terpsichore where tax cuts for the rich-- in particular Bush's tax cuts-- are over *fifty times* greater than the total amount Bush requested for new education spending. "No-Child-Left-Behind", my rear end! After all, *we* aspire ourselves, absurdly, to reach that topnotch specula-positis peak where *we* can also acquire tax-dispensation on empty grounds (An aspiration 99 percent out-of-touch with reality, and not qualitatively different at all from a ghetto black kid's contempt for schooling, as his agenda-- a *pfahn-young-mayin's*-agenda-- toplists out at shake'n'bake in the NBA). Don't we watch controlled network TV on the edges of our seats to see if the executive with whom we identify on *The Apprentice* (ironically, one of the few official apprenticeship programs in our country) will be hired or fired by the-- now founding, again foundering, then floundering, ever-repulsive-- Donald Trump? And it is heartily network-assumed that we *will* identify with at least one of these shallowly bumptious obsequiositors. Add in that cute regressive tax structure of ours (Tables 1 through 3) and its loophole "shelters" (the mega-rich need oil well *shelters*?), our easy allowing of large companies to evade taxation by "headquartering" themselves in palmy offshore island havens like Grand Bahama, the Caymans and Granada (where under Reagan we actually *invaded*-- and now you know why); and we are the only developed nation to so collusively wink at this monkey-business-- to obliquely behind-the-back promote it. Why? Because we love it, the great "Individualist" criminality of Our BigBoys-- we want in! The American Dream: *I want MY monkey business too!-- I'll pray for it to come true-- in church* (For an eye-opener, again see Table 2). And what monies remain-- yes, we're so rich booty does yet remain-- that flows also into those "Welfare" subsidies for "Individualists" like King Cotton farmers, four billion each year; and into no-strings tax breaks and other incentives to corporations-- Mercedes, Toyota, Walmart, A K Steel-- to locate here-and-there (approximately fifty billion per year), often even promising *no* tax payments, none whatsoever, nor managing any agreement on job creation. Nor job maintenance.

>*Wasn't that the point?-- job creation. And job-keeping.*

If you don't have jobs you don't have anything. You might not even be in the mood to watch Jay Leno.

One argument frequently put forward by Republicans, and no few Democrats for that matter, is that other nations, like Germany, do not invest anywhere near as great a proportion of their national incomes in national defense (See Table 13). Instead, as I've written, those other nations funnel euros into social welfare and infrastructure (Germany, 50 percent of GDP, France 60 percent, U.S. 37 percent); and, true, sometimes the Europeans do divert funds toward corporate subsidy-- as with France's Atlasing-up Alstom, which built the super-train TGV. But we plough away, techno-cavemen, into laser-guided missiles and bunker buster bombs and bunker buster research (*bunker-buster research*!?) and worldwide military bases, aside from our own domestic ones, in: Iraq, Afghanistan, Cuba, Greenland, Australia, Germany, The Philippines, South Korea, Bosnia, Colombia, etc. And will it be very surprising if pretty soon our Right presents to Congress a much-needed proposal for an anti-anti-anti missile missile missile? Our defense budget is larger than most national budgets, we boasting an Army or Navy presence in one hundred twenty of the one hundred eighty nine member countries of the United Nations! But the whole question is, as is the whole purpose of this book, just what American Greatness and Democracy (and *toilets!*) is it that we are defending?-- when by most civilized-humanitarian standards we are already less great and less democratic (and less rich) than other democracies. And they, those other democracies, they don't even seem obsessed about "defending" their democracies. Boy what slacker-nitwits, huh-- not a bunker-buster bomb to their foreign, greenhorn names. Not a cabinet-level Homeland Defense Department.[*] And, counter to public belief, with such defense "allocations" we really do not spend gobs and wads on foreign aid-- because we're spending so volubly on defense *against* foreigners. Fact, veiled-over like an Afghan lady's berka: We couldn't really,

---

[*] More than $300 billion in new spending has been added to the Pentagon budget in less than three years; and the "war on terror" will add another $885 billion to federal deficits in the next ten years (Center for Strategic and Budgetary Assessments). More than enough here to develop good public school programs in academics, or vocational programs across the nation; or to finance a system of universal health care for some time to come.

effectively, rid Afghanistan of the Taliban; so those concertina face-wires yet imprison their women's features. Hell, we give less by proportion of GDP to assistance in Africa or impoverished Asian countries *than any other Western nation* (France donates the most). Didn't believe *that* one, did you? So we are not just domestic pikers, but pennyante international Scrooges in the bargain. By not spending on societal ills-- ours and others-- that we are coming less and less to *recognize* as societal ills, and then even *regard* as societal ills ("You know: that's-just-how-life-is."-- such sort of Rumsfeldian aphorism) we are making ourselves less and less great and less and less educated and less and less democratic and less and less admired, and more and more disliked, and more and more dangerous.

Then hated?

Then pitied?

Except, we think, Envied. At least we think we think that-- until we THINK.

Then we think, We don't care.

Social Alzheimer's.

International Social Alzheimer's.

But we do care.

TABLE THIRTEEN

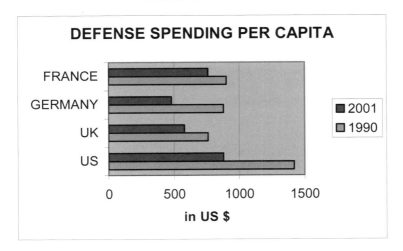

Source: http/www.nato.int/docu/review/2002/issue 2/english/statistics.html

Remember President Bush's annuncio that we were attacked because the terrorists quote "hate freedom"? But the terrorists didn't attack nations *more* free than ours, like who?-- Canada or Denmark or Sweden? (I'll mercifully not name all the others). And I can't believe that any terrorist worth his maldirected-jihaded-salt wakes up each morning with the refrain, "I *hate* freedom!" He probably wakes up and reads the morning papers, like you and me; only foreign news-sheets, ones that report more worldwide incidents; and so the terrorist-- believing he *loves* freedom?-- absorbs information on the order of what I'm relating here.

And the more dangerous and disliked we become aren't we are apt to become in reaction even less and less democratic? Less and less civilized. Looks sure like: Circular Cumulative Causation. Note: Americans, flattened-out by work (or no-work, and/or flimsy edjacayshun), watch "whatever's on" television. Sixty percent of us do that, roughly eight hours per day. In Germany it's only twenty percent; in France, seventeen percent. Not so many flickering screens through the windows as you wander and investigate the avenues of Europe-- which you *can* do because walking is nice there, as a shooting or stabbing or robbery is far less likely to be just around the corner. Far less. FAR LESS! They talk, in groups there, in Europe. Inside. Outside. Cafes. Pubs. Civic meetings. Lectures. Whatnot.

Now science: As we emphasize Defense Spending, the United States has begun the descent towards losing its global dominance in critical (non-defense) science, medicine and innovation-- as in energy; the environment, and in the investigation and curing of disease:

> Item: Ratio of number of cows France tests *each week* for Mad Cow Disease to the number the U.S. has tested in the last *decade*: 7:6.
>
> Item: Antidepressants such as Serzone (Bristol Myers, Squib) have been connected to liver damage and death. Our FDA permits Serzone's sale; Europe and Canada ban Serzone.
>
> Item: Our percentage of patent grants is losing out to Asia, and to Europe.
>
> Item: The top science journals publish fewer and fewer Americans-- now only 20 percent. Europe surpassed the U.S. in the mid-

nineties as the world's largest producer of scientific literature.

Item: Our share of science Nobels is falling to a share equal to the Stockholm and Oslo winnings, individually, of Britain, Japan, Russia, Germany, Sweden, Switzerland and even New Zealand.

Item: In March of 2004 Euro scientists announced that one of their planetary probes had detected methane in the atmosphere of Mars, a potential signal that alien microbes live beneath that planet's surface. This comparatively mega-finding made headlines from Paris to Melbourne, but not here, even in *The New York Times*, where they print "All the news that's fit to print" (We were too proudly bombarded in America by colorful 3-D images from our own rovers cutely caterpillaring the red planet while the first of the two Euro-probes did fail to enter Mars, or to communicate that entry.

Item: More ambitiously, Europe is seeking to dominate particle physics by constructing the world's most potent atom-smasher, to debut in 2007, while we'll be obliterating atoms at MIT and Johns Hopkins and Berkeley and Livermore "the-old-fashioned-way", with what?-- the sub-atomic equivalent of tenderizer-pounders and cleavers?

Item: Coup de grâce: The brain drain *to* America, that pride of our intellectual gravitational attraction, drawing Calcuttans to *our* Cambridge (Mass) and Canterbridgeans (Cambridge, England) to Cambridge (Mass) has now begun to rebound and reverse course: American scientists are booking graduate (and undergraduate) round-trips to India (the IIT), to England, to Germany. Secondary price: Our venture capital flowing out, to

these other lands. As some flippant-
wiseacre sage predicted, it wont be
America, but France which becomes the
nation where "*test tube babies* are surfing
Google." Or India. The recalcitrant-proud
French may not call it Google, but,
what?-- *Le Google.* "

So, back to school, mah fella 'murkins: Except, private school just,
unfortunately, lamentably and unfairly, has to be considered in today's state-
of-the-nation, if a parent is to feel his child will become a responsible, stand-
up, human being, much less an educated one who might fulfill his hopes, and
not just-- here it comes again-- getta edjacayshun. Or worse, just drop out--
as our dropout rates are shooting up (pun barely intended). And if an
American kid does drop out? Hold the cellphone. Lotsaluck. We have, in
contrast to Europe, lackluster alternatives at best: little formal vocational and
apprentice training, as Head Start programs continue to wilt under the recent
administration; and as Pell Programs for crafts and basic college and basic
college equivalents for the poor fade away. Sure we do have our prison-
alternative, as I've said-- more prison "establishments of alternative skills
and learning" than any other Western country. It's practically a societal
directive, an economic funnel. The Other American Conduit. But that's
another story. Sort of. No it's not: Forty-six percent of American eighteen
year old dropouts receive no other skills-- zip. They learn nothing. In
Germany, just *one* percent receives no compensatory skills-- *one percent!*--
as vocational training carries no stigma. Scarcely any. Quite the contrary,
vocational training is often preferred there, and in France. It can be
encouraged. If that's what a child wants; if that's what he likes, that's what he
should get. And Euro-corporations participate, voluntarilly-- most
companies employing more than ten workers train apprentices. This cooperative human-tooling-up is at the heart of the German "miracle" (dimmed
as it has been somewhat by the recent world downturn)-- and it is crucial to
France's survival. But now, here at home, domestically, consequentially, we
are talking at upwards to thirty thousand dollars each year, for each child, if
he or she is to succeed at escaping hardcore untrained America and be lifted
off to acceptance at a good university-- even forty thousand dollars-- if he
(or she) is to succeed at "life", and not be relegated to our disastrous "mean
and ugly"-- and so, *un*Godly-- "safety net". Or prison. Which American
safety net would not be "ungodly", a pathetic dole, if we did incorporate

realistic training into it, vocational and apprentice training, as other advanced countries do, with good job placement as the light at the end of the tunnel; all so our welfare would not be eternal, miserable, humiliating, infuriating-- to public and recipient alike-- and a dead end (if not cut off, "terminated", before the real dead end of life-- termination itself). With their picayune substance we have even made mocking travesty of these phrases: "safety net"; social services; Welfare: Loser chump change. A life-flunk.

Now, at the risk of being a broken record-- Not-in-Germany. No private schooling. Not-in-Europe as a whole. Okay, barely any; as barely any is needed. So, no expense incurred for the average parents. You may have heard tell of the famous German gymnasia and the French lycées. The gymnasia are not paraphernalia-gyms where you monkey on monkey bars and clamber ropes and dribble "roundball" and spike volleyballs and totter one-legged on the "horse". The German gymnasia are the equivalent of the American high school, although they additionally cover the first two years of what would be college in the U.S. They are good too, even as the worrywart Germans do agonize these days that they are not good enough. "We worry at a very high level," boast-complains one headmaster after having visited America and been witness to our Very Low Level. A full eighty-eight percent of German pupils have said they wanted to do well in school (81 percent in France; 66 percent in Britain; and in America?-- only half of the students interviewed gave a damn: doing well in school sends out, in too much of our nation, creep-vibes). I myself have observed how a French kid, or a German, or a Swiss, will know Saul Bellow's works to some extent, Philip Roth's, Updike's, Pynchon's, Melville, Shakespeare, etcetera-- even if he has not completed gymnasium and earned his *abitur* or baccalaureat (France). An American kid-- are you kidding?-- he/she will not be familiar with *his own great writers*, except Stephen King (forget "composers"-- except Kurt Cobain-- forget artists; forget Günther Grass and Thomas Mann, and those other "esoteric" alien schmuckos like Goethe, Joyce, Flaubert), this even if said American kid *has* completed high school, even with a string of straight A's. Even if he/she has completed *college* and gotta-edjacayshun! -- on what?-- the inverse relationship between stocks and bonds pricing and the calculus of the interest rate; the marginal cost and marginal revenue curves intersecting at a firm's microeconomic production-sales nexus; how to run a meeting while coming off optimistic-tough-sincere-confident. This "kid's" familiarity with "his" Shakespeare or Germany's Goethe will be limited to *Cliffs Notes*-- at best.

The average literacy rate in Germany and France-- of those over age fifteen-- hits at an unbelievable (to us) *98 percent*. Man! That is slightly higher than America's 70 percent[*] ; and France Loisirs, the major book club, sells some 26 million books per year-- one for every two Frenchmen! Compare that to America's highest volume book clubs, which sell perhaps one book for every thirty Americans (and that's in a damn good year; and that's with "kitsch" quality wares). And next time you're in Europe, cop a gander at the magazine racks in kiosks and train stations as well as in bookstores. The thickness of *The Economist* dwarfs *Time* or *Newsweek*, as does *L'Express*, *Der Spiegel* or Germany's *Focus*. One reason-- a relatively obvious reason-- why Americans are so pandemically obese ("You people are *dick*," a German taxi driver once said to me, meanly-happily, as *dick* means thick means fat) is not that we have a fast food culture-- that is consequence, not cause-- but that we have, as I've said, no true essential education. No food for *thought*, if you will. Dulled-out with few *inner* resources (rather, undeveloped resources: why, for example, jazz and Woody Allen and Phillip Glass and offbeat films like *My Dinner With André*, are more appreciated in Europe than in their land of origin [Jerry Lewis I'll hedge-off on]), what "appealing" dregs you've got remaining here are MTV and M&M's and Eminem and "raves", and the everso aptly named beef jerky, "aristocratic" George Bush Père's favorite food. You have a substantial American electorate (usually the ones owning the undemocratically heavy, malproportioned state electoral votes), that "electorate" passionately greedy to select one-of-their-own, not some smartypants "candyass" who got A's (Or, hell, even B's, unless the B's are in Business), as they do elect in "effete" France, or in smug "cold-clinical" Germany. No, we are attracted by, even soldered and galvanized to, politicians who pulled down their "gentlemen's C's" and who are now of course fervently *for* edja*cay*shun. This esteem and respect for statesmen, even pseudo ones, certainly influences the German and French body of voters: They do look for politicians who at least aspire to higher ground, a more world-aware viewpoint (even the corrupt baksheeshers do this); so these foreign electorates *vote*: they actually trouble themselves to travel to their precincts (some distant) and enter a booth and

---

[*] The average reading level of a soldier in Iraq is at age eleven.

pull levers or drop cards; and they perform this act at an astounding rate, one and two-thirds greater than our pathetic American "democratic" forty percent (sometimes fifty percent; sometimes thirty-five percent).

WHY WE COMMITTED ATROCITIES AT ABU GRAIB (THE IRAQ PRISON) THE LINGUISTIC VIEW

(or Why "Our Finest" call Guantánamo "Gitmo")

The photographs show it all, the torment and the abuse. But they do not show the language. They do not let us hear the Senators on the Foreign Relations Committee torturing the last name of the assistant Secretary of Defense, Cambone, pronounced in the Old World Kam-bohn-ay (and in ethnic sectors of the New World), abusing the good secretary (who really wasn't so good in truth) by calling him Cam-bone, as if it's some damn minstrel show: *Cam-bone, Cam-bone, How you doin'?* Cambone himself is born-here American and so is not offended-- he seems to know no difference; he seems not to know or care that his grandparents and those generations before in the old country who came here with the rope tied around their olive sacks were *Kam-bone-ay*, and proud to be Kam-*bone*-ay... The good Senators-- with their own Americo-butchered Old Europe names-- they inquired about the rules and directives at "Abugrub", and Cambone-Cambone answered flatly. But there were no Arabs present to say, Please, if anything, if nothing else, Please respect our language, and then perhaps you will respect Us: The torture prison in question here is Ah-*boo*-Gra-*yeeb*. And there seemed to be no correcting Arab-Americans present, or European, or Asian-- as everybody else in the world knows (from the most illiterate Karachi squatter to the wealthiest shiek) that Al Qaeda is not, as *we* say, Elkhidea-- like a parlor game at the Elks Club-- but Al-Ka-*yee*-da. We don't even require a decent waiting period of, say, a generation, before we squash and squish a name into a porous linguistic sponge. *Kinder* becomes "kid" as soon as you cross the ocean, and *tout à l'heure* becomes toodle-ooh-- becomes, now, "toodles". The American pronunciation is the linguistic compactor, the shock'n'awe, the bunker-buster vowell-bomb, not just of language, and of name, but of what is profoundly thriving within these-- *attitude*. Respect. Tradition. History. Dignity. Knowledge. All alien is a mishmash to us-- *t'was mimsy and the borgroves*-- all foreign is meaty beef become bouillon become gruel. We have simply destroyed the vitality and beauty, and thus meaning, and thus music, of name, and word, and work, and calling, and thus of vision, and so of attitude. And once these are smothered and snuffed by The American Indifferent, by edja*cay*shun, our native accent dullificator, once you are pronounced by The American Glottus, you are merely grist and mumblegrumble and 'I dub you Dull: Torture-fodder in Abu Grub (*Why the* fuckin *hell not?!*). In Ver-*sayles*, Indiana or *Nay*-pulls, Florida. Or, as the natives call Washington, with their local DC accent (white accent though)-- Wash-tun.

Back to point, please: Those German gymnasia, they are free, as are the roughly equivalent French *lycées,* one significant reason (aside from un-insane Defense expenditure) being that they spend one-third less on sports than American high schools. Recently, when inadequate tax revenues forced Schwarzenegger-California to cut back on high school sports in Alameda and Contra Costa ("Against Cost"?) counties, the students went up-in-arms: "Without sports we'll wind up in jail!" Huh? Strange linkup-- they actually did holler it; but the kids apparently regarded this school-sports connection as incontrovertible logic, as necessity, as inalienable and unsunderable constitutional right-- natural and spontaneous. Was such idiot-entitlement merely American-assumed, or was it taught in their high schools?-- or inculcated at indignant home? Another species from, say, French students, who veritably demonstrate for more, better, *studies*, more homework to trounce lurking idlenesses, not more hoops and balls and Nikes and end-zone wiggle-waggles in-yo'-faces. And the French kids demonstrated too for harder teachers, even as they already tote up to ten kilos of textbooks to school each day-- which is over twenty pounds, which is over twenty times the *one* book-pound their corresponding American sluggard-student carries (if he must)-- he who will dribble off the round-ball he *does* carry, to jail, after the No-Sports Default robbery (Seven-Eleven?) he *does* commit in compensation (*Weren't mah fauht, yoannah: all that tahm own mah hainds!*). Note: Many Euro-gymnasiums have-- how about this one?-- no "gym-nasiums". Yet Germans, as you know, with no school gym-gymnasia, are pretty damn good at sports. It's not in the genes, I don't imagine. Sports go on *in the Community*.

And your child is not likely to be attacked in a sportless *gymnasium*, or sportless *lycée*, forgodssakes, or outside one (by a fellow student carrying Stendahl with no time on his hands), even if the school is dead-set in a downtown urban environment. Especially if it's there; and I have walked by them plenty. No attacks by the deprived progeny of the "safety-net"-deprived and rightfully angry (See Tables 14 and 15). I must admit to the sunny stirring, a nostalgic sensation from the fifties, of seeing children, and not the sullen unpredictable future-fighting, as they enter or leave a school in the center of a Euro-city, as that experience reaffirms the civic as a centerpiece, a nucleus, a Life. And in such a world one's child is not likely to fall into, or be pulled into, The-Wrong-Crowd-- the Big Parent Worry in American schools-- as there isn't much of a Wrong Crowd: The wrongest might be a kid who can speak fluent Turkish and whose parents work like hell in the family neighborhood *doner-kebab* (I know I'm stereotyping, but *doner-kebab* is the most popular speed-lunch in Germany; it far outsells McDonald's, as it's better than the Big Mac), and said Turkish kid's idea of muscling is simply to hoist iron in his subsidized apartment building's basement beside the washing machine. So the wrongest isn't even Wrong (Sad to say-- but say I must: It is a different story in some French suburbs. North Africans, unassimilated, unhired by fearful employers, are as justifiably angry as ghettoed Americans, even though they receive far greater state support. They are a smaller "cohort" than the American-rejected, but one does wonder what will become of them. At least, for now, they're gun-less. Mostly.)

TABLE FOURTEEN

THE SAFETY NET

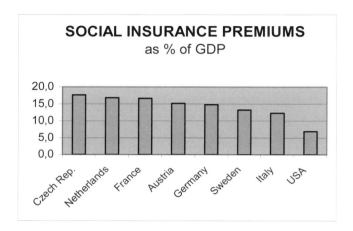

Source: OECD

TABLE FIFTEEN

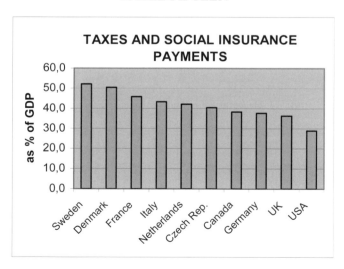

Source: OECD

Apropos of lifting weights and the American school-fear of physical violence: In police stations in our nation, especially the larger ones, there does seem to be invariably a weight room, a well-equipped stronghold motif (tax dollars) with officers of the law pumping away on barbells as if these law-enforcement-officials are defensive linemen for the Boston Patriots preparing to protect the civilian backfield of Back Bay Boston. Pumping-up, ostensibly, to handle the day's dangerous suspects; or worse, bulking up because they are in-these-times in thrall to a bulk-up monster cop mentality. Now we all know that the British "bobbie" is a gunless lawman, and the French Foreign Legionnaire-capped "flic" always seems a touch comical, Chaplinesque and indifferent; but it seems churlish of me to own that even *Germany's* police stations are now quite pacific havens, thoroughly unmuscular oriented. Often, by comparison with American officers of the peace, the German *bullen* look boyish, and girlish; and in the two German stations I have visited I have witnessed no weight rooms, although my eye was caught by what seemed to be a chess room in one, with a Bobbie Fisher book (translated, but Bobby still sour-faced) resting by a board. Chalk all this up I'm sure to the lower level of violence in Europe-- even with (another sad-exception-caveat) the recent attacks by some young Muslim French Arabs on Hasidic Jews-- old ones too; and the very sporadic skinhead assault-upcroppings in Germany and Switzerland; and "hooligans" in England-- at big-rival soccer matches. In general however Europe does remain far less violent than America; and the lower perceived threat of head-banging, stabbing, stomping and shooting sure cuts down on reciprocal head-banging police tactics, prep espantoon drills at the station or Police Academies of Europe and their gunfire readiness. In Rome, I the intruding wisenheimer just came out and asked at central police, "Say, where's the *weight* room?"-- and a mesomorphic Danny DeVito led me over to the WAIT ROOM, where people were, well you guessed it-- Waiting? No, I have never seen a bobby, bull or flic posted outside a European high school. But I have seen many American cops poised (fake casual-nonchalant) by the fences of ours. At youngster middle schools too (And I wasn't malingering) ... So: it should have constituted no great flabbergast then that our "finest young soldiers" should not be "our finest young" whatevers but rather our education-deprived undrafted "volunteers", our prison-avoiding (and chump-work-ducking, and dole-dodging) joinups who became rather easily tantalized in Iraq, in Afghanistan (and in their crudely diminutive nicknamed, respectless "Gitmo"?) into becoming our handy-dandy-- and substitute (for *us?*)-- fun-loving torturers. After all, they didn't have much organized sports after duty; and few tomes on Reinhold Niebuhr. Or Ghandi.

Upwards, onwards, to university: Let's resurrect our long-forgotten German Euro-man visitor to Northern California. Had that bruised and abused tourist been not Deutsch but French he might well have vacated his vacation by now, so enfuriated he bagged the whole venture, turned tail and flew to a hospitable (for a Frenchman) Club Med or a former French colony, like Martinique. But now let's say our German's "heimat" is Heidelberg, the home of Germany's oldest university; and he visits Berkeley. Two university towns. Despite San Francisco Bay's natural, geological beauty, on the crafted, architectural human beauty front Heidelberg has to take the gold hands down-- although nature did not deal Heidelberg much of a bad hand either. Of course matchup is hardly fair. Heidelberg dates from before the renaissance (You've seen the romantic duelling features like *The Student Prince*), so you cannot with decent justice stack up a facade of American clapboard against your template of jugendstil and baroque. Apples-oranges, sticks'n'bricks. So our decent Euroguy allows for that. But: Berkeley sure does win on the campus itself, no sweat, as Heidelberg doesn't even *have* a campus. Being twelfth century, the university is mixed among other buildings, public and private. Like NYU; like the Sorbonne; like Berlin's Humboldt University; like most European universities. And Euro-man is impressed-- he loves the Cal campus (no matter the American college campus was the brainchild of a French architect, Joseph Ramée); he walks and hikes the great Cal campus, wooded hill and valley, and wishes he'd been fortunate enough to attend there... But then, uhoh, there looms Telegraph Avenue; and it sure is no Hauptstrasse, Heidelberg's Main Street. Berkeley's seamy Telegraph, although it boasts two great bookstores-- Cody's and Moe's-- will make you zigzag and/or dash for cover. Helterskeltersville. The bumming, the egregious sixties' time-machine insanity ("love"-eviscerated however) of hair and whacko-jabber and threat, the incipient-seeming danger. Heidelberg's main street, by contrast, is a kind of student-tourist Fifth Avenue: jam-packed, fast-paced, shopping high-end and low: life-crowded, but not dangerous. The Berkeley campus is undeniably wonderful; like so many American university landscapes it flowers with that castles-on-the-hill mystique. But universities are for life-training, aren't they? And life-training-- on-the-job-experience-- mightn't that best be accomplished within Life? The campus at first entices, conjures, spellbinds; it surrounds the neophyte freshman (and this German visitor of ours) with its stadiums and field houses, with football, fraternity and sorority houses; it's an idyll of immortality, of eternal youth-- of these-are-the-best-days-of-your-life-you'll-remember-them-always Delusion. And I am certainly not ridiculously suggesting we abandon the campus. But it is true that you may be condemned by that prevailing magic-mist to become a frat-boy for all of your ensuing non-frat *man* days; and if too many adults go through life on that narrow callow path, well . . .-- you know who you get. On the contrary, the university campusless-in-the-adult-world, that is a university that is-what-it-is, a university: not a kaleidescopic schmorgasbord pleni-versity, with sports. With un-university university-Distractaversity. When you study physically within-The-Adult-World, sandwiched among commercial buildings, isn't the osmosis something of a civics course in itself? Or at least a more plausible, possible, preliminary one? You may even be more motivated to fix-up-the-world, as you may see more readily into-the-world. Even without books and lectures, you may perceive that the world needs, you know, *fixing.*

It always does.

It always will.

Even the purported dimwits competing in "swimsuits" for the Miss America title always aim their sights high: at World Peace.

And, oops, forgot: the university is FREE in Europe. There's that enticing, unwonted weirdo word exploding again like a shock cigar. *Free,* dude-and-dudette-parents. Well, to a considerable extent. And doesn't that egalitarian ideal keep popping up here?-- like it's got this near-theological status.

Okay, I'm sorry-- I misrepresented: $350 to $435 per year in France: What?-- a couple less liters of wine?

Okay, one or two hundred pounds in England: Sliding scale, depending upon the remuneration-rumor-promise of your major-- your chosen profession. And that's even for Oxford and Cambridge, sportsfans.

And, broken record again: this deal is accomplished without the aid of college football, or even *fußball* (soccer) and their profits-- if there are indeed any proceeds in America after the mega-stadium and top-line equipment outlays and sweetheart deal "stipends" and "scholarships" for jocks (I hereby advocate that we be honest-- at the redoubt of honesty, the university-- and abandon the oxymoronish *athletic* scholarship, in favor of the accurate-honest *jock*ship), and top-line prostitute payoffs for these "students". These jockshippers: California, by the way, even including non-academic dispersals, spends more on its *prisons* than it does on its state universities. Parents in effect pay for lockups and college athletes by paying those exorbitant college tuitions. As with the *gymnasia*, and even counting in British university rugby and regatta, sports are simply not integral to overseas education, on philosophical grounds and of course because the halls of learning are embedded among all those commercial structures (What are they gonna do?: "Okay, Fritz, you cut left at *Das Wursthaus* and I'll fake kick it to you. That parked black Jaguar XKE is the goal."). So, in Germany, or in France, at Heidelberg or the Sorbonne, your son or daughter will not find a glandular case diffidently sprawled out next to him who can "slamjam the roun'ball down into that *hole*, man"-- better than Kierkegaard ever could, even if he stood on Heidegger's (skinny) shoulders-- and then that jock-shipper be hangin' from the basketball rim with your basic primate bravado; he who on "scholarship" in, say, Business Law class (as it is always *some* Business course, isn't it?) asks the prof, "Uh, like, sir, my-*man*, so the *moan*-ies of the deceased, they be goin to the *hairs*?"

Alright, I do deny here racism-- I seriously, adamantly, deny it: The problem is obviously American Social, not American Genetic; and jocks aren't *that* dumb-- inherently (many). But they do always major in Business. If not PE. And have you ever been captive to a lecture, a bafflingly inde-cipherable "enterprise-zone" disquisition by ex (and super-white) athlete Jack Kemp? "Republican wise man" they actually call him, who was once all star quarterback for the Buffalo Bills. Actually, old Jack's heart is in the right place, but please, mercy, just a *partial* Jack lecture: We try, but we can't handle the whole betwisted, contorted, shpiel.

Back to Europe: So thus, four years in "Uni" in Europe with no tuition, or tantamount to none. And very few "elite" tuition colleges. A savings of approximately anywhere from forty thousand dollars in a state university here in America to one hundred thirty thousand in a private college, as in the Ivy League. Then, graduate school-- advanced degrees? Free in Europe, to those who qualify, by test and interview. And, my dear American-egalitarian-deludeds, if you haven't put two-and-two together, let me clue you: This all means that *European* universities are less class-based than American ones. Far less. This means *Europe*, not America, has greater social mobility; and America, not Europe, remains upper echelon, an inflexible pyramid, mucked in-- to Americanishly coin a phrase-- societal stagmire. University demonstrations in Germany have come equipped with placards declaring, "ELITE FOR EVERYBODY"-- and yes, a professor in France or Germany is seldom subjected to those often puerile, and less helpful than helpful, "helpful" student evaluations (German college joke: What can a prof do without suffering serious scholastic consequences? Answer: Burn himself alive during his lecture [Germans aren't too humorous]); and yes, our major American universities are often better endowed and fitted-out, though not necessarily better taught. But oh the price of our pricing: Our poor stay poor stay poor.

TABLE SIXTEEN

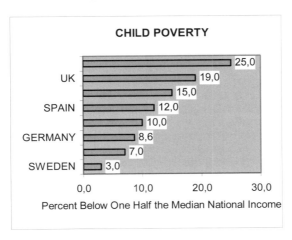

Source: Luxembourg Income Studies

Additionally, our lower middle class stays lower middle. They don't get to benefit from what our best universities have that are The Best. Really our lower-middle class does honker for the most part at lower-middle-- in the community college system-- and there it remains ahonkering, unprepared for and untempted towards serious thought-- political or philosophical or (need I even venture?) "poetic". But prepared they are, and ready they be, chomping-at-the-bit, to "graduate" and *Make it in Bid'ness*: More Republicans in-the-making* -- a self-fulfilling prophecy. No, self-fulfilling Program. The Great American Treadmill.

And ah yes: Even those European university students who do decide to major in Business or economics, who care most about material success, these European young people still tend to know, unlike their American Business major brethren, some decent smatterings of literature and philosophy. Some training in real thought does, intentionally, come their way. As I commented earlier about European CEOs, Euro-students don't become narrow technocrats, upgraded Amway salesmen and bookkeepers. By the way, I have scarcely encountered a German woman, or a French one, who has not "taken" piano as a *fräulein* or as a *mademoiselle*. But, true, few men; albeit not so far down in the music-appreciation cellar as the micro-scopic number of American men-- with *any* instrument (save guitar-- and dunderhead guitar-miming [guitar invisible]-- and old '78 platter-spinning for beat). There has in fact been a recent influx of American MBA students-- and other American students-- *to* European universities; and this constitutes quite a turnaround, as European exchange pupils' interest in America has fallen by almost fifty percent. The 180 degree change is not just bargain-basement economizing either, but the worldly-culture factor, pretty consider-able now: a broader Euro-education might well lend a leg-up when these MBAs-- and others-- head off to work today all globalized-ready for the once-hinterlands. Yes, sure, utilitarianism is utilitarianism, the pragmatic may lead and rule here, not kulcha-love; but more culture-awareness might have *some* awakening effect ("Ohmigod, you mean there's MORE!?"), which might even, conceivably, enhance the levels of Business. Perhaps in the near future you won't so readily overhear a president smirk-bragging with a John Belushi twinkle (or, far worse, a George W. Bush snicker of shallowness) that he has never read a book-- even if he has maybe perused one or two; and then cutting-in some impoverished writer-hack (so contemptibly naive as to have majored in *English*) to ghost-pen three hundred pages for him of his most

---

* And quite contra, for important example, stem cell research. Until, that is, someone in their own family develops Parkinson's or Alzheimer's; or diabetes. Then the "Republican" becomes a tad less Republican.

significant-meaningful life-events where-he-learned-a-lot. I mean, isn't that like climbing through your professor's office window in your college days the night before an exam and ripping-off the test questions?-- and then selling them!... And then becoming student body president, and delivering the valedictorian address on ethics and honesty (*Pro* ethics and honesty, not cockily con).

Here an event from 1990 springs to mind. It should have embarrassed Americans, but it merely amused us. Well, those few of us who read the international pages: The then Prime Minister of France, François Mitterand-- a pompous prig in many respects-- alluded to a scene in a Saul Bellow novel to then President George H. W. Bush, (Bush Père) *who had not only not read Bellow, but had never heard tell of the bum!*-- our only living Nobel laureate fiction writer at that time. Well, why should Bush have heard tell of Bellow?-- that highfalutin non-fact stuff ain't Real Stuff like the CIA and Oil, so it's not worth the made-up pages it's printed on (Then, for under- scoring you can watch a dual press conference teamed by bumbling Bush *fils* and articulate Tony Blair. Nuff said?). And, did you know that France leads the world in Nobel Prizes for literature?-- not four-times populous America (In truth, few French authors are as purposively inscrutable as Derrida). And did you know that American publishers bring out yearly less serious books, *in absolute numbers*, than does England or France, each as I say with less than one-quarter of our population? Or Germany, with a bit more than one- quarter. No surprise then that Europe possesses far more bookstores per capita than we do-- these treasure houses; just walk a street there, a random street, and you'll see that. Wait, wait-- I'm wrong though. An exception has to be made here, for those ubiquitous, and smarmy, and annoyingly dis- ingenuous, but oh so entrepreneurial, How-to's FOR DUMMIES-- the literary equivalents of rap and hip-hop. Big agent business there-- and they do have a few of those cribbies in Europe. A few. But, you know, no agent is even *required* in Europe, unless the book is a potential mega-blockbuster: fewer middlemen then swivel-chairing between author and reader to deter- mine whether or not a work has publishable worth, meaning money worth-- not intrinsic worth. Sales potential is considered in Europe, of course; but it is not towering over, crowning the graph as in America. Now, you go walk yourself into the English language aisles of a German or a French bookstore, and you will discover perhaps two to four hundred titles-- and that's minimum; whereas you stroll the German or French *aisle* (singular) of an American bookstore-- even a good bookstore-- and, well, *you will uncover no such aisle!* A shelf, perhaps. Perhaps-- for French and German together. Ten to twenty books, if you're lucky. Probably theme-mixed. Some merely texts for language learners. Not exactly your well-roundedness.

L'EXCEPTION FRANÇAISE

A major chink, however, in the French university story; an irony-- good and bad-- that I am compelled to present. It revolves like a curious carousel around specialization, verses generalization. The top 65,000 students in that nation that prides itself on the wide-encompassing knowledge held by its students attend *Les Grandes Ecoles*, where they are trained-- and trained specifically-- in one of the three areas that pretty much take care of running the nation. There is, first and foremost, The National Administration University, ENA (*L'Ecole National d'Administration*); then *L'Ecole Normal Superieure* (for general cultural knowledge); or the topnotch school of engineering, *L'Ecole Polytechnique*. Fifty percent of the students at these *Grandes Ecoles* are the children, not of any elite, but of plain ordinary citizens-- an admirable arrangement, and far less elitist than America's Ivy League snob aristocracy of student legacies waving their birthright credentials in lieu of their unimpressive grade credentials.

This organizing of intensive learning, this French zeroing-in on what should be zeroed-in-on is impressive. But one does wonder about the diminishing marginal returns to such a setup, where specialization is inevitably the outcome-- and in a profoundly generalist-admiring and appreciating culture. This especially among the "elite" who will be guided in their specific areas towards conducting all the significant affairs of La France. Centralizing education, as the French do with their bureaucracy, even egalitarian centralization, can cause obvious problems: not least a monolithic worldview; a myopeia on the (sometimes annoying) order of "l'exception Française".

BRAIN FACTORIES

Percentage of all Graduates
in Science and Technology

Europe:-----------------------------------26%
Japan:----------------------------21%
US:---------------------17%

Source: European Commission

Anyway, my theme, my theme: Over such backbreaking economic school costs in our America, *that Europeans do not have to endure,* one might justifiably in this nation suffer a nervous breakdown. About 26 percent of Americans have been judged to have mental illness, compared with only 4 percent in Shanghai; and about 18 percent of Americans seem to be afflicted with anxiety disorders, versus 12 percent of the French.

TABLE SEVENTEEN

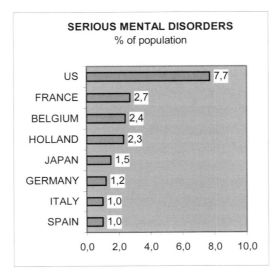

Source: Journal of the American Medical Association;
World Health Organization

No doubt over our school-dragooned shell-outs many Americans experience more of even what might be called "normal garden variety anxiety": I have seen a clever TV commercial where a father deposits a squirrel into his son's room to drive the boy bonkers as he crams the night before his SATs. "If he goes Ivy," the father sweats it to his wife, "we're toast." The commercial is for home refinancing, an ultimately negative practice (nothing's free) you never hear about in Europe. As American "toast", Ivy League or no, you can't earn enough; you can't save enough to pay the flimsy-jiggle-toilet-reflux re-fixing plumber (Vide my Introduction). So? Lord knows what you do, you ordinary person, you. But I'll tell you what the *nation* does, the nation-as-a-whole: Borrow, baby, borrow: Great rich America's development has been financed in the last decade especially by foreign saving (As I've said, foreigners *save*)—i.e. foreign investment in American firms and Treasury notes: To the extent that now the financial stability of our country depends considerably on even the central bank of, where?-- *The People's Republic of China:* (See Table 7 again, and button your lips, folks: this is a big hush-hush). Correct me if I'm wrong, but mightn't indebtedness to *China* kaibash our clout a trifle when it comes to a Taiwan support initiative or leaning with our weight on trade? "Okay, you Chinese, you stop bowldlerizing our Nellie and our P-Diddy and our *Titanic*, or . . . Well, okay, uh, pretty puh-leeese. . . ?"

Heart problems?

And say you do succumb to something rather cardiac?

U.S. A LAGGARD ON BENEFITS, STUDY FINDS[*]

The United States lags the rest of the world in providing paid time off for illness, maternity leave, vacations and other benefits that are critical for working families, a study has found.

The project on Global Working Families at Harvard University this week released the first comprehensive report comparing government policies that guarantee employee benefits in the United States with those in more than 100 other countries.

[*] *The Boston Globe*

It found that the lack of federal support for workers who care for children and elderly family members means that the United States falls short of government protections available in other industrialized countries like Germany as well as in less developed countries.

The U.S. government, for example, does not require employers to provide paid time off for illness. As a result, only half of American workers receive sick time. In contrast, *139 other countries require paid time off for short-or long-term illnesses* (italics mine), according to the Harvard Study.

"While we think of the U.S. as a leader in many fields, we are enormously behind on every single kind of measure protecting working families," said Jody Heymann, the project's director and an associate professor in the Harvard School of Public Health and the Harvard Medical School.

U.S. policy failures affect not only those in the lowest-wage jobs but also middle-class families, she said.

"The majority of the middle class can't count on paid parental leave when they need it, paid sick leave when they need it, having the ability to address the sick needs of children, elderly parents or other family members," Heymann said.

Neil Trautwein, assistant vice president for human resource policy at the National Association of Manufacturers, responded that having the government require companies to provide benefits would reduce employers' ability to hire, create costly bureaucratic red tape and foster abuse of the benefits.

So how DO those 139 other countries do it?

Anyway, let's say you do succumb to some event rather cardiac?

In Old Europe you go to a doctor, no debating it, no cheerfully-bravely convincing yourself you are a weakling unbrave hypochondriac and so shouldn't go to any wealthy-man DOCTOR. In Europe you *go*, as you are insured: The right to good health care is regarded as a basic right of any civilized society; it is-- how shall I put this?-- sacrosanct (Except here: cost-benefit-analysis). Good chance in Europe you even (Get this) *walk* to the doctor (or bike), as that's healthier; and in any case it's just *what-you-do*. I'll get to European insurance in a moment.

Everyone knows of course the incredible story at home base in "opulent" America, so bizarrely worried as it is about Defending itself. *"Americans get substandard care for their ailments about half the time* (my italics), even if they live near a major teaching hospital... The inadequate treatment," says Dr. Elizabeth McGlynn, a Rand Corporation researcher (publishing in *Health Affairs*), "leads to thousands of needless deaths each year." Most of us are now imprisoned in HMOs (Humungus Murder Operations), if we are fortunate enough to carry any health insurance at all-- or be carried by it-- as a full whopping thirty percent of us do not have *any* such insurance. Thirty percent! That's ninety million people, sports-fans, approximately as many as vote in this democratic land of less-voters than any other supposedly-serious voting lands-- to which lands we are prepos-terously presumptuous enough to send *our* "experienced"-voting-observers like the well-intentioned Jimmy Carter. You know, my fellow citizens, even Taiwan now has national health insurance. Now, a goodly proportion of that deprived American-uninsured "cohort" clutters emergency rooms, right? You've seen them when you insureds have gone to Emergency with an Actual emergency, and you've been darned put-out, haven't you?-- angry, since you've had to wait doubly long, triply long, quadruply *long*, with your Real Official Emergency, and now you are waiting eternally *along with THEM*, rubbing elbows yet, with these, well, annoying unfortunates, with their Routine uninsured runny noses, right?-- all amidst the screams and shouts (and radios) of these, our "uncivilized"-uneducated-uninsured; though many are civilized *and* educated. (Teaser, but true: In 1995 Fidel Castro was in Harlem, in his ever-ready seemingly painted-on fatigues; and seeing what Harlem desolation he saw Fidel offered to send medical help *from Cuba* to Harlem. New York's mayor Giuliani of course rejected the humanitarian help of el Presidente). . . And oh those solemn-ominous smoldering, threat-ening, waiting room-cluttered SILENCES. As if it's a crucial series for the Stanley Cup, the hockey championships, vicious fights have tended to break out in these ERs, even among the fight-hindered, frustrated, broken-limbed and the (cardiac or pulmonary) short-of-breath.

Smash-cut to contrast: Smooth, calm, uncluttered, efficient, polite, European Emergency rooms are what they should be-- soothing. I know: I was ambulanced to one: Crone's attack.

So: Since our uninsured cannot pay the American piper, the American cost is passed on to those of us who can pay, meaning insurance companies' rates balloon (even those of crumbum HMOs), meaning then the least profitable customers get the axe, meaning Us-- meaning *more* uninsureds crowding-up emergency rooms, *more* fights among the unfightable sick, more card-scrutinizing as if these are hanging chads, and rejection as if these are hanging chads, more beleaguered physician curtness, culminating in *more* enrollment in perfunctory-- and peremptory (and curt)-- HMOs, which one might say are our American parallels to our newly launched American free-enterprise prisons-for-profit-- which aren't "free-enterprise": they're state subsidized. Again, Circular Cumulative Causation-- that on-the-money term coined by the Swedish sociologist Gunnar Myrdal to describe how the rich countries evolve richer and the poor poorer. The Spread and Backwash Effect, Myrdal also called it. So, backwashed, and let's say horn-swaggled, you are obviously, seriously, constrained; then you are enervated; then you may ultimately become palpitation-ridden, having been beset-upon by the skyrocketing Mach II costs of The One Element meant to make your life easier and more relaxed and unbeset, and unpalpitated: Insurance. I mean, *that's what the word MEANS*: Surety. Reassurance. Safety. A Civilized Invention. You have chest pains and pressure. Angst, probably, you tell yourself (and being American-diseducated you likely pronounce angst like "gangs"-- but leave me be not a total snob); you convince yourself that your discomfort is anxiety, surely-- you'll just stay at home. Or, hey, it's simple indigestion, right?-- no doctor needed-- or more adworthingly modern, it's "acid-reflux", though not that that stuff's the greatest either, the esophagus not being any penny-ante piece-of-cake pushover. . . But, you know, what if it is *not* psychosomatic?! If you are one of the dwindling brotherhood of American fortunates not constrained by an HMO, you call your general physician, perhaps an internist. Not unusually, you may have to wait a few days for an appointment-- unless you pester and harangue-- in which case, of course, you may never get in to see even the janitor. If you are not on an HMO, perhaps you call straightaway a heart specialist, a cardiologist. Again, however, you might have to wait. Maybe two weeks. Maybe not. Maybe three. If you are on an HMO, your general physician at the Humungus Murder Operations will have to *refer* you to a cardiologist. Then, you commence your week (to three weeks) wait. Then the cardiologist proceeds.

Note: Percent of American doctors who admit to not telling a patient about a treatment because the patient's insurance did not cover the treatment: thirty-one percent (Percent in Europe: Zero. My guesstimate-- based both on European insurance and European bluntness). Some revelation here. Obscene revelation. We truly are a Third World Nation. But hey, let's Defend America from all those Unfree Envious. . . Or at least let's educate the depraved terrorists that we are as deprived as they. . . Or, perhaps they know that.

CHART TEN

LIFE EXPECTANCY (2000)	
1. Japan	81.3
2. Sweden	79.9
3. France	78.7
4. Italy	78.6
5. Austria	78.3
6. Germany	78.0
7. USA	76.9
8. Poland	73.6
9. China	70.6

2004: U.S. -- 19th. Just above Costa Rica.

Source: UNICEF

Did you know that even in the Middle East most citizens are covered by health insurance? Didn't know that one, did you? The dictator-president-shiek provides for medical care-- Khaddafi, Assad, Mubarak, even Saddam did. So, maybe we can hire terrorists to smart-bomb only our HMOs? Oops, forgot the collateral damage. Okay, scratch that. Chalk it up to frustration (Please, Patriot Acters, don't come now and confiscate me).

In Europe, sure now you know this: Firstoff, you are possessed of health insurance. Oh those lucky "Old" Europeans with their antiquated ways. Everyone is covered. Germany had the first overall blanket shelter--

Bismarck in 1881-- to fend off threatening pesky uprisings. Now *there* was some keenly intelligent defense spending: insurance for others as insurance for yourself. First, there is basic government insurance (In France, the *Caisse National d'Assurances Maladies;* in Germany, the GKV: *Gesetzliche Kran- kenversicherung*); then there are a range of statutory but semi-autonomous insurance agencies; and, counter to American mythology about "socialist" Europe and endless red tape, there is also private health insurance-- not that the government provisions are particularly paperbound.[*] Yes there is also European private insurance, and it will allow you to see certain specialists not available by state coverage (and receive hospital care in a special (well, elite) wing-- often with room balconies); but for the most part, except in special cases, every patient in Europe can see any physician (Germany now has instituted a ten euro co-pay for non-private; but this small co-pay is not required every time one goes to his doctor [our American way]-- it is only for the first visit each quarter). You call a physician in Germany, general or specialist, and it is extraordinarily rare that you will not be seen on-that-day. *On-that-day!* Mark them magic words, Yankee. I have remarked to my Ger- man wife how medical appointments in Germany are like the old Henny Youngman joke: The patient calls: "When may I see the doctor?" The doctor's assistant seductively responds, "So, when can you get here?" Take note: this efficiency recognizes that we are dealing with *illness* here-- not aluminum siding salesmen-- conceivably a life-and-death deal: Availability of the doctor does not mean that he is incompetent and sparsely patiented, and thus on his knees for business. It's not like a first date where they're trying to show they're just *toooo* popular. It's *Medicine*, man! No need to play hard-to-get.

Now, if it's your heart-- you've got those boom-boom palpitations, or fibrillations. *Something*, and chest pressure like you just swallowed the von Hindenberg-- rest assured: even your general physician or internist in Germany is equipped with the requisite diagnostics: echocardiogram; stress EKG-- by stationary bicycle or treadmill. Equipped, and he knows how to

---

[*] Those smarmy Republican TV ads in '93 dissing Hillary Clinton's federal health insurance program-- Sam and Suzy, or whoever-- these were misleading political axe jobs; and I hope that those actors hired to play Sam and Susie (or whoever) have lost their coveted Actors Guild Health Insurance by now, and are suffering on HMOs.

use these, does this plain generalist guy. Specialization is to a great extent now an American disease. Or rather, *over*specialization: Few American docs know anything anymore beyond their increasingly diminishing microscopic bailiwicks, and they seem to hold it unprofessional and cloddish to venture an opinion beyond that organ or limb or artery or epiderm; and might this misdirected smugness (or protectiveness?-- malpractice insurance has cata-pulted in America too), might this jealous safeguarding descend in the end to one obscure capillary? But to quote Adam Smith, the divinity of American conservatives, of laissez-faire individualism, "The division of labor makes men dumb." And while I'm at it let me adapt in attitude the words of an Adam Smith contemporary, the irascible tell-it-like-it-is Samuel Johnson: *Sir!*-- Specialization is the last refuge of a *scoundril*. Of course tetchy sage Johnson was really inveighing against that other dubious scoundrilism, "patriotism"; but the motifs touch perfectly, especially if we convert the epithet "scoundril" to "incompetent", or "coward". Certainly, unarguably, it is an achievement to take pride in that early America led in the creation of specialized equipment like Eli Whitney's cotton gin, and the streetcar, and the flush toilet, and the traffic light, and the radiator, etc.-- all easily operated advances, all improvements just waiting to happen; but these innovations came about precisely *because* our people were so *un*specialized: You cannot even invent a specialized widgit unless you are already a seasoned, savvy generalist of widgit-possibilities, of the stages leading up to the widgit-in-question, and upwards from it. A Big Picture Person. Which generalists Early Americans happened to be-- Jacks of all widgit trades. By pioneer necessity.

Okay: Let's forget the medical tests in America, reassuring as these might be. Right-off-the-bat forget, that is. It's as if hereabouts you've got to *earn* those big techno-babies: *Show us you are sick!* Impress us. Sick or no-sick, you have got to wend your way through a kind of medical-frat paddle-whack initiation for your diagnostic reward. Once you have achieved your craved appointment with your internist or, to continue our example, cardiologist, if he/she decides to test you-- well, *he does not have the equip-ment*. It costs far too much in America. Plus, his office rent is a killer-bankrupter (as his landlord has to pay for *his* health insurance and *his* kids' college), so your American physician's office space is too small for all that diagnostic clutter-waste rigamarole. Like his landlord, *he* has to send *his* kids too to private school and private college, doesn't he?-- so *they* will be able to afford health insurance and drugs-- and not become disc-spinning DJs talking fake Rasta-Jamaican. So here you witness the social fear-consequence of our failed social structure, which is a consequence of our failed economic structure, another consequence of our individualist laissez-faire failure at Community. So your poor American doctor, bereft of the requisite technology, stuck in his shrimpy office-- and stifling his stowed-up hostility that he is so damn stuck this way-- well he *can* at least have his assistant take a stationary EKG in default. This he does have. But hell, the stationary EKG doctors even have in their offices in Bangladesh!-- and the stationary EKG is tantamount to nothing diagnostically (Though not-nothing for your pocketbook-- or your insurance company's spreadsheets, if you have said company); the stationary EKG means little, as it may indicate your heart and arteries are fine, *if you always lay down like a couch potato and never labor a muscle to move to munch a pretzel.* So now if your physician does decide to promote you to further advanced testing, here we go again: referral to the hospital techno-wing (where, with the super tubes and megaglobes and laser lenses and batteries of buttonry and lighting you realize you are a poor unfortunate baboon who knows *nothing* and deserves, apparently, less), all distressing moreso with those whitecoaters superfast-purpose-striding, so otherwise unwonted in America (the old-cold-grim-perfunctory) so un-Americanly outside *Chicago Hope* or *General Hospital,* where folks are melodramatically dropping dead every urgent episode (ratings); that spare and pallid tile; the other patients (unshaven) being wheeled with glucose swathes plugged into their forearms, tubes up the noses; the disheartening dress-cubbyhole curtains; the *fleur-de-lis* splotch design sick-dude gown-of-cheer-despair you've got to don, with your rectum hanging out in back, and you yourself unable to *tie* it, bunky-- and you pathetically calling, "Uh, Nurse, uh, could you please come in here a moment?"-- so even if you are healthy, now you are feeling pretty miserably sick and humiliated, at conceivably death's indifferent door, just at a time when you least need dark shadows cast-- even though you may well be perfectly well.

Whew. Is it ironic, or really quite logical that American health care costs as a consequence of such out-of-office test situations has gone, not down, but *up*? $4887 per person spent in our country; $2000 per person being the world average; 12.1 percent of our GDP; 8.1 percent in Germany. This is American Efficiency? And, with less basic care, doctor's office care, people will get even sicker here (My internist in Bad Herrenalb actually makes house-visits). . . Or now, wait: You lucky beseecher, your blood pressure is measured at a shameglorious 220 over 140, and you are referred straightaway to the cardiologist. No introductory hospital diagnostic invasions for you. Congratulations. But no, wait; actually you're not so lucky: Cardiologist Backlog-- one week, to two. To three. Conceivably four (Sounds like a "*Monopoly*" board game, no?). Unless, *Wait-- genius light bulb!* you actually *engage in a heart attack.* Or, understandably, and you've got my sympathy here, *fake a damn heart attack.* In which case 911's your ticket. Again the agony of Emergency in an American hospital with those faultless underclassers relegated solely to same Emergency for the sniffles-- or for gunshots. The good old psychotic screaming. Or faked psychotic, for some dispatch-- or for desired ejection back to street level and its "normalcy". Or the eery psychotic silences: Those nutcases; and does Emergency *hire* these crazies for effect?-- as a clever (diabolical) treatment firewall? Guys like Kramer on *Seinfeld.* Then, ohLord, the thirteen-year-old jolly peppermint-stripling "aids"-- our cheerleaders for Ole Miss. Man, it's worse than trying to win the attention of your waiter in a newly touted Thai-French-Cubana restaurant.

And, is it me, folks?-- or have you noticed that of late physicians' offices in America have become a tad the scruffiationalish warrens? The fuzzballed carpets, the iffy floors, the scratched-up cabinets; alien hair strands, pugboogers on the exam tables of indeterminate origin best left unspeculated upon; and, I'm afraid to say, again, the "help". And, I'm afraid to say, politically incorrect as it may (of necessity) be, the linguistically-challenged "help" (What in heaven's name are they *saying* to you!?). Not the most assuring quality to confront when you're seriously help*less*... So helpless, perhaps, at long last, you *are* sent straight-off to a hospital. In Germany, the average stay is seventeen days. In the U.S., eight. You may be discharged while you are still internally, uh, *bleeding*? If you discern a certain klunkiness within, don't fret; it's only that you may be harboring in your peritonital cavity-- they are after all so harried and hurried here-- a scalpel or retractor (100,000 cases of such in America per year-- and that's *reported* cases: Post-op schrapnel. In Germany, I've seen a proud report of 1,000 [An over-proud report of a perhaps over-proud-trying nation? Possibly].). So, does our briefer-dispatch-hospitalization indicate that Americans get well quicker? Now, what do you think, Leroy? Alright, perhaps our reassurance might come from knowing-- or rather the more blissful not-knowing-- that American medical students are now being subjected to old soap opera videos like those of *ER*, to study from George Clooney and his actor colleagues how to *act* more like upstanding, confidence-projecting, care-giving doctors-- the joke now having been reversed from when that actor on a TV commercial for aspirin (or whatever) physicianlyesquely admitted, "I am not a doctor, but I play one on TV." So now it's, "I am not an actor, but I am a doctor who plays an actor who plays a doctor on TV." (But George Clooney, et al, have played unconscionable criminals too).

Well, here again-again: In Germany one *does* feel relaxed in the doctor's office (Unless, that is, you are a Mister who adamantly objects to being addressed as a "Herr". In which case they will of course call you Mister). As each patient enters the waiting room he or she politely greets the other waiting patients-- "Guten tag"-- and the chorus of "Guten tags" responds. Nice humane counterpoint in illness. A smidgeon robotic, but Nice-- especially when you're under the weather, as it conveys that minor chord of we're-all-in-this-fragile-woe-together. The Blues, kind of like. White Deutsch Blues. Then: The calling of your turn really *is* your turn-- you are not tricked into the transitional waiting-examining room, a fake stage two. You actually see the physician. And, lo and behold, he/she is less perfunctory, plain kinder. You are not hurried, shuffled, cut-off in mid-complaint, as by the too-often wall-eyed American doctor, as the German doctor is not pressed for time by a harrying Humungus Murder Organization (Germany has now one of the world's highest doctor-population ratios-- 3.2 per 1,000; compared with 2.2 in the States); you are not hassled over insurance matters, even in bureaucratic once-paperwork-pious Germany! And, needless to say, as it is Germany, you could probably eat off the doctor's floor. Well, hyperbole, sure, but you catch my drift. Is it hypo-chondria that induces Germans to visit a physician on average 11.5 times per year, whereas the American goes 5.3? Confidence, perhaps? In preparation for this book, I called various German medical specialists' offices, and American ones. I talked to people, as everyone is at one time or another, a patient. I have as well my own experiences, including the tossup of being at once impressed, and then put off, and then amused, and then annoyed, and then, well, *allured* by the uniformization of German physicians and nurses and technical assistants, the ubiquitous crisp whites, even down to the clean pure reassuring (or comical) socks and infernally-heavenly (white) Birkenstocks. It's like you died, but ever so sweetly expired-- "passed"-- and floated on up to the Nordic Pearly Gates where they all glide on the most immaculate of cloud-sandals. What can I say on that score?[*] For good or ill. What follows are the results, abbreviated, of this my personal unscientific research:

Neurology: It is I suppose irrelevant to my argument here, but I must say that it is both daunting and invigorating, and somewhat diminishing of any symptoms to be confronted by a six foot tall blond neurologist named Heidi-- in starched-crisp white getup and towering *comme il faut* in her white "Birks". But, complaining of (fake) headaches and (concocted) dizziness, there I was: No fantasy, no back room video. Pinch me. Heidi did not do any pinching; but, smiling, she did perform the usual manual proofs, and those needlepoint poke ones-- fingers, toes, arms, legs, eyes-- whatnot-- to determine any neurological deficits. And then, smiling, she led me to another room, where, smiling, she ran the echogram on the corotid and other cervical arteries. Then to *another* room-- I mean, she had serious *space*-- where an assistant, smiling, (and white Birkenstocked) conducted an electroencephalogram. Now I am aware that Germans are driven by an inordinate fondness for machinery, for electronic systems, and for certainty. But in America, as I know from personal experience, these diagnostic procedures are not even *available* in most neurologists' offices, if in any; they would be farmed out to a hospital: The Old Waiting Game. The Impersonality Routine. Your fellow waiting nuts and worrywarts. It is obviously far more reassuring, and relaxing, to have sophisticated tests performed by your own doctor-- in his/her offices. Smilingly. Also, Doctor Heidi ululated her best "Goot" after I passed each test. And that too felt awful nice.

Orthopoedics: After an auto accident in Heidelberg (unfaked) I suffered considerable neck pain. I had been rear-ended, and violently, not by a Michael Schumacher-mockup German, but by an American serviceman in

---

[*] A semiotics being (or buff) could have a field day here: German doctors are sarcastically (but reverentially) known in Germany as "gods in white", while American doctors, in their sportscoats and suits-- or just plain buttondown shirts of Oxford broadcloth-- ought be known as those whose position *they* respect, and perhaps try to emulate: Businessmen in suits. Or CEOs.

the only sixties' era Mustang I have ever lain eyes on in Germany. He was stationed at our Army base there and had been obliviously blabbing on his cellular, an activity illegal in Germany as you drive, whether it's oblivious blab or crucial blab (By the way, they call a cellular a "handy", believing this to be a chic Anglo usage). In America, whiplash is of course a serendipitous windfall; most physicians and attorneys have to stifle their sniggers to take whiplash seriously (Some lick their chops: the rent, the kids' prep school and university). In Germany, however, there are no great auto accident lotteries: you pick up a pittance, so unless there is severe pain most victims do not rush off to the doctor to build up their "pain and suffering" cornucopoeia. Or to the local scheister lawyer (*Scheiße*, by the way, means shit.). Thus a German orthopod, when visited, *takes it seriously.* The physician I saw was-- and this is a combination not unusual in Germany and France, and therefore not derogated as quackery-- a mélange of orthopod, chiropractor, podiatrist, homeopath and herbal whatnotistry. He also performed acupuncture, acu-pressure, and laser treatments-- smilingly (He was indeed a little elfin fellow-- your basic Rumplestiltskin, or Cantinflas as Peter Lorre). Anyway, he used the Alternative methods when the usual, routine western anti-inflam-matories, NSAIDS, did not work. Or were working harshly on my stomach. Why trade whiplash for an ulcer? Especially if you really HAVE whiplash (And really have an ulcer). As I am fortunate enough to be covered on my wife's German health insurance, I was not worried about prescription drug costs; although in Germany, as in all of Europe, pharmaceuticals are not nearly so exorbitant as in America (and Germany has the highest drug prices in Europe). They ring out at approximately one-half to one-third the price. Sometimes even down to one-fifth. Thus no sticker shock at the drug counter; no dangerous "economizing" cut-backs on your own meds-taking. So, one-stop-shop at the orthopod. American specialization out the window. I myself am not a particularly suggestible fellow (except when I suggest myself suggestible), and in the bargain I am suspicious, dubious, cynical-- and, conceivably, sporadically, negative-- so the non-Western treatments did not work on me: apparently they require some degree of acceptance-- and cockeyed hope? But I was impressed by the orthopod's knowledge, con-ventional science and other, his easy, genial, confidant, *gestalt*; his presence as a clear-eyed man who would attempt to surround a problem, rub his chin and attack it from all vantage points. And I was impressed by the time he took. We humans are ridiculously complicated, our nuances are still unfathomable to us-- mind and body, body and mind and body-mind and body-body and mind-body-mind, you name it, we've got it (or we know where to get it, haha). Western medicine-- or should I say *American* medicine?-- does acknowledge these complications, even respects them; but we do not thoroughly *treat* them. Our functional, pragmatic history has led us to be, despite ourselves, rational technologists: Deweys and Pierces galore. Kneejerk, we proclaim our parameters, our *ceteribi paribi*, and we specialize within those yardsticks, in order to feel "scientific". It's sort of like feeling you *have* to wear a *yarmulcha* at a Bar Mitzvah-- or you will go blind; but you might settle, if pressed by the Rabbi, for some colorful contemporary talisman-beanie like a bad black (or Islamic-- well, Nation of Islamic) dude would wear. Yes, we are very nuanced creatures-- unfathomable.

Footnote: The orthopod, in his role as podiatrist, did prescribe for me foot orthotics ("You have just about everything wrong with your feet," he said, "a man could possibly have." What my feet had to do with my "whiplash" is a conundrum, but it does show the widebody *weltanschauung* essayed by continental doctoring). Now I've had custom insert arches made in America: you sit, you raise your foot and they glob on plaster for a mold. These have never worked for me, they have indeed made my neck and back worse. But this orthopod fellow had me stand upright in a kind of kiddie sandbox, so my feet pressed down their imprint as the arches would naturally when I'd be upright, standing or walking. I mean, who needs orthotics that are terrific for when you *sit*? These Euro-orthotics created from the sandbox impression worked. How come no American podiatrists do this? Or orthopods. None I've visited anyway.

I guess because you stand in *a kiddie sandbox*-- and that ain't "scientific".

Urology: When we poor sorry males achieve a certain age, we are obliged to get once-a-year, along with the general blood workup, the PSA test. My count was high. Most likely this is nothing. Our prostates expand as we age, so they produce more prostate specific antigen, which registers in the blood. But it can indicate cancer. Or a constriction of the urethra. The German urologist gloved himself, made the usual urologist jokes, and did the usual probe. Fine. Same as in America: that rectal blastoff as if you're being rocket-launched to the moon (although my American urologist is funnier). Whoopdedo, worst over, I figured I was done. No: He led me to another room (lots of German office space again) and did an echogram-- prostate-bladder-kidney. I'd never had one of these done in America. Probably because the urologist in America had no echogram equipment. The German urologist sat and watched the screen as it registered its fancy hi-tech isobars and bloop-bleeps, like a submarine sounding for an enemy destroyer. Again, as in America I'd have had to be delivered over to a technician in a hospital diagnostic wing. The week wait for such test. Or two. Or three. The waiting room crazies. So most American urologists do not send you for this reading. But, look, it's There! It Exists! *Science!*-- Charlie. In the German doctor's office, the himself-administered echogram-- he smiling-- was fine. I was fine.

Ear-nose-throat. The ontolaryngologist: With a concocted complaint I went, for my survey. The specialist softly placed a toplike trapezoidal gismo at the entrance to each ear, unintrusively-- no pain. It was either a plastic gismo or a hard rubber gadget; as usual (for Germany) it was pure white as your basic cueball. It also resembled a gyroscope-- a kiddie one from a Five-and-Dime. "Pressures equal," he announced, "in both ears." I was certainly glad my pressures were symmetrical, although I had never known this was a measurable phenomenon, of import or not. And of course I had never before seen such an instrument. Again, as a benighted American patient-denier accustomed to deteriorating American medical practices-- and of course in the dark as to their deterioration-- I felt like your basic aboriginal wandering mist-eyed from Ayers Rock or the Amazon into an only-before rumored Bwana civilization: Lord, what wonders! Then, total-equipped as was every other German physician, he had an assistant perform a hearing test in a soundproof room (Some American ontolaryngologists, I hear, do possess this equipment and can afford an assistant to operate it. Some can; but not *my* ear-nose-throater in Berkeley-- and he is considered The-Best-in-The-East-Bay.). Next, with echo paraphernalia the doctor did an echosinogram. Wrinkled isobars; bleeps; bloops-- all appearing on the slender screen (hi-def) as arid as elephant pachyderm. "Perfect," he said. "No sinusitis." No need to take an X-ray of the sinuses, which he could have done, as he had such equipment-- which my Berkeley ontolaryngoloist also does not seem to have (special visit to special X-ray place. Special wait, ancient *Time* and *Newsweek* dealing with Princess Diana's accident and possible royal involvement). Then, with a narrow-radius flexible laser tube, after spraying a local anaesthetic, the German doctor gazed down into the labyrinth of bronchial and trachial passageways (no feared gag reaction). To the best of my knowledge, none of these implements-- not the top-like pressure gauge, the echosinogram, the laser endoscope-- is present in the cost prohibitive smallish offices of American ear-nose-throat doctors, except I guess for those new-formatted designer medicoes for Beverly Hillsers like Barry Diller and Steven Spielberg and CEOs (especially CEOs of HMOs-- who wouldn't be caught dead using an HMO).

Same story with the opthalmologist (I lied that "my eyes hurt."). Great big multi-roomed offices. Specialized wonder equipment I had never experienced before. Neat sweet shy assistants. Whitenesses and Birkenstocks-schmorgasbord and gliding billow-winsome walks. I, barbaric American heaven-eyed, infatuation-eyed, all wonder.

The dentist, you guessed it: same story. Although I was afflicted this time with an authentic tooth problem. Bicusped. Pain shooting from tooth upwards, to temple. Spacious uncramped room (He had three). Space age chair operated by remote. Muted overhead lighting as in the starship Enterprise, or an operating theatre. Or Houston Ground Control. A slender TV screen swivelled around to face the patient, me (one foot distance), to show the projection of his X-ray ("Roentgen", in *Deutsch*) in full-blown enlargement, high-def. And, by the way, again no precision-expert specialization. You need a root canal?-- I did-- you are not shunted off to a pricey endodontist, as in America: referred to a specialist who is even more pricey than your pricey non-specialist dentist. The German dentist performs the German root canal. He has done many. Look, specialization is of course important-- if it's necessary. Don't get the wrong impression: I'm certainly not trying to badmouth fine-honed expertise. After all, who wants brain surgery from even a good podiatrist or a world-famous proctologist? Or even by an orthopoedist. But specialization just does too often create its own habit, then its own momentum, then its own necessity and rationale, and then that necessity snowballs into a requirement-metaphysic, a creed, a law. And a snobbery-- pricing to match. My unspecialized root canal went well... And, let me say, this German dentist had some serious measuring implements that made me feel again I was from The Amazon or the Galapagos: holding tools, placing tools, shiney mouth maneuverers the likes of which I, well...

The pharmacy ("*Apotheke*" in *Deutsch*, like Shakespeare's apothecary): No wait at the *apotheke*. No line. No, Come back, please in two-three

hours. Or tomorrow. No mistakes, as the pharmacist is not beleaguered tally-
ing out pills-- fingering and shaking and sliding and counting (and phum-
phering) the damn capsules and pellets as if he's in quandried turmoil,
badgered and flurrying over a shuffle of abacus plugs-- as he/she distributes
the little buggers into little tinted plastic bottle-cups, which really have no
why or wherefore. Really, *why the damn bottle-cups in our America*? In
Europe the physician merely writes out in his prescription the drug name in
one of the three or four amounts packaged uniformly by the pharmaceutical
company, and the pharmacist just hands over to you the apropos box. That's
it. Ten seconds, Myron. That's why there's no wait, no line. A swift modern
transaction, at anywhere from two-thirds down to one-sixth the American
price (Canada, one-third to one-quarter? Ask any-lucky-body residing across
our tier from Washington state to Maine). Within the Euro-pharmaceutical
box is a sheet with all the info about your medication (true or not is another
question-- as it is here in the U.S. as well). And, by the way, in the rare
situation where the *apotheke* does not have your pill container in stock in the
prescribed quantity, he will order it and *it will be delivered to your house
later that day.* Even if you're not elderly. And I'm not making this up.

And, as I've said, it's cheap, a bargain: easily less than half what an
American pays (at its most expensive worst). Not that that matters: everyone
has insurance (Our insurance biggies could lobby [lean on] our pharmaceutical biggies... I suspect-- if they so wished).

And I should add: there are *apothekes* on almost every block; *les
pharmacies* the same in France. They are far more frequent than phone-
booths, which must be interesting evidence of something (the medicinal
verses the conversational), aside from the interesting evidence that competition can exist in "social welfare Europe"-- small business rivalries-- while
there sits rock-hard the Oligopolies in America, thoughtlessly accepted
oligopolies too, of one drug counter (invariably now in a huge variety-type
mart [few American dedicated-drugstores]), per three square miles--tops-- in
our land of "laissez-faire".

Medical Shangrila in Europe? Well, to me, the American Aboriginal.[*]

---

[*] Rank of the U.S. health care system among the most efficient in the world: 37.
  Source: World Health Organization (2003)

Modest Proposal: We in the U.S. might dock pharmaceutical firms at a progressive or regressive rate, dependant upon their uncontrolled rate of profiteering-- we do top the rest of the industrialized world on drug prices, as if you didn't know. Any company producing a drug setting back any of us, say, $200 for a one month supply, which sells at a sticker-shockless, say, $50 (56 euros) in Europe, will be forced-- by the FDA?-- to reduce, along with the price-tag of its drug, its chief officers' salaries to, say, $50,000 per year. The major stockholders will surely be scandalized; that is, until consumer-demand kicks in to the healthy level where it should have been resting in the first place. Chief officers' salaries may then ascend to a decent -- yet generous-- $l50,000.

Not the accustomed millions!... The self-justified millions.

The biggest danger here really is ignorance. Our native ignorance of the fact that we are not enjoying The Best, but our believing, somehow, that *We-are-enjoying-The-Best*. We have just become a passive accepting people who yet believes the PR that we are an active never-satisfied people. As I just said, if we do not reside in our northern tier, from Washington state to Michigan to Maine, and so can zip up to Toronto or Vancouver or Quebec-- where those immoral Canadians who believe in Gay Marriage and decriminalized marijuana also believe in decent drug prices-- if we cannot just hop up there to Canada, we simply, obediently, go on and on purchasing unexorbitant medications at exorbitant, gouged-out, prices. And, *although we do know that we are paying more*-- and *because* we know it-- in some mysterious nether region of our denying-deluding American cortexes we come to believe "our" medications, expensive as they are, *must therefore be better*. QED. Our Valiums and Viagras and Zantacs BETTER, than Germany's Valium or Viagra or Zantac; or France's Valium or Viagra or Zantac. Or England's. It's the *same* chemicals folks! (With good education-- and not edjacayshun-- we would know that.). It's even the same companies! It's nowhere near the dodginess of those anonymous "generics" with which we often are allowed to cavalierly dose and console ourselves (after a patent runs out), we not knowing the generic source from our-- well, you know, it could be Bangladesh or Bangalore (Sure, you could investigate generic pill origin through your pharmacist; but you wont. And Google does not present such info. And Google's soon-to-be search-engine competitor, a new branch of Microsoft, will certainly not tell you pill origins-- if it knows). And anyway it's a certainty that your pharmacist doesn't know pill origins himself.

They don't teach Suspicious Cut-Rate Supply 101 in pharmacy school. Your poor pharmacist is just an *employee*: Low salary, for a professional school graduate-- unless he/she slaves twelve hour shifts-- *counting out those damn PILLS*. Your overworked pharmaceutical coolie. And since those other, "benighted" Old World countries believe more in government control than we "individualists" do, our government (read, Republican) argument that we cannot be sure of the *foreign* pill quality because those countries don't have *our* kind of FDA (so we prohibit importation)-- well, that specious, pardon my French, SHIT, is, well, obscene. . . And this is the same, isn't it?-- with toilets, tires, roads, electrical grids, cars, doctors, etc. Nor are we aware that, counter to what might be the decent approach, the Normal international (civilized?) give-and-take, our executive branch has recently attempted to lean on foreign governments (read, European) to *raise* their prescription drug prices, so that, what?-- *We* wont look so godawful bad? This the ultimate Machiavellicized "competition"-- with lead-lined boxing gloves. No, it's *restraint* of competition. Restraint of enterprise. By we "free-enterprisers". It's conservative Individualist " Corporate Welfare.

Sure, I know: The drug companies need the big bucks for Research. Right? Their argument: Out of every one hundred thousand molecules screened in their labs only *one* becomes, advances to, a new drug-- after about twelve years of work. Fine, if true (Our government *gives away* to these firms most government-science discoveries). But that firm-research truism is plastered often in, at minimum, half-page ads (sometimes color; sometimes full-page) in major papers. But the US citizen shouldn't have to foot that research bill-- and its expensive rationalizing PR bills-- if indeed it is a true bill and not your basic bogus bill-of-goods. Our government also gives steep tax breaks for those "research" claims (And who are the auditors certifying those claim-amounts by Eli Lilly and Pfizer, etc?-- Enron's mendacious Arthur Anderson and Co? Or a mendacious "Professional Accounting Firm" colleague-competitor?). Drug firms live in a "fools' paradise". Except-- it isn't *they* who constitute the fools, now, is it?

And paradoxically it is that American heroic Solo-Guy bent, our myth history, that is in part the cause of the American physician's reluctance to incorporate the newest-tech diagnostics into his practice. A *hee*-row, an idolized figure, the American doctor has been trained in the American medical school training hospital to stay up three nights (and days) running *while treating people. He* does not need gadgets and gizmos. He's Davy Crockett and Daniel Boone at The Alamo-- but not as Davy and Dan'l were sitting in their legislatures (see Chapter 4). He can rely on his manly-savvy powers of observation, his educated sleepless eyeballs swimming and eyeballing (not measuring) in the hypnogogic world of half-dream, while he labors diligently-astagger over life and death. You rely on those damn sleek *Euro*-med Gizmos, you lose your stand-up edge-- PILGRIM.

Sometimes this does work out well. And economically. Sometimes it does not. *Oft*-times it does not.

But of course it is also the money. Repeat, m-o-n-e-y. The German doctor is not hardpressed by Humungus Murder Organizations. Not yet, anyway. He is not bevexed by that urgent felt need, as in damaged American society, to pay for private schooling and private universities for his kids. The German (or French) doctor is not beset by another miscreant of overhyped (and poorly understood) "laissez-faire", mega-malpractice insurance, the offspring too often of scheister (read again "laissez-faire") lawyering; though the offspring also of hero-Pilgrim doctoring. . . And HMO harried doctoring.

Well, as I reported, those German doctor offices do tend to be larger, less cramped; and French offices are roomier too. They can accomodate all that, you know, EQUIPMENT. Smaller countries-- Montana size Germany. California size France. Yet more room? Weird.

By the way, Americans tolerate lower rates of life expectancy than do the citizens of France, Germany, Britain and Italy, and of course Scandinavia (see Chart 10). Aside from the aforementioned failings of our insurance and medicine, our pensions have some blame here too. Even if our layaway nest-eggs have not been recently shipwrecked or shriveled in "laissez-faire" corporate misdoings and the stock market bubble, our retirement benefits still pale on average compared to what Europe-in-general sets aside (See Chapter 5 and Appendix 1). That is of course long after we have survived our higher infant mortality: eight babies younger than one-year-old die for every one-thousand births in America. In France, only five; Germany, five; Italy, six; Britain, six. Prenatal care-- and postnatal-- here in the U.S. does not stack up, timewise-allowed in maternity leave, in diagnostics (three paid sonograms-- France, one in America), stay at birth in hospital (French or German-- five days, compared to the American two[*]) and the aftercare is

---

[*] And longer, safer hospital stays are not limited to a "birthright", as they keep patients in hospitals longer in general, post surgery, whether it be for gallstones or

more intensive, after release: "*Liberté, égalité, maternité*", one more French motto. . . My impression also is that Europeans are stronger. Than Americans. Literally. Physically stronger. Muscles, Backbone. Grip. Women as well as men. I have performed no studies in the sinew department, not arm-wrestled with any French or Germans (even with women), but I have noticed, anecdotally, randomly, an uncommon Euro-strength, compared to an average American's, in the hand-shaking, the congenial, ubiquitous embracings where my ribs have been squnched-- by ladies. Impressionistic stuff?-- and/or a consequence of the health system? Genetics? Child-rearing? Less worry? Or is it their obsessive *walking*? And better shoes. And bicycling. And less fear, ie, attitude. Perhaps all these, benign and besetting, are why we, in The-Land-of-the-Free, we Solo *Hee*-rows, are becoming relatively shorter and shorter and shorter and shorter and less appealing (See again Chart 8). And sicker.

I would in fact love to see a study on sleep comparisons between Us and Them: Duration and depth, REM and non-REM, plus sleeping pill consumption-- a pretty fair index of worrisomeness. I have, however, found no such studies.

I should, however, mention that, as with industry, physicians in Europe are prevented from billing more services, or from billing too much, by oversight committees of peers: doctors and Sickness Funds. Same with hospitals and clinics. Must I reiterate?-- Not True Here.

An addendum here about the German *"Bad"* system. An important note: *Bad* towns, a scattered network of country spas, are nonexistent in the states, except for those rare sequestered Camp Davidlike retreats reserved for the rich and powerful. As I've said, my wife and I live half each year in Bad Herrenalb, one of the two hundred or so *Bad* towns sprinkled around Germany-- mostly in the south of mountains and forests-- and also in Austria,

---

cervical discs or hemorrhoids-- as is the case not just in Germany, but in Canada, France, even China-- ie, all over the world. The reason is obviously to guard health, to safeguard against infection and relapse. Again, here, the cause of our failing is not merely American insurance, but the Old Glory individuality hero-myth-- bragging rights: "We'll have you out in two days," yodels the cowboy American surgeon to the cowboy-hopeful American patient-- "even if you've still got our retractors hanging on in your belly, haha-- just kidding."

Switzerland and the Czech Republic (It is only an English language joke having it that there are good and bad *Bad* towns). The first spas were Roman baths implanted by the Caesars in the first century AD, and you can still see the sunken stone pillar and bench remains of some (The largest are in Baden-Baden, Wiesbaden and Rottweil.). *Bad* towns and villages vary in what clinics they offer: ours has a colossal hillside orthopoedic-heart-neuro-logical rehabilitation settlement, and a psychiatric clinic-- which is less a corollary of the American mental hospital (or the German mental hospital, for that matter) than a getaway for the *kurschatten* (spa romancers; plus psycho-and-art-therapy). And let me say here that I have found Europeans to be more romantic than Americans-- even those practical minded *sang-froid* demeanor Europeans who mock American naiveté and pride themselves on their non-Hollywood romanticism. Whether it be that they have more time, less work hours, less Puritanical baggage, or okay, more tradition, Europeans dress and act in a kind of unembarrassed romance-polarity. You can see this "*ganz spontan*" in any cafe, a natural performance by quasi-art-pantomime. To be primitive about it, men posture as "men", straight of body, firm and deep of word; women playback as the assessing, bemused judiciary. Bass clef and treble, little ambiguous alto and tenor in between. An old dance. *The* old dance of the molecules, this throwback with its built-in animal magnetism. This holds true even among "liberated" leftists, socialist or Green. Unisex is played out only by teenagers yet glued to *Amerikanische* MTV: *Kibbitz für die kinder*.

In addition, in our spa town there is the *"Evangelische" Gemeinde* (Lutheran: *Evangelische* does not translate to Evangelical-- of which sects there are few in Europe). This *Evangelische* structure constitutes their com-munity center for all of the state of Baden-Württemberg: a long-winged Black Forest hill edge compound where lectures and performances are offered. There is a meditation retreat (Vipassana)-- again hillside; a town center where exhibitions and more performances are scheduled; a ski slope, complete with lift (one bench, three-seater), and trails for Nordic; a sheer granite cliff, the Falkenstein, used for rock climbing and super viewing; and of course the *Bad* itself, the therapeutic thermal springs. It is housed in a modern glass-spanned roundabout, the mountain waters in a lagoon that wends it way from inside to outside the building. People bathe outdoors in winter, surrounded by snow and kids on sleighs. Within, treatments and massage. Physical therapists locate their offices about the town park, which contains the spa and a miniature golf course. And *fußpflege* people, literally foot carers. And psychotherapists. German health insurance pays for a one month to two stay at these treatment havens (only with a recommendation from one's physician), and upwards of six million Germans take advantage of them each year-- although recently with the European economic downturn (which paralleled America's) they have reduced their payments. Of course one can pay for oneself. Obviously, these *Bad* towns could not have evolved out of a culture that did not prize the healing powers of nature; nor out of a sensibility that was not communitarian at its core. Still, in the most "*schicki-micki*" (German for fancy-schmancy), Baden-Baden, it's not quite so rawbone: there is the neo-classical gambling casino at the plateau of a central hill (sportscoat essential for gambling solemnity), next to a classic amphitheatre, with high-end Champs Elyssées type shops and cafes leading up to it. Doubtless it's reassuring for a citizen to know he has resort to such old-timey oases if need be-- even hokey and rigid as they may seem; even abused by the plain healthy, as they famously are: I know a German woman, a self-confessed slacker and abuser, who somehow wangles a *Bad* prescription from her internist every three years (visits are limited to that period) really to go hunting for Herr Goodbar. Well, with her conventional six week paid vacation leave from work in a bookstore (this is yearly), and/or her up to eighty-four weeks "sickness" benefits (full pay for the first six weeks; then 80 percent pay for up to the next 78 weeks) she can afford The Search. I presume she is not the norm. I know she is not the norm. . . I also know that the German government is cutting back some on all this; they are not forking it over quite so heftily-- even as recession recedes: With the new competition from Asian industry, times have begun their unpitying remorseless change.

One hopes that they will not change so much.

7

BE FAIR

A voice echoes, Be fair. The Voice has been building up, rumbling up, a kettle drum: Come now, the avenging ostinato, there are better features in America than in Europe. There still are. The world has learned from us. *Us*. First-off, there is under the circumstances a peculiar and perplexing survey result. In response to the statement, "I often give more to my job than is demanded of me, it's so important to me that I sacrifice a lot to it"-- guess which workers were most in agreement. Not the assiduous Germans, at 43 percent; not the dig-in stiff upper lip Brits at 48 percent; not the self-possessed (and not-inconceivably mendacious) French, at 52 percent; but *we Americans*, at 66 percent. Two-thirds of American labor is either more loyal to the job at hand than the rest of the world, more responsible, more work-identified-- or more brainwashed into such American Delusion, and/or suspicious of the suited-up interviewer (and such person's possible contact with the boss?-- there being in America few unwounded muscle-unions.). In any case, confusing, doubt-casting results, considering everything I've been tackling for the last six chapters. . . And then there is the fact that despite far higher voting percentages in Europe than in America, this performance does *not* hold for the general EU parliament: voters in each country don't care so much, yet, about the European "Nation", and their turnouts in the thirty-to-forty-five percent range show it (a big factor is that there is barely any political EU publicity or advertising). Not surprisingly, nations remain nations in Europe: it is hardly a united monolith, even by telescoping, magnifying eye. So now, conscience and research forcing me, I will go with what's better here at home.

I'll start off very small. Take our bandaids-- plain American bandaids. You walk into a Schlecker, the German drugstore, which is not to say *apo-*

theke (or pharmacy), and you purchase a box of bandaids. The German psyche can be so controlling, so fixated, so overwhelmingly determined, that in the case of these *pflasters* you get bandages that glom on even along the sides of the center antibacterial coating; so one had better apply that gauze protection with serious, deliberate, not unscientific, caution: if you miss, and a sliver of that super-adhesive has been easily-accidentally pressed onto your wound, gird yourself when it's stripoff time, especially as the stickum on German bandaids is major league world class Superbowl allstar *stickum*: It could brace and tether an Apollo spacecraft on reentry. It would adhere through a battle with the dust and asteroids of the rings of Saturn. It-- oh well.

The milk cartons. Ours pop open easily. Sheerest breeze. Some of our milk cartons these days are even plastic "bottles" with twist-off caps. No problem. Whereas the German milk carton is a bear. It is as securely fastened as a German bandaid; so when you squeeze to pop the cap open, you may not be able to. So you squeeze harder and harder, until you rumple and eventually squash the carton itself, and milk squishes out of various unpredictable fissures that you have inadvertently effected, and through which you are now condemned to awkwardly pour your milk, watching errant dribbles milken-white your fingers, your tablecloth, table, floor, breakfast partners.

Newspapers: The German dailies and weeklies are good and variegated, from the *Time*-like *Der Spiegel* across the spectrum to *Die Frankfurter Allgemeine, Focus*, and, among others, *Die Zeit*. But the French, being centralized in bureaucracy and attitude (and Paris location) may display the same monolithic worldviews, whether they come across in the government-oriented (Right) *Le Figaro* or the leftish *Le Monde*. French stance is French stance. America is much freer of opinion, wider, more a political rainbow.

Let's try highway paving (and repaving). Obsessive Germany is always at this. I mean *always*. I mean endless. Robotsville. Surreal worker ants. Well, when they're not enjoying one of the many non-work, non-robot days off. Germany being at the center of Europe all those double-trailer trucks are crisscrossing the country like crazy-- the English over to Austria, the Polish down to Spain, etc-- so the roads wear down rapidly; you truly would not want any other, non-efficient land but Germany to be straddling mittel-Europe: the appropriate fixer-up nation stands there, literally lubricating the wheels of the EU. End result, a smooth drive, safer even if superspeedy. But!-- you the auto driver are not considered in Germany during repaving. It is usually performed during daytime work hours, which are of course the main *driving* hours-- *because they ARE work hours!*-- of the road repair people as well. In America such toil-- when it is finally mañana-mandated, and with, sadly, cheaper, less durable materials-- it is at least considerately accomplished late at night or in very early morning, when there is sparse traffic. German unions just have that more clout than American ones-- which of course isn't saying a whole lot. The German worker is not going to stand for roller-paving and grunt shovel-smoothing on a highway at 3 AM, in artificial floodlight, when a normal human being should be sweetly under the covers dreaming of Tuscany or Florida. Thus at three in the afternoon, when you are driving from Cologne to Berlin, on a perfectly durable road (to an American-- pothole-inured as he is) you may suddenly find yourself caught up in a one hour *stau* (traffic jam), while the pampered German road worker labors alongside you with diligence and magnificent indifference-- to render that perfectly durable road *even more durable!* Though, to be fair, I must say that German radio has found a neat way to break into your CD playing *The Well-Tempered Klavier* and warn you of the impending, looming (ten kilometer) *stau* (Not that advance warning would matter: few alternate routes). Or, your interrupted CD might be playing one of the popular songs of the day:

Stau, stau, staun auf der autobahn...

Now: Let's say it is Saturday night at 9 PM. You suddenly see one of those clever TV ads, *Got Milk?*-- and you realize that you haven't. Zilch milk. You foray out on your quick mission to Safeway or Grand Union, maybe pick up a Ben and Jerry's in the bargain. Germany?-- forget it, until Monday morning. The stores have closed-- not that they have Ben and Jerry's anyway. The best they stock is this undistinguished brand called Mövenpick-- (which, for you hoops fans, is illegal in basketball-- haha.). The German stores have closed at 4 PM on Saturday (in some towns, 6 PM; in some 2 PM; in some, midday), and certainly *not* to reopen on Sunday. This restriction is based on the lingering clampdown observation of the sabbath in a nation that no longer observes the sabbath: almost no one goes to church in Germany anymore: You could bowl down the central aisle of most German houses of worship on any day and knock not soul one off his pins (except in the Turkish mosques). But this limitation of store opening hours is loosening (They are aware it couldn't help but increase employment -- thus spending, thus more employment, thus more taxes-- thus continued social services at a high rate; thus more business support; thus continued Social Democrats in office). . . Although, in the German supermarket, or the French, or Dutch, *you will have to Do Your Own Bagging*, as the cashier is a dedicated cashier-- strong union again-- and the concept of specialized "baggers" has not been conceived of as yet across the Atlantic. And it wont be (although bagger-work might provide more employment-- as with our nation's WalMart): *But What!?-- Cashier-And-Bag/Cashier-And-Bag/ Cashier-And-Bag-- Eight hours!? Ich denke nicht!* Plus, on the employer side, it would constitute an added store expense (though not-so-much, if the store followed our union-inimical WalMart). And, by the way, it is incumbent that you the customer bag your bag super-*schnell*, Charlie, as the next customer is breathing down your neck. And you bag in a bag that You have had to *purchase*: None provided freebee. Or you could BYO-- a nice cloth bag (Good for the *umwelt*-- the environment: influential Green Party again). And then, insult to injury, you may not be able yet to pay with a credit card, in many groceries (though again they are catching up). Almost like at the gas station, where there are no gas tanks extant with credit card inserts. None I have seen anyway. To slide your card you actually have to *walk into the office*. . . Where they might be having a sale on, let's say, German driving gloves. But only if said sale has been specifically state-allowed: No sales at the retailer's own discretion or initiation, mind you. Might help the economy, sure, but at the expense of your rival gas station down the road (I hear this also may be changing).

You go to a restaurant here in the states. It's lunchtime-- you order only soup. You receive a nice (plastic) basket-full of rolls, or at the very least slices of bread. Good for crumbling and ersatz-crouton dunking, if you're of that kind. In Germany, forget bread-- well, *free* bread-- and a normal person cannot fill up on soup alone, can he? (Of course this story does not hold true in France, where you do get bread, plenty of bread, your fill of French-proud sliced baguette). Then, later, at German-restaurant dinner, the same damned glaring "*brötchen*" lacuna: No bread complimentary. You must humble yourself and *ask* (Unless it is an American-style German restaurant). In one cafe I asked for ketchup to spice up my schnitzel

-- a no-no, and sure I knew it. But I am an American, and sometimes I, proud-perverse creature, do enjoy teleprojecting my nationality. Anyway, the waitress responded to my schnitzel-ketchup-entreaty by fetching and bearing a red-checkered squeegey, which she unhesitatingly squeezed, once, twice, thrice, all the while waitressly eyeing me for orders as to when to stop squeegeying away. When my bill came I learned that I was being docked for the accumulated, and well-clocked, ketchup-squeezes. Metered ketchup, like mile-fractions in a taxi. Why this parsimony of condiment prevails in Germany I have no idea (It goes unheard of in France). That German ketchup-clockery was not a penalty, I don't think (for being an American?); but there ain't no other *mot juste* for it but, uh, cheap. The Germans are certainly a glass-is-half-empty people who guard against even losing that half-empty glass in its entirety; whereas the French are a people who will honk away at you that their brandished glass is, even if not fuller, *finer*-- than yours. . . Onwards: That cheap ketchup-clutch is also like the screen-lessness of Euro-windows. The *fenster* and *fenêtres* may be routinely double-paned for winter insulation, but the screwball things don't have *screens*: You wish to read on a warm, sultry summer night-- maybe because you cannot sleep and you have no *milk!*-- and you do your reading at the risk of West Nile Virus, because they've got in Europe, as we do in the U.S., mosquitoes and other buzzy-winged biters, but they've not got, unlike us, *Screens*. I don't get it, as screens do not set you back so many euros: *Get screeens!* Actually, I do get it: its the influence, the inertia, of having-- and having had-- older houses with older gate-like windows that do not accommodate so easily the modern screen. But this is not excuse enough. Not, anyway, for the likes of Me.

Actually, regarding this peculiar bread-and-ketchup-control I do have a notion: It's that tension I spoke of earlier, having to do with the individual verses the community. In our America, individualism works its way into catering to-a-*person*. An "*in*-dividual"-- which when you hone in on it is a strange tongue-and-groove of a word. *Not*-divided: In the U.S. we are *not*-divisable dudes by constitution and belief; a holy certainty makes best for citizenship and patriotism, a righteous unambivalent passion makes for instant goodness and decency, when (unfortunately) just about every theme in the world-- no, not "just-about", but *every* issue in the world-- is, bar none, chock full of ambiguity and shifting nuance-- or *divid*-uality. Multi-*divid*-uality: So in Europe the ketchup-craving-Individual may be at the mercy of the non-ketchup communitarian. . . Which communitarian can sure go overboard:

Frankfurter Allgemeine Zeitung

Bread and ketchup, *please!*

And now, ladies and gentlemen, for the piece-de-resistance: You go to rent a flat, or purchase a house, in much of Europe. In much of "older" Europe indeed, you don't purchase a house. A house is not a home, a flat is a home. Despite the EU, they are, country-by-country, smaller lands-- so this will always be true: whether by habit, by predisposition, or by constraint. In any case, you walk into the kitchen of your prospective residence in Europe and you discover quickly that, well, the kitchen is an *area*, not a kitchen. Not yet. For as you look around, you are confronted by the barren: pipes poking out of walls, as if you are in the engine hold of a destroyer. There is no sink in evidence, no stove; wires may also be unattached Medusas-- with tragic implications. You have to purchase the missing fixtures, have them delivered and installed. A true pain in the ass American. Yet ironically, perversely (compensatorially?) there is a superabundance of TV satellite dishes; and it is a history-discombobulating farce to observe all those space-age receiver bowls aimed at the heavens from atop even countryside half-timber houses dating back occasionally to before Goethe or even Dürer, and almost to Joan of Arc-- along with the cognitive dissonance you get, especially in France now, of vast countryside (American style) "hypermarkets", with their garish billboards. And Warning: When inside someone's house in Europe, do be on guard for those wicked beauties, the Euro door handles: they aren't round softie knobs, like ours, but long kidney-sabres, which can gore you good as a bull. More no bread. But, damn, they are solid things.

And then there is the SMOKING. An American friend visited me; at my favorite cafe in Heidelberg (named Hemingway's yet) she inquired after the Non-Smoking section, while I abjectly cringed as the waitress responded with *sang froid* (or Icey Deutschey style), "Non-smoking? *Raus*." Or, outside (*Raus* doesn't have to mean, as in the World War Two movies, "Get out!"). But oh lord, that SMOKING. In cafes, in supermarkets, in train stations and train compartments, in houses, at universities in classrooms and offices, in banks, on trams and busses and in Hospitals! (in designated areas)-- by *doctors*! The wild Individualist American has listened to government warnings (We can still picture the fierce, golden-shoulder-braid uniformed, unyielding mannerist-beard physiognomy of C. Everett Coop, although he is long gone as Surgeon General), but the "civilized" sophisticate government-regulated European (the communitarian *un*-individualist European) has scofflawed and snubbed at the cancer evidence. This is a strange twisteroo, and it deserves further investigation; though I suspect it has something to do with a certain fatefulness of a people who have lived through too many wars and holocausts and have perversely decided that in smoking's case comfort means not prohibition, not forbearance, not habit-breaking, but permission: Just be human: Have a peccadillo. Have a foible. Allowance. Laissez-faire as chill-out in the psych arena. Perfectability as a juvenile disorder: we Euroers sneer at this anti-puffing Americanization. Same reason we (they) don't drink de-caf. Or low-fat lattes (Yeah, try asking a cafe waitress in Paris or Berlin for a low-fat de-caf latte-- with soy milk).

Raus!

Other reason? On America's plus side and Europe's minus: The American Individualist is trained, whatever else, to *Take Responsibility*? Whereas the French, for example, are trained to ward blame off-- to push it afar: We had rented a car and driven from Bad Herrenalb to Paris, parking on a small crowded side street just off Boulevard Saint Michel. When we returned our rental's locks rebuffed our key: someone had attempted to jimmy a door lock and steal the car, but our Lupo had a feature whereby all keyholes in such situation shut down: We could not enter our rental and return to Germany. We called the French offices of our EuropeCar; we complained, but like our auto locks the customer service *madame* resisted us with, "*I* did not harm your auto, sir. *We* can do nothing." "But you are EuropeCar," I replied, as furious as I was uncomprehending; "You are the same company we rented from in Germany. Surely, for goodwill, you would honor Germany EuropeCar's-- " "Sorry," she cut me off unsympathetically; "you are *German* EuropeCar and *we* are *French* EuropeCar." EU, where are you!?-- the twain would never meet? "This would never happen in America," I inveighed; and the French "customer service" lady did not respond. She was bored with my insipid (childish?) business ethics lecture. So: my wife and I used a coat hanger (from our hotel) to break into our *German* EuropeCar, as four members of the French *gendarmerie* watched in indifferent (not even curious) merriment during our two hours or so of sweaty auto-criminal incompetence-- abandoned as we were by the French division of the same firm we had patronized. Overboard nationalization, or "community" (government) support may have been the indirect culprits here—i.e., French EuropeCar had some public funding? And so it didn't give a hoot about capitalizing our Americo-Deutsch "Goodwill"? Just conjecture, mind you; or perhaps it was just overboard French self-justification with a dose of French self-dispensation; or all of the above. "We always assist *French* EuropeCar renters here at EuropeCar," the manager of the German offices swore to us when we eventually returned (We'd had to break open the gas tank latch as well-- with an aghast French peanut gallery at the gas station-- we tugging at the thing like bears prying ajar a car door in Yellowstone for some corn flakes). "Please don't judge all Europe," the German manager seemed to be pleading, "by our neighbors across the Rhine-- even if there are no longer any travel borders."

But did the Germans really help the French?

I wouldn't venture renting a Franco-EuropeCar and faking a breakdown with it in Germany to make the necessary (anecdotal) research.

And finally, regarding American opulence, whether it be delusion or reality, I have to mention that despite the economic and institutional poverty we seem to have visited upon ourselves, the U.S. is surely the richest nation in two ways: A larger share of Americans-- except for the Japanese-- do receive at least some community college education; and secondly we are richer in our variety of cultures, of people. You cannot find, anywhere in Europe, or Asia for that matter, such a wealth of communities, of ethnicities -- of food, of attitude, of music, of literature, of churches-- in other words, of Life. We have not banned, as the French have (well, Chirac), the wearing of Muslim veils by students in our public schools-- or, as in some German *länder*, veil-wearing by the teachers. Our American language is informal, and when its informality is not sloppy ("dudn't", wudn't", "whassup") or insulting (gooks, chinks, kikes, beaners and Alis), it enjoys a happily-loose incorrectness, stocked as it is with clever-quick Yiddish and Spanglish and "Blacklish"-Ebonic slangs like "shakne'n'bake" and "chump-change" and "schmuck" and muchacho-machos and *la vida loca*. Same with our comport-ments. Our easy shuffle-dawdle walks can come off as diffident as they can affable and unpretentious; same with our stances, with those heaperies of bearing, those plain-guy slumps and hunchbacks at the slouched-over American thorax. Such that when we the victors met with the defeated Iraqis after the first Gulf War (Desert Storm, not today's ambiguously-named Enduring Freedom) it looked on TV as if *their* generals, with their dignified high postures, were the winners, and our generals, in bedraggled schmo motif, had lost.

Yet (surprisingly and not-surprisingly) our music has intoxicated the world-- from blues to jazz to rock and rap and R&B-- a curious (even per-verse) consequence of our talented variety serendipitously mixing it up with our social deprivation-- both our talented and (chutzpahishly) untalented deprivation (as evidenced, for one example, by Snoop Dog's not off-key but utterly keyless rendering of his Sinatra version of the song *New York, New York*-- and it sure looked like no joke: the rapper was seriously *trying*). And like our music, our jobs often exhibit a certain way-station freedom: a wait-ress in America may be an actress, whereas in Europe a waitress is more than likely now and later, and ever, a waitress; a cook in America may hold a PhD in classics, whereas in Europe a cook is a cook is a cook. "They" are often locked in place-- and they seem to want to be, often. Our humor, fueled by our variety, is richer and roomier than Europe's-- by miles-- and coated with American optimism and brightness, it can enjoy making fun of itself. Whether it's Jewish humor, the "Take my wife, please," of a Henny Youngman or the Woody Allen, "I don't mind dying; I just don't want to be there when it happens." Or American-Irish: A drinker with his flask in his hip pocket falls off his bicycle leaving a pub; he feels wetness swamping his rump. "Oh lawd," he swears, "let it *please* be *bluhd*." A Puerto Rican American janitor is upbraided by the building manager for not showing a visitor to the elevator. The janitor wryly indignant, explains, "Is not my chob, man." But in Europe, humor is constrained, and fragilely, by national identity (and the German humor is simply constrained: water there, yes; but it must be bucketed-up from some deep-down, mold-encrusted cistern). With Euro-humor you don't bear down heavy-hard on your own (vulnerable) self-image, your own traditional, community self-dignity. In Europe you desperately fear being pinpricked like a balloon. A German holding two PhDs will pompously, seriously, call himself Doctor Doctor (and he will do a well-vetted doubletake when you smile at that-- as if you're "dissing" him and he maybe should quite challenge you to a Heidelbergian duel.). No, rather than the confident self-jibe the Germans may mock the Poles (as lazy and dumb). The French mock "les froides Allemandes" (Germans). Italians send up everybody icey north of them, especially the *Tedescos* (Germans), while everybody north of them has at the jabbering Italians and their nifty clothes and skinny-tight pinch shoes and inveterate "low-class" (both sexes) ass-pinching. But our American humor is kindly, cheerfully, self-directed. We're the Pillsborough Doughboy. European humor is tirelessly, and meanly, Other-aimed. Cruel-verging, similar to the merciless French and Italian city driving, that fender-bumper mode of the challenge, the callow take-no-prisoners.

Let's put it this weird (and not-weird) way: Europeans feel superior-inferior, while we Americans feel inferior-superior. American individual-ism's best face, its open face (yeah, like that sandwich we invented), its no-myth face is American variety. Its Ellis Island origins. Our inferiority become superior.

Annex: Comeuppance too: Amazingly, even French TV is copying American TV. One of the most popular shows over there now is a sort of Reality *HeeHaw* production where Grade C French celebrities perform farm work (and "perform" is the word) like delivering a kid goat and shoveling bovine manure. And German TV now airs a show where celebrities (again, Grade C) become servants for plain humble country folk, cooking and shopping for the "bumpkins" while couturiered-up and designer-styled, Claudia Schifferesque. This after British TV has announced an *Apprentice* show of their own, with the iconoclastic entrepreneur Sir Alan Sugar (who?) in "The Donald" role. And now plans are underway to "laissez-farie"-up France-- partially, partially-- by the government's selling shares of-- likely small however-- Air France, France Télécom, Gaz de France and even Electricité de France. And, *dégeulasse*, the French are getting fatter, especially the "McDo"-chomping teens... Then: amusingly, certain German and French CEOs have recently been captivated by the bright idea-- *in*-dividualist idea-- that they ought to mimic certain infamous American CEOs-- only not on the good entrepreneurial cholesterol; rather the bad: After Mannesmann's takeover by Vodaphone, the senior managers of Mannesmann and DeutscheBank have awarded themselves spectacular extra bonuses, like our Kenneth Lay and Jeffrey Skilling Enroners and Dennis Kozlowski Tycoers; and Jean Marie Messier, the disgraced former head of Vivendi, is being pursued for stock "irregularities" of $1 billion by the French judicial system. This corporate selfishness has been unheard of until now (in Germany; not however in mischievously corrupt France, entertainingly corrupt France-- even expectedly corrupt); still, its volume does constitute a rather strong breach in the usual community system, the accepted national business ethic. Euro-CEOs really may be watching too many repeats of *Dynasty* and *Dallas*-- like our "new breed" med students patterning themselves after the stars of *ER* and *Chicago Hope*.

But there is something else, something quite serious, stemming from our hang loose ethnic variety: Tolerance. Despite our American culture-failings, our "humungus", "awesome" education gaps, our Babbitt-"bidniss" reverence, we do not as a rule kick over Jewish gravestones, as seems to be the current case in Europe, and the past case reduxed; we seem not to attack the yarmulchaed and great-coated Hassidim; we swastika synagogues at a re-markably microscopic infrequency. Whereas in France today, this monu-ment-clobbering has again become a problem[*] , with the Gaullic Muslim and the Gaullic far Righter, the followers of Jean Marie Le Pen; and the Neo-Nazi cueball-heads in Germany (whom, unlike in America, they need to

---

[*] French Jews are emigrating at a volume greater than at any time since World War II.

keep in check by stringent law). In the U.S. we certainly have once had our "strange fruit" hanging from southern trees, to quote Billie Holliday-- and it is ironic how great melodic songs can come from misery as well as from love (Actually I suppose it isn't ironic at all). But nowadays, even with our de facto segregated education and its mean consequences, still, we are better here. Not economically, no; but socially. We're fairer.

And now for the ultimate in Be Fair, be it with a facetious twist-- Table Eighteen.

TABLE EIGHTEEN

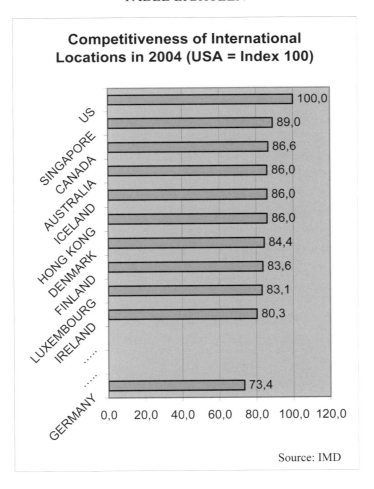

If you are an adept of the IMD (Institute for Management Development) you will rank favorable business climates on, well-- guess what?-- favorite business desires. You will prefer to establish your enterprise in the U.S. for many of the same reasons I have raffishly-yet-seriously preferred to wonder why anyone would want to establish, not one's business but one's *self*, in the U.S. And Singapore. And-- likely-- China. Of the ten most valuable global brands in 2003 (Source: Interbrand) eight were American.

1. CocaCola	6. Nokia
2. Microsoft	7. Disney
3. IBM	8. McDonald's
4. GE	9. Marlborough
5. INTEL	10. Mercedes

And Nike consistently outsells Adidas.

And Wal-Mart is the world's biggest retailer and largest private employer.[*]

And GE (lobbying congress like crazy for every tax break it can get) is the world's largest company-- period.

Perhaps this is why German CEOs are acting like our guys?

Perhaps it explains, in part, why these CEOs are recently calling out for American-type 40 hour weeks for their plant workers (although our "forty" is more like forty-five), drawing out the Western Europe 35.

---

[*] Although WalMart does systematically keep out union employees (See Chapter 4). It cannot however de-facto close-shop in Germany, Britain and Japan, where tackling unionization is de-jure illegal-- with enforcement. And WalMart's women employees are suing it for job discrimination: especially significant as *most Wal-Marters are women.* We in America are so nice and equanimous and unclass-conscious that most ex-WalMarter employees-- not excluding the union-dismissed (trumped-up, not union membership as reason)-- still shop at their alma mater, WalMart. Well, it is cheap, and they may be on Welfare. Or contemplating it... Which, however, might not be so bad as being one of the Third World sweatshop workers used for-pennies-for-years by Nike.

8

STREET WALKING

But fairness is a two-way street. Tell the whole story. Like, simply, streets: You can't walk any street in America. You know what I mean.You'd be suicidal to go the pedestrian route on Any Streeet U.S.A., as you'd be daring homicide right in its amoral angry face; and I can imagine some perverse Larry the Lip oddsmaker happily quoting you risk-ratios like a life insurance underwriter on the various precarious venues of our various urban grids. But you *can* walk the streets of Europe. Saunter the cities, ambulate yourself as trusting and wonder-eyed as some Forrest Gump. Try any street. Well, just about. Well, Western Europe. Developed Europe. "Old" Europe. That is, if you avoid some suburbs, like Paris's *Gouette d'or* (Gold Nugget) and the by now ironically named Belleville-- which are approaching our urbs for danger. But gunless danger; relatively; thankfully. So far.

To capture the most obvious, galvanizing example, so enthralling it has become the archetype of Developed Difference, a Paris stroll should do: mosey the Seine's banks, by sculptures and prized architectures, arabesque and brocade and balustrade and cut stone masonry, and ornamented facades, and the endless rows of book stalls. This places you a universe away from some ill-advised promenade along the smoke-belched East River (you just wouldn't suffer to do it-- unless you were on Ecstacy) or even the Hudson's well-benched Riverside Park in New York City-- which really isn't half-bad; or along the business skyline of downtown Lake Michigan in Chicago. And certainly not the muscle beach of ugly-squalid-brutal-hip Venice in LA (the Lower East Side by the Pacific). Or even unique Fisherman's Wharf in San Francisco, exotic with its crabs and seals and speaking otters and cultivated colorful funkissimo in sea air (but basically still ticky-tack)-- and its bay-close Alcatraz (The Parisian authorities had to put a halt to McDonald's golden arches being swooped over a building where Picasso and Matisse once purchased their paints-- and perhaps their painting pants. This though *it was once only an art supply store*. And it wasn't even that now).

Another scene: An inveterate hanger-outer, I confess to schmoozing in two cafes, as after morning's writing I crave, not exactly hang-out companionship, but at least real *faces*. The two cafes: The French Cafe in Berkeley, ridiculously-inaptly named, and *Das Krokodil* in Karlsruhe-- well, also absurdly named. My German wife calls my Berkeley "hang" a hole-in-the-wall, which it surely is. Even proudly is. No amount of self-delusion and mental decoration could transform my Berkeley cafe from its tortured-tottery unmatched wooden chairs and wobbly Formica tables, unmatched too-- even in height-- and sloppy-but-friendly Mexican counter guys into *Das Krokodil* with its broad "*stamtisch*" tables and neatly designed and woodworked counter and its appealing waitresses-- none of whom are actresses-in-waiting nor therapists-in-training and in-waiting; they are simply *waitresses*. And food (albeit no bread with the soup: slices are metered-out, extra). These two cafes have similar clienteles, the over-the-hill gang: intellectual solitaires, artists and musicians, yappy or mute-depressed, and aged-retired academics; and simulacrums of these types-- aspirers to what-beats-me. They are all of course getting older, and lamer, and canier, and now and then once bites the dust-- to deader; and, sure, you still expect to see a deceased him-or-her hobble on in any day now, with aprocryphal reports of the groovy Afterlife, all hunchily under the transom humming some Janis Joplin Song or Country Joe (himself; with a "Fish" or two) or a Grateful Dead remainderer. Indeed, to peek for the first time into my Berkeley haven, even with its clique-camaraderie and its fly squadrons circle-buzzing, kamikazees over antiquarians strumming guitars in their three blues chords (and looking very intense about it) you might believe it ought be renamed The Cafe Depresso-- The End of the Road Redoubt. Whereas, into *Das Krokodil* an errant businessman might wander, for lunch, mistaken but not so terribly misplaced (or disappointed), and nobody sane would ever slip into The French Cafe for a midday meal, or even a mid-afternoon snack. Honesty does force me to say, however, that Berkeley's French Cafe might not veritably be so inaptly named, as in France-- especially Paris-- there are socialist cafes and conservative cafes-- conservative *philosopher* cafes, not conservative businessman cafes-- and philosopher-philosopher cafes, and musician cafes.

Not officially, of course. . . Business cafes would not, by definition, *be* cafes: they would be *les bistros*.

   "The passage from the big to the little is what makes Paris beautiful." That from Adam Gopnik's subtly intelligent book *Paris to the Moon*. That passage says it: that at once sudden shifting, that slender-yet-great trans-formation, is really what makes *any* city beautiful (if the city can manage it-- I might amend the Gopnik line that slight way). When my wife was a graduate student in Munich I decided to set out and learn that city, by foot. I covered the Schwabing district, which is part university, part upscale, part Greenwich Village; and Giesing, which is a middle-rent Soho. And the magnificent museums of the town center, these, as with the libraries, not yet budget-snipped into some days closed, unlike our American museums, libraries and post offices. *Oh our post offices!*-- now so often shut on Saturdays-- and/or Wednesdays-- with one employee berthed (or fox-holed) behind his/her projectile-proof cage window, surrounded by two empty-cage spots (fired coworkers?-- forced early retired?): Then, Lord, those post-weekend Monday PO *lines*: Neither in France nor Germany in a post office have I had to cool my heels for more than a few minutes-- if at all; and they manage other functions there, various forms of credit, pension and banking: Three to six counter spots, three to six counter workers; rugs sometimes, warm furnishings; picture postcard racks. The relaxed (understated) absence of bulletproof glass! More like a color-coordinated poster-decorated travel agency. Post Office Paradise! Whereas in American post offices these days, forgodssakes they are often unequipped with even the appropriate rubber stamps. I went one day to send a book from Berkeley, and the lady embedded behind the (bulletproofed) counter informed me, "We don't have a Book Rate stamp." "Huh?--this is a post office," I said, "you mail *books* from here." She replied, "You're telling *Me*?," and then she hand-scribbled, on the large package, Book Rate-- which of course I could have done at home, and my parents probably did do at home during World War Two. Well, at least she didn't have to borrow my pen. That week. But were we in Senegal?!

   I digress-- can't help it-- the subject made me do it: Back to Munich and my walk tour. I was leery of heading south and east, towards the Turkish neighborhoods, thence to the reputed skinhead warrens. But I did want to see these areas, as I wished to be able to inform friends back home of my bravery undaunted. I recollected how, when I'd lived in Greenwich Village in the seventies I had hit upon the bright notion of my doing a piece for *The Village Voice* on being a plain white nebbish dude traversing, alone, the black streets of Harlem. Not Mister Brave exactly: I'd had more in mind a kind of serio-comic set-to about this Mister Magoo, me, loping oblivious, dum-de-dum-dum, across 125th, up Lennox, and so forth. A winner break-through piece, in the optimistic know-nothing vision of a young writer in his twenties. But, to mix Falstaff with Alan Greenspan (and how more unlikely could you get?) where the rising Reality curve intersects the descending Paranoia curve, feets do your business: I came off the A-train and began walking. Male black huddlings got to me. I recollected how white bicyclers in northern Central Park were de-biked by strings, near-invisible and tied taut across the curving park bikeway, tree trunk to tree trunk; then these hapless ten-speeders were unburdened of their cash and credit cards-- and *only* these if they were lucky (I actually knew a victim who had once remonstrated with muggers to allow him to keep two cards: one, library; the other his driver's license, so that he would not be compelled to languish at the derelict DMV-- where he even might encounter the familiar thieves again). So: Don't stare at anybody, I coached myself, as I snappy-busy-poked up Lennox Avenue: Staring, that's threat, Jack-- or it's wary fear, a cornered pussycat: Just Don't *Stare*! Then, overthinking, I forced myself to abandon my semiconscious-- and latent-- run-walk in favor of this ersatz saunter-lope, slow-cocky as a halfback after a good run, as absurd as that looked on a skinny-ass (terrified) white writer. But *wait*: Now I saw that I was actively *not*-staring-- overly, overtly, *not*-staring!-- and damned if *that* couldn't be interpreted as arrogant. Above-it-all. Mister SuperWhite. Okay, don't stare, don't *not* stare. Don't run-walk. Don't over-slow-cocky non-run-walk-walk, like those wildlife nuts who go to Alaska to hang out with grizzlies, turning their backs on the great bears to illustrate they TRUST the unpredictable one ton creatures which have been morally unschooled in inter-mammalian ethics. At least these environmentalist-nutcases are oblivious when they're bear-hugged, indifferently-crunched and eaten. Act Normal.

Good luck-- there *was* no Normal. In a non-normal world there exists no normal but absolute non-normal. I got myself back on the A-train to The Village. Feets did their business. *Village Voice* piece kaibashed.

True, nothing had happened. Zero. But the danger was palpable. That is, imagined danger abraided the skin (and esprit) of a man who had seen enough TV reports, read enough newspaper items; a man who was now observing, from inside, the litter, the tumbleweed bags, the wine bottles, the overburnt ribs aromas, the street-strewn mattresses (with people on them), the boarded-up windows of ghost tenements and once-beautiful brown-stones, the unemployed, bored, plain-awful *lurkingness*, the-- to him, *Me*-- beaten mean blank voidish All. Of great New York City just above great Central Park. The slow smiles that could mean and not mean a smile? An Israeli somehow plopped down into Gaza City; a Palestinian-- with lumpy backpack-- entering the Knesset or a Jerusalem synagogue. That perverse pride we take here in our Darwinian (again, *social* Darwinian, not Darwinian Darwinian) manliness. And we do have an investment, a bedeviling-twisted and relishy stock too, in our roughness. It's shown, paraded-out, in more than enough of our (exported) movies (and TV), the wildcat cop leaping over the overflowed garbage can in the hell-worldly back alley urban manhole world expunging its manhole fog (and again, Why don't European manholes exude that bleak smoke?); the mendacious *kvelling* of the American tourist to, say, a Parisian: "Hey, in New York I carry a '357 Magnum in my cutoffs"; as if to say, "Hey, sure, you got beauty, but we got *balls*-- and balls'll out every time, you fop with your chartreuse scarf, you Brie-nibbling surrender monkey, you."

Munich: I gathered my parcel of courage and walked a predominantly Turkish area; I even braved the chancy-touted skinhead lands west of the main train station. Surprise: Not much litter and loiter. No gutted, emptied-out lots; no storefronts hollowed and abandoned; no stoops-bunched leering hopelessness of eyes and mouths. The same outdoor fruit and vegetable stands and kebab parlors and kiosks you see in other neighborhoods. "Good energy", as the New Agers (stupidly) like to say. Little to stoke the old American paranoia; or the recent American paranoia. Except, well, for the occasional self-imposed baldie nonchalantly leading his Pit Bull on his studded leash. No cops even (See Table 20). But the downtown sidewalks are widewalks in Europe, three, four times more broad than ours, as they are meant for leisure-and-business, not business-and-business; so you are not cramped-in; you are not forced to bump shoulders, a male-provocative act, a pre-punch threat of rhinos on the Serenghetti, even when the bump is unintentional (Though is it ever that?). And wide sidewalks (or side widewalks) allow not only good walking-- thus good exercise without its being *prescribed* EXERCISE-- but bicycle lanes: thus good exercise without *its* being prescribed EXERCISE; and those protrusions of Plexiglas awnings leaning far out over storefronts, so that one might walk block after block dry in rain or snow. Good for *stadt bummeln*, literally "town bumming", but really window-shopping. And the outdoor cafes are often five tables deep, even in "bad" neighborhoods; which elbow-roominess can foster an environment inimical to ugly moods, to violence. Now it may not constitute politically correct feminism, or in some ways be conducive to modernist New Era personal development, but mothers are out, all over town, shopping, cafe-ing, or with their children, women's-job-work being not so essential for even a below middle-class family to keep afloat; as Germany spends a great deal on family support (Table 19)-- Community:

TABLE NINETEEN

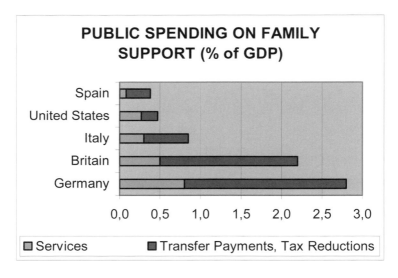

Source: OECD

And by the way, those widewalks I mentioned; they allow those sturdy yellow baroquey-scalloped phone booths-- real *booths*, plastic huts really-- that Americans find so quaint and cute, particularly as the phones in them *work*, and the smell abiding is not suspicious reek, the coin return slots (although most are simple phone card inserts) not gunked with unpleasant viscosities. Same story even in Kreuzberg, the notorious low-rent "bad-hip" and Turk quarter of Berlin. Same in Strasbourg, France, across the Rhine from our Black Forest house, where the Islamic underclass becomes not Turk but Algerian and Moroccan. Unfortunately though, I do have to say at the risk of dereliction of journal-duty, this easiness I'm depicting does not hold for those Algerian-crammed suburbs of Paris, *les quartiers chauds*, or the "Chicago" district of Toulon in the south. *La France* harbors 5 million Muslims (far more than any other European nation), many employed exclusively in street gangs-- but outside the inner city: a considerable *faubourg*-gulag that tourists never see, and even the French themselves seldom confront. *Affiches* of graffiti like "fuck la police" on the walls of mega housing developments, block long foundry things (A cartoon in *Le Monde* once depicted a suburban ghetto schoolteacher instructing her Arab charges in French declination: "*I* want to burn a car; *you* want to burn a car; he, or she, *wants* to burn a car." (Of course in the U.S. the tutelage might have gone, "*I* want to shoot a cop, *you*...). The French schoolmistress is also emphasizing to her class that they not overlook the correct Gaullic circumflex in *brûler*-- to burn-- as France is a stickler for proper language. Now these sub-Mediterranean warrens can obviously be scarey sites; but they really are peanuts when stacked up against the well-armed badnewslands I have seen of Baltimore, my home town; Pittsburgh; D.C; San Francisco; Oakland; L.A; New York-- *our* ghettoes being fully weaponized.

FLASH!-- This just in: Most of our NFL football players own guns (These athletic brawny bubbas claim that they are frightened of fans).

EDUCATED ASSUMPTION: I could walk into the locker-room of Bayern-Munich, the UEFA *fußball* team, break into their lockers and probably find not even one picayune box-cutter.

In a recent year, handguns murdered in the following countries--

New Zealand	2
Australia	13
Japan	15
Great Britain	30
Canada	106
Germany	213

while the United States, the victor, easily garnered the Gold: 9,390!

That's 45 times as many gun slayings as in our closest competitor with its population meagerly one-third ours.

TABLE TWENTY

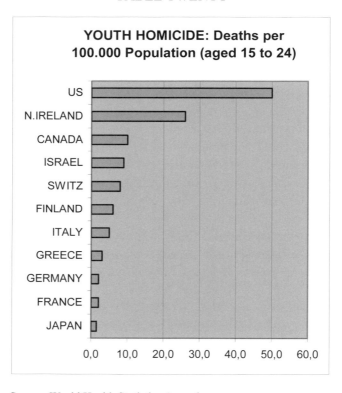

Source: World Health Statistics Annual

Our world-beating GDP might well be called: Guns Dangerous People.

Or: E+EP+SP+NRA+AM=GM. Economic Poverty plus Emotional Poverty plus Social Pathology plus American Myth plus Charleton Heston equals Gun Murder.

And then there are the courtyards. Ah, in many inner cities of Europe courtyards prevail. Through brass archways or partially open gateways, or vaingloriously left ajar ones, these *hinterhöfe* present glimpses of a kind of communal privacy, a group cultivation, behind even aging wornout residences-- sometimes those even collapsing. Again, quaint stuff to an American. *Un*American stuff to an American, unless you happen to be of the upscale fortunate in Manhattan where, as on MacDougal Street, there exist a few exclusive, uh, "*mews*". The rule in our American cities, the standard evolution, has been the linear, which tends to be the factorial, the impenetrable row: the rear windows of an apartment facing, and sometimes not so distantly, the rear windows of an apartment on the next street (where Jimmy Stewart [or Christopher Reeve in the remake] might witness a murder). But one's European courtyard windows alight *on-the-courtyard*: An inner-outside haven, sometimes with garden, sometimes with attractive buildings that do not even front upon the city beyond, and so are never seen -- and enjoyed-- but for residents. A private-but-yet-public (or public*ish*) wealth, in even an unwealthy dwelling place. Obviously the courtyard began as "commune" housing in the medieval castle court; but design can create mentality, adapt it-- the credo of Frank Lloyd Wright (and of everybody now)-- and changed mentality then creates even better design: another extending of family; of mutual aid, mutual obligation. Ninety-six percent of the French keep close ties to family; ninety-one percent remain close in Germany. Amazing numbers, to an American: Because of that modifier "close", Americans are relegated to the cellar of "family", at forty-two percent. But I don't need such stats: I merely observe my wife's attachment to her parents, to her brother and sister-- calls, visits, dinners: *anhänglich sein*, the Germans call this. Staying tied (Truth is, the an*hänglich sein* sometimes drives me, Mister American, quite nuts.). The profoundest aims of government can be attested to by the aims of that government's people, and by their affections. Even if these aims make up a ladder that can never be fully scaled.

Now perhaps I'm being naive; not only romantic but over-romantic, chimerical. Utopian. Still I would venture that, globalization notwithstanding, there is a subtle difference between European and American commerce. Buying and selling is unmistakably buying-and-selling-- trade for profit (The doctrine of Comparative Advantage, to economists: You produce what you make better, and I do likewise; then we exchange, with cash differentials reflecting our goods' market values). But trade has always seemed *more* to Americans-- even with the Puritans-- a *means* to life, a kind of pragmatic workout, an in-order-to: The original intention-- Life-- gone, forgotten. Oh it is spoken of alright, but the American praises of Life, the exhortations to Live, are words that are bizarrely unkennable, curiously flat (even when *sung*) and unplummable when focused on in our country. Life?-- Duh? At best our LIVE words may mean the thrills of sky-diving and bungee-jumping on your day off from BUSINESS (as compared to Europe's two days off), or billionaire Ted Turner's America's Cupping, or billionaire Larry Ellison of Oracle America's Cupping. Though brave, adventurous, thin crêpepaper as soul stuff, two-dimensional. So, today's brightest kids in America, the non-science-oriented ones, growing up in the native demi-soul-vacuum, tend not to major in literature or philosophy but Business. Literature and philosophy by and large seem musty curioes of "reflection", or some region weirdly "interior" (*God, get outside yourself!*), peculiarities best left-- such antiquities-- to the girls, and to the boys who in college we once cruelly labeled "pears", the "sensitive" broad of hip and narrow of clavicle and suspiciously-spooky-smart of brain.

In Europe, however, the bustle of goods and money still does seem to be held as only a part of life, not a route *to* it-- whatever It is. French chefs can attain the status of concert pianists and movie stars, not because of food snobbery, or food-profit, but because food is a serious part-of-life. The average Euro-town will have, unlike in the U.S., at least one highly regarded restaurant (although it may be closed from three until six); a good bakery, not a chain franchise (although it may be closed from midday until three); a pharmacy, not a drugs section of a "drugstore" or a variety store, but a devoted place of medicine (as *we* used to have-- with Mister Jones the pharmacist whom you knew and trusted); a bookstore sits in the average Euro-town, not a rack at the Safeway of Romance and Murder and Caper (although the bookstore may be open only...); a fresh produce store; a grocery (although...). It's *Here,* Life-- or rather, it's *There*-- naturalness in its design and evolution-- its plain growth. A kind of group breath-- *"Savoir Vivre"*. You see it, trace-and-fiber, even in the big cities: how Amsterdam's red brick row-houses are not squealched and suffocated into an uglified ghetto crumble, as in Philadelphia or Baltimore; as canals and streams, once no longer commerce-useful, are not, for "efficient" street transport, concreted over mercilessly, as in the infamous case of the Canal Street of what is now yuppily called Tribecca (Manhattan)-- where try as you might you will not unearth any meandering canal; you see Life, the group breath, in the small Euro-town downtowns, which are not-- as in America--

functional square brick and rectangular pale white cornice; as in the French small towns where the *cafe*, if one does not exist (unlikely), it will be created by town subsidy-- or even by national subsidy. The countryside is given, allocated, more than its share in France because it is seen as a source, a root, an origin of lifestyle to be preserved. As with the courtyards and cafes and streets, European stores are simply more attractive; even the large ones are more comfortably slow-paced yet alive; and a lot of them remain so, even as Life changes, as Life Americanizes with our exported low-overhead bare-bones WalMarts and Home Depots and McEverythings and (Americanized-McSwedish) Ikeas. Brilliant and debilitating, we multi-faced Americans. But touchers?-- no-- not outside of Hollywood (Well, TV interview Hollywood). But in Europe, people do touch, people do hug-- even, really *men* (they even cheek-buss; even *men,* even truckers and construction guys), without the skittery curse of homophobia; people can bump into each other without anyone feeling his "space" has been "invaded". Life is not barebones.

Actually (and I do hesitate to reveal it) this part-of-life attitude goes also with an activity we Americans are indefatiguably, and quite against nature-- even our own nature-- trying to stamp out, as if it's the munificence of birds and beetles. What it happens to be is Prostitution. As you likely know, "working girls" are legally working in parts of Europe. Even in our humdrum Karlsruhe there exists (thrives) a little Amsterdam: a street (well, a block) of lady-shop windows; in effect, showroom competition. By design, or coincidence, this block runs cattercorner from the university (my wife's) and across street from the largest Volkswagen dealership (ours). Say what you will about the oldest profession (which it isn't: hunting-and-gathering is), prostitution's lawfulness provides at least for more, affordable, health service for these women and girls (i.e., free), less furtive-embarrassed skulking to the doctor, and less abuse-- like robbery, and slavery: No "bad" German pimps prance in superbrim felts; no cruising "John" cars with chagrin-shouldered hunters pursued by cruising hunter-hunter cop-cars-- the police become predators who will in America confiscate, impound (and then *sell!*) the "John"car. No vice squad officers taking kickback-- bucks or barter. No Byzantine squalor: these "shops" put one in mind of hairdressers' salons, and the street is even polished cobblestone, in a *fußgänger* zone. And-- no small accomplishment-- teen pregnancy rates less than half those of America's. You may not wish to partake in the exploitation of women optionless or earning for families left back in the less developed world; or, ricocheting between your hormones and your morals like Alexander Port-noy, you may be excruciatingly ambivalent. Even a good man can be ambi-valent-- especially a good man-- whatever a "good man" is. But Europe, as it has come to recognize relativity in gender, does also recognize relativity in Goodness: Gay marriage is nowadays performed all over Europe; it has neither to be cosetted in shy embarrassment nor belted out in egregious righteousness over the TV news. It is, just, simply, like any other marriage. Almost (While the French people are overwhelmingly pro gay marriage, their current Gaullist government is against).

TABLE TWENTY ONE
ACCEPTANCE OF GAY MARRIAGE

United States:	24 %
France:	65 %
Denmark:	82 %
Netherlands:	80 %
Germany:	80 %
Spain:	80 %

Poll by IPSO (2004); and *Elle*

And if Europe in general recognizes relativity in goodness, what does America recognize? Or not recognize.[*] Denial: World Class: We have The Best This and we have The Best That. Well, true, our *sitcoms* are best— whatever this means-- and our cop shows; and our actors (by sheer opportunity for role variety-- as English is WorldSpeak), although our actors' acting is projected onto screens in less comfortable theatres in America than in modern Europe (wider-softer seats over there; thicker sound-blocking walls between the plexes); our space-tech is topnotch (Who but us could send a spaceship over two billion miles to Saturn orbit?-- albeit with Euro-

---

[*] Certainly not relativity. Shadings of truth in our nation are more likely seen as the first refuge of the impotent: Comically, if a Democrat wears an Old Glory stickpin, like Joe Biden, a very ethical senator, he is perceived not as a patriot but a copover, a copycat Republican-- a lilly, phony patriot. What we recognize in our land of staunch Affirmation really is, paradoxically, non-Affirmation. Denial. Actually, by definition, we don't so much recognize Denial as exhibit it.

pean help. But for how many years longer we will lead here is a big question. First, there is our super deficit; secondly, the Fundamentalist "majority" may easily, adamantly, decide that space exploration is un-Biblical); our-- and now I will use our most-abused-word-- "energy" is best, our religious hope-driven energy; and our ambition-energy. And our terrified-of-bankruptcy-no-safety-net-energy. Quite a bit "buts" still here, really. But-- there are those Best "buts" too: What about those afore-mentioned postal workers? Have you noticed that often the mailman doesn't even pick up your mailable mail anymore when you've got the red flag on your box raised up and lifted? Has that complicated signal procedure dating back to Millard Fillmore been deleted from postal training school, as too time-wasteful? As too much sacro-cranial bending?-- and therefore insurance rate elevating, e.g. lumbar issues. They (Sure, yes, here I go again), *they-pick-the-mail-up-in-Europe*-- where postal employee work is regarded as, not social-resentful failure-work, but plainly Your Job: not looked down upon. Even garbage pickup is not derogated; it's okay: You do your job, not your grudging chore, you Serve-the-Community. What we here at home now seem to do is, we lower taxes, thus receiving less services and shoddier, rottier infrastructure; and then, being discontented with the rot and shod which *We* have generated, and therefore needing personally *more* wealth to pay for private unrotted services, like Fed Ex or UPS, or private schooling, or private garbage pickup, or just better US Post Office service-- we vote down taxes *further*! Insanely, We vote Right, angry at Left (or even Center), for the unenlightened license we have given Right: Guillotine the messenger. The downward spiral of laissez-faire in its angry unenlightened mode that, unenlightened, heads down darker, darker, darker-- as we merely possess (mostly possess) edja*cay*shun, not education. Who would deny that psycho-social wealth is more profoundly important and essential than, well, wealth-wealth? (Actually, a lot of Americans would). And so here in the United States you get the surly, resentful bus driver-- resentful for his low-stuck place in America's ladder-climb myth-- this driver who will grudgingly, harrumphingly (if that, and not out-and-out furiously) direct you to the bus stop for the appropriate bus-- you having wrongly committed the venal sin of boarding *his* bus-- while even in poverty-worn India, a country with some social cohesion mixed with a not inconsiderable social-religious rift, a kindly direction will be given by your Bombay city busman.

Now then, your Mister Plumber?-- who charges here like a neuro-surgeon, right? Again, not in Europe (I'm sorry-- and by now I'm in sack-cloth. I believe sackcloth *is* still made here in the U.S.). Ahyes, the American plumber: he cannot come for a week, at least. Nor the master electrician, if he wants to come *at all* for your piddling domicilic job: Hell, *he's* got Private Service bills to pay!-- for *his* children and *his* health. And, you know my broken record: they do come in Europe, *that day*. Somehow, they manage that decent-- needed, civilized-- service. Normal Operating Procedure. They come without bellyaching about it. They're polite. Somehow. The natural, civilized, *politesse*. Thus in Germany, or Switzerland, or France, or Austria, and lord knows where else, you don't have to nervously rely on one of those RotoSchmoto 24 hour schlockster "services" with their "experts" speed-trained the day before. I mean, Have you *seen* those American Roto guys?! Don't they resemble those characters hanging out at the Greyhound who unnerved our European traveler way back in Chapter Two? Do they carry in their Rotovan, along with snake and vacuum and multi-wrench, a semi-automatic? Well, it's America-- these fellows weren't really public school trained for anything (tax funds, tax funds); these guys are happy--well, less *un*happy-- to have acquired their pseudo-plumber positions with pseudo-plumber outfits. Except, they are "trained" by their superiors to get it done snappy, your leak, your short circuit: there's profit to be made. Community satisfaction, uh-uh-- not in the bargain. What's a *Community*, dude? Look, I'm glad these guys have a job, even if the job is a racket. But funny thing is, you know a lot of these men can't even *vote*. What, you ask? Why? Well, because we democraciers undemocratically *deprive* people of the vote: people who have served time in prisons, if convicted of a felony; and many of these RotoSchmotoRescuers do come from that segment. Still, they have served their time, they've paid their bigtime penalty, and they certainly understand sheer Need. And before you laugh, this door-slam in the face of once-jailed voters is unlike in Ireland, Spain, Switzerland, Poland, South Africa even (why Nelson Mandela finally could win South Africa's presidency) and Canada (And our vote-depriving sure helps keep our unimprisoned Right in power). Such American "democracy" can make you lay back and mutter. And wonder. And mutter.

Hey, be a relativist. Don't be a Denier. Give a guy a chance!

Then-- endless apology, but I am compelled to go the litany: It's for our own good. So, then: the subway ticket machines don't work in America, say one-third of the time. You know that. I mean, try sliding even a new-pressed dollar into one of those gizmos in San Francisco or New York. Recall the grousing cue-crowd forming behind some sap who can't get his dollar inserted; you see that predicament repeated and repeated, more than when you don't see it-- it's an American subway commonplace: NAMOP (Normal American *Mis*operating Procedure-- to supplant our ancient world war SNAFU-- Situation Normal All Fowled Up). BUT: In Berlin, in Frank-furt, in Paris, the euro note slips in "like a champ", as if it's as lubricated as a good condom; it practically reaches out and grabs your euro from your fingertips, even if the bill is mush-crumpled as if it has been sunken in a Rhine flood (I've performed this test). And the parking meters *work* in Europe; I've never seen one to fail. Nope (as you know) in the good ole Best States of America: half of the damn meters here are at any one time on the fritz. Half of them have bags and baggies smothering their heads by frustrated-- yet of course gladdened-- parkers. Hey, who makes these unreliable wonders, our American conkoutimajigs? American gizmos that were once The Best.[*]

And not recognizing all this reality-- or recognizing it and dismissing it-- is nothing other than The Big D: Psychiatrically Clinical Denial. It is as if we know deep down, in the subliminal lobes and cavities, that we do not have The Best. And, as I've asked and asked, How could we not know this? And how could we not resent it? We are a lot of things, but we are not stupid. Actually, we are quite, strangely, smart. But oh We are Superior. It's astounding, our credulous "superiority". We desperately dig our fingernails in on the reality-cloak like a man hanging from the edge of a building's roof; and such a crushing load of hold-in/hold-on has great consequences. Ameri-can violence. The Hatred Americana. Our Go-Your-Own-Wayness. So, listen to this one! Most of the feral Nazi literature now circulating in Germany, where it is illegal (reasons obvious) is printed in and mailed from, not Austria, not Bavaria, not South Africa, but from our U.S. I suppose the Euro-Nazis don't mind the awful wait-time/down-time in our post offices; the penned-in, unstamped, Book Rate. A lot of denying, repressed, "indi-

---

[*] The revamped diminutive for Out-of-Order ought really to be updated from the Europeanish "on the Fritz" to the more lately appropriate American Bob or Bud: *The machine is on the Bob. . .The machine is on the Bud.*

vidualist", hate here. The old superior-inferior.

In his seminal book *Bowling Alone*, the sociologist Robert Putnam calculates that American involvement in civic and professional associations, and in political ones, has plummeted since the sixties by about 25 percent. Whether it be the Kiwanis or the AMA or Hadassah or (most sadly) the PTA, we don't join up, we don't engage. Putnam creates a figure exhibiting his "guesstimated" causes of the decline:

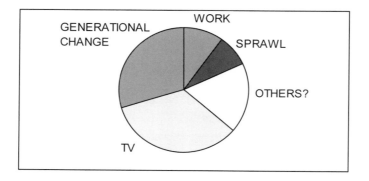

In Europe, with civic engagement in less decline-- if it is in decline at all-- I would speculate thusly:

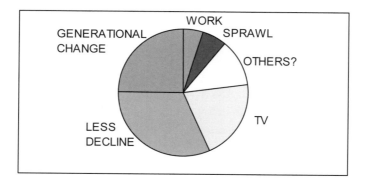

Generations do seem to change their attitudes less dramatically in Europe. As I've shown, a steady, respectful tethering maintains to one's "*heimat*", which is an old town, not a nucleus-poor "burb"; work hours, as I've shown, are less stacked-up; mall-and-sprawl is less diffuse-- when it even exists. And television there is not the be-and-end-all, as it has become in America.

In Germany 35 percent admit to watching *fernseher* indiscriminately; in France, 27 percent are passive-obsessive viewers; but here at home *60 percent* of us nowadays glue ourselves to the screen and, not even embarrassed to admit it, we say we watch "whatever's on" our multiplicity of surfable channels. Well, over there in the EU they do keep up that living involvement of Community Doings: Church groups; bus tour groups; union groups; citizen groups; lecture groups like the old American Chatauquas. The yet agonizing experiences of Vichy and the Third Reich continue to exert profound influence: so people read; they try to be active, to not fall into the trapped repetition of a passive (and horrific) History. Voting; involvement in issues. With *lichterketten* (candle marches, or processions)-- or without the candles in France-- out into the streets: on environment; on energy use-- solar and windmill (the Greens in coalition governments); on international affairs like Iraq. Express. Listen. Think. Influence: The government wont dismiss you or ignore you, nor will Big Business--as has by now come to pass in America. And come to accepted pass. The government *is* you. . . Or it is Out, and therefore Not You: Elections can be called for. Over There.

The Greatest Divide today is perhaps, as the pundits say, between The West and Islam, an echo of the medieval Great Divide-- of Mohammed and Charlemagne. But a more subtle, and in some crucial ways more important distinction may lie, not between locomotive and caboose but between the two racecars zooming at the head of the track: Capitalism Civilized and Capitalism Benighted. Or, if you find it more tasteful, more palatable, Capitalism Cooperative and Capitalism Atomized and Alienated. And a victory for the latter is an eventual loss for all. Citizenship is at its heart about participation, commonality; and this, a sense of the general welfare, can sometimes course through Europe as if it is its spine, its armature. In America we have now come close to three centuries from our strong, original communitarian origins, rounded past the naive Individualism of the industrial revolution, and now it's time-- far past time-- to head back home to Community. Time to, as economists are fond of saying, "fine-tune" our freedom. To no longer blindly defend our illusionary American "wealth", but create a true wealth-- of People. In health, culture, comfort, and community, as well as in actual economic-- Gross Domestic-- wealth. We need not copy Europe-- we cannot-- our origins being set distinctly, and our histories having been driven along different paths. To us it seems outlandish and comic that many Germans, apartment dwellers, own *schrebergartens* outside their cities, horticultural cabins where they spend weekends digging, mulching, three meters from the adjoining *schrebergarten*, their neighbor's plant and flower paradise. Or we Americans watch amused as a great and unwieldy-hectic body of the French-- apartment dwellers too-- swarmingly abandon Paris each weekend for similar reasons (the French have more country homes than any other peoples) clogging the *autoroutes* like perverse, drugged (and angry) ants; and that architecture-obsessed Paris is the home of the largest, most frequented, most uncomfortably people-crowded and humid-close greenhouse in the world. We Americans are different, yes; but isn't it time we conquered that tired, and tedious bravado? -- overcompensating for our plain-folk origins-- so that our structures *work*, and our interactions *work*, so that positive connections may adhere, and "bowling together" we may craft our own new beauty. When you drive through tunnels that are dim and disintegrating before your eyes, and over roads and bridges that clobber away at you and your shocks and your tire treads, where your electricity, your energy, is as unreliable as is your toilet, and your TV shouts its ads so divertingly and frequently with so little respect for your taste and your discrimination, your ears may soon enough turn to tin.

But "Life is with People"-- a Yiddish proverb. In a huddle-- speaking, singing, listening.

The clarion cry-- *"Let's fix it!"*

Appendix 1

Old Age Cash Benefits –
as a percentage of GDP

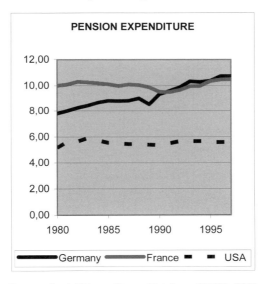

Source: Social Expenditures Database OECD, 2001

Year	France	Germany	USA
1980	7,79	9,99	5,18
1981	8,01	10,09	5,65
1982	8,24	10,31	5,64
1983	8,43	10,25	5,91
1984	8,66	10,18	5,75
1985	8,81	10,11	5,55
1986	8,78	9,97	5,50
1987	8,82	10,08	5,46
1988	8,99	10,03	5,44
1989	8,53	9,87	5,41
1990	9,32	9,52	5,38
1991	9,59	9,50	5,53
1992	9,87	9,67	5,66
1993	10,33	9,95	5,68
1994	10,27	9,98	5,66
1995	10,36	10,34	5,62
1996	10,73	10,46	5,60
1997	10,73	10,49	5,60

Appendix 2

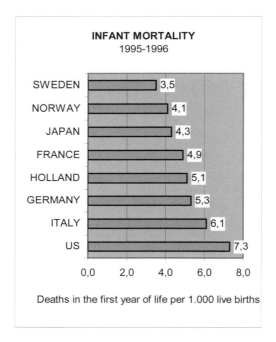

Source: Industrial Nations: United Nations Demographic Yearbook;
U.S.: National Center for Health Statistics.

Appendix 3

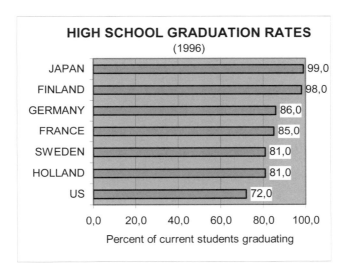

HIGH SCHOOL GRADUATION RATES
(1996)

JAPAN	99,0
FINLAND	98,0
GERMANY	86,0
FRANCE	85,0
SWEDEN	81,0
HOLLAND	81,0
US	72,0

Percent of current students graduating

Source: OECD.

Appendix 4

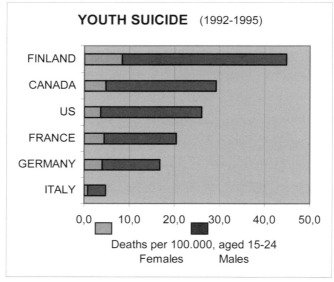

Source: Industrial Nations: World Health Statistics Annual, 1995, 1996;
U.S.: National Center for Health Statistics.

Note: 1995 U.S. date presented here for comparability purposes

Appendix 5

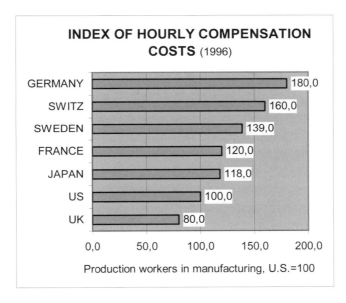

Source: U.S. Department of Labor.

Appendix 6

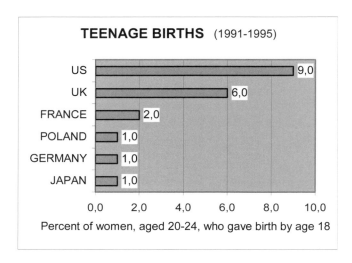

Source: Alan Guttmacher Institute.

SELECT BIBLIOGRAPHY

John Ardagh *Germany and the Germans*

Associated Press "Michelin to Cut 2,900 Jobs" *International Herald Tribune* 6/5/04. "AirBus Signs $7 Billion Deal With Gulf Carrier" *IHT* 7/20/04

Luigi Barzini *The Europeans*

Elizabeth Becker "WTO Rules U.S. Tariffs on Steel are Illegal" *New York Times* 11/17/03. "Push for a Trade Deal" *NYT* 7/25/04

Katrin Bennhold "In Germany, EU Parliament Elections Attract Little Voter Interest" *IHT* 6/4/04

Richard Bernstein *Fragile Glory: A Portrait of France and the French.* "Universities Hope to Recapture Lost Eminence" (Germany) *NYT* 4/8/04

Bloomberg News Service "Airbus Wins China Order" *IHT* 6/13/04

Daniel Boorstin *The Americans*

Robert L. Borosage "The Kitchen-Table State of the Union" *The Nation* 2/2/04

Boston Globe, The "U.S. A Laggard on Benefits, Study Finds" 7/28/04

Alan Brinkley *The Unfinished Nation*

William Broad "Americans are seen losing their scientific edge" *IHT* 5/3/04

Anke Bryson "Not Working for Economic Reasons" *Frankfurter Allgemeine Zeitung* 6/18/04. "Savings Up". *FAZ* 5/28/04. "Shakier Positions" *FAZ* 6/4/04

Chris Buckley "Furniture from China Draws Anger from Rivals: Loss of U.S. jobs sparks talk of sanctions" *NYT* 1/30/04

Business Week. "Stars of Europe" 6/7/04; "Waking up from the American Dream" 11/03

David Callahan *The Cheating Culture*

Doreen Carvajal "Job Losses: A Tale of Two Unions" *IHT* 6/16/04. "Michelin Offers Guide to Save Jobs" *IHT* 7/14/04

Gordon Craig *The Germans*

Sabine Delanglade *"La croissance introuvable"* L'Express 5/10/2004

Jonathan Denby *France on the Brink*

Ed Diener and Eunkook Suh, editors: *Culture and Subjective Well-being*

The Economist: *The World in 2004:* Steve King *"A la recherche de l'entente perdue"*. Sophie Pedder "Corporate Scandal in France: Getting Messier". John Sparks "The Power Game". "France's Creeping Americanisation" 6/26/04. "Taxing the Poor to Pay the Poor" 4/3/04. "Special Report: Financing Universities-- Who pays to study?" 1/24/04. "The Price of Prudence" (Risk Aversion) 1/24/04. "Reality Television: Down on the farm (What a celebrity TV show says about French attitudes to rural life)" 5/8/04.

Jeff Faux and Larry Mishel *Inequality and the Global Economy*

Kim Phillips-Fein "Texas, Inc: Taking Privatization to Extremes, A New Law Ends the Public Sector as we knew it" *The Nation* 1/5/04

Niall Ferguson "Money or Survival: America's Quest for Global Dominance" *Newsweeek Special Issue*, 12/03

Thomas Friedman *The Lexus and the Olive Tree*

David Garland   *Crime and Control: Crime and Social Order in Contemporary Society*

Adam Gopnik *Paris to the Moon*

William Greider *One World, Ready or Not.* "Under the Banner of the 'War' on Terror" *The Nation* 6/21/04. "The Serpent that Ate America's Lunch" *The Nation* 5/10/04.

Alfred Grosser *Geschichte Deutschlands seit 1945: Eine Bilanz*

Hakim, Danny "Carmakers Feel Pinch of Pollution" *NYT* 7/27/04

Harper's Index "Chances on any given day that the only 'vegetables' served in a U.S. public school are potatoes: 50%" 10/03. "House Republicans thrice rejected an amendment to upgrade the U.S. electrical grid" 10/03. "Ratio of the number of cows France tests *each week* to the number the U.S. has tested in the last decade. 7:6" 3/04. "Rank of Costa Rica and the United States among countries whose citizens live longest: 18,19"; "Rank of the

U.S. health-care system among the most efficient in the world, according to the WHO: 37"; "Percentage increase since 1999 in U.S. households in which there was hunger due to poverty during the year: 22" 2/04.

Michael Harrington *The Other America*

Gardiner Harris "Drug Firms Seek Antidote for Unpopularity" *New York Times* 7/8/04

Bob Herbert "Sending America's Best Jobs Offshore" *NYT* 12/27/03

Melville J. Herskowitz *Economic Anthropology*

Stanley Hoffmann et al *In Search of France*

Richard Hill *We Europeans*

Hajo Holborn *A History of Modern Germany*

Brad Holst "Resegregation's Aftermath" *The Atlantic Monthly* 7-8/2004

Will Hutton *A Declaration of Interdependence.* "The American Prosperity Myth" *The Nation* 11/7/03

Ronald Inglehart *Modernization and Post-Modernization*

David Cay Johnston *Perfectly Legal: The Covert Campaign to Rig Our Tax System to Benefit the Super Rich-- and Cheat Everybody Else*

Tony Judt "The World We Have Lost" *Newsweek* 5/31/04

Michael B. Katz *The Price of Citizenship*

Aaron Kirchfeld "China Boom Powers Piston Producer" *FAZ* 2/6/04

John Komlos *"Wie Gross Werden Wir?"* *Die Zeit* 5/04

Jonathan Kozol On American public education. *The Nation* 5/3/04

Charles Kupchan *The End of the American Era*

Felicia R. Lee "Godliness is Next to Wealthiness, Study Finds" *IHT* 5/12/04

Mark Landler "Oil Prices Spur Europeans to Seek Alternatives" *NYT* 6/1/04. "Angst as 'Made in Germany' Loses its Luster" *NYT* 4/8/04

Peter Lindert *Growing Public: Social Spending and Economic Growth*

David Moburg "Unions in America" *The Nation* 9/15/03

David G. Myers *The American Paradox*

Serge Mallet *La Nouvelle Classe ouvrière*

John Markoff and Jennifer L. Schenker "Europe Hones an Edge in Technology *NYT* 12/12/03

Donald G. McNeil, Jr. "Mental Illness, the Global Affliction" *NYT* 6/3/04

Paul Meller "EU Signals Support for Rescue of Alstom" *NYT* 5/18/04

Marc Miringoff and Marque-Luisa Miringoff *The Social Health of the Nation*

Curtis Moore and Alan Miller *Green Gold: Japan, Germany, the United States, and the Race for Environmental Technology*

Gretchen Morgenson "Are CEOs Worth the Millions They're Paid?" *IHT* 1/27/04

Jim Motavalli *Breaking Gridlock*

Bobbi Murray "Money for Nothing" *The Nation* 1/8/03; 3/8/04

New Economic Foundation, The 3/04

New York Times, The "Health Care in U.S. is Poor half the time" 4/6/04. "A Defeat for Clean Air" 12/8/03. "The Case Against King Cotton" 12/9/03

Joseph S. Nye, Jr. *Soft Power*

Otto Pflanze *Bismarck and the Development of Germany*

Otto Pohl "Environmentalists Push a New Lever: Globalization" *NYT* 7/5/04

Karl Polanyi *The Great Transformation*

Katha Pollitt "Do You Feel a Draft?" *The Nation* 6/7/04

Michael E. Porter. *The Competitive Advantage of Nations*

Robert Putnam *Bowling Alone*

Saritha Rai "Outsourcing Backlash may be Easing in India" *NYT* 7/13/04

Steven Rattner " U.S. Interest Rates: What an Increase Can't Hide" *NYT* 7/2/04

John Ratey and Catherine Johnson *Shadow Syndromes*

Reuters. "Nanotech Investment Urged" *IHT* 6/30/04. "Labor Confederation Critical of U.S." *IHT* 6/10/04 "Protesting Likely Cuts at Siemens" *IHT* 6/18/04. "Daimler Chrysler Executives Pledge to take Salary Cut" *IHT* 7/20/04

Michael Roth   "Mother of all Machines: (German) Machine-tool makers have top global standing" *FAZ* 5/7/04

Charles Schumer and Paul Craig Roberts "Exporting Jobs is not Free Trade" *NYT* 1/7/04

Joseph Schumpeter *Capitalism, Socialism and Democracy*

Joe Sharkey.. "What Carries 800 Passengers and Takes 3 Days to Unload?" *IHT* 4/7/07

Amity Shlaes *Germany: The Empire Within*

Fred Siegel *The Future Once Happened Here*

Eric Solsten, ed. *Germany: A Country Study* (Federal Research Division, Library of Congress)

Werner Sombart *The Jews and Modern Capitalism*

R. H. Tawney *The Protestant Ethic and the Spirit of Capitalism*

Time-CNN Poll "George Bush Most Admired American" 4/03

Gregory Treverton *America, Germany, and the Future of Europe*

Louis Uchitelle "Changes in U.S. Workforce Make Accurate Data Elusive" *IHT* 1/13/04

United Nations *Human Development Index, 2003. World Values Survey 2001*

Ian Urbina "Voltage Still Poses a Threat in New York" *NYT* 2/7/04

Katrina van den Heuvel "Commentary" ("Hunger is epidemic in Ohio"). *The Nation* 12/22/03

R. Veenhoven *Happiness in Nations: Subjective Interpretation of Life in 56 Nations*

Loec Wacquant *Prisons of Poverty*

Amy Waldman "In a 'Brain Gain' India's Westernized Emigres Return Home" *NYT* 6/25/04

Fara Warner "New Realism at U.S. Carmakers? Big 3 Vowing to Regain Market Share and Focus on Profit" *NYT* 1/7/04

Max Weber *Religion and the Rise of Capitalism*

Curtis White *The Middle Mind*

World Economic Forum *Ranking of Business Competitiveness, 2003-2004*

World Database of Happiness 2001

Gordon Wright *France in Modern Times*

Eli Zaretsky *Capitalism and the Family*

INDEX

FOR COMMENTS TO THE AUTHOR PLEASE CONTACT:

americaneditions@aol.com